# STAND UP, SPEAK OUT

# STAND UP,

**Estelle Zannes**
University of New Mexico

**Gerald Goldhaber**
State University of New York—Buffalo

# SPEAK OUT

## An Introduction to Public Speaking

**Addison-Wesley Publishing Company**

Reading, Massachusetts
Menlo Park, California • London • Amsterdam • Don Mills, Ontario • Sydney

The title-page photograph and those on pages 16, 30, 37, 64, 86, 104, 130, and 226 are by Marshall Henrichs.

All other photographs, except those carrying specific credits, were provided by Tom Zannes.

*Second printing, May 1978*

ISBN 0-201-08987-4
BCDEFGHIJK-HA-798

The authors wish to express their sincere appreciation to the following people, who reviewed the manuscript for *Stand Up, Speak Out* and gave constructive comment and suggestions.

Jon A. Blubaugh, University of Kansas
Diana Corley, Black Hawk College
Jo-Ann Graham, Bronx Community College
Paula Michal, El Paso Community College
Daniel Munger, Western Illinois University
Sandra Nickel, University of Missouri
Christopher Rollins (student), Western Illinois University

# PREFACE

From the police sergeant briefing his officers to the alcoholic at the AA meeting, from the corporate training director teaching new managers to the teacher training new students, from the stewardess demonstrating the oxygen mask to the waiter or the car hop reciting the menu, from the five-year-old girl selling lemonade on the street to the 75-year-old grey panther organizing senior citizens to protest social security procedures, from the cradle to the rocking chair, millions of people regularly stand up and speak out.

From Aristotle's day, the timeworn principles of public speaking have remained stable. In *Stand Up, Speak Out,* we explain and apply those principles to the daily situations in which most people find themselves when they give public speeches. To discover and document these situations, we have gone into the heartland of America for examples of speeches, occasions, and audiences. We have surveyed and taped hundreds of speakers giving hundreds of speeches. Most of our illustrations are taken from nonclassroom assignments. As teachers we accept the friendliness and availability of student audiences, but we remind our readers and colleagues that they are only one type of the hundreds of possible audiences people in all walks of life can and will address.

Our book differs from most contemporary public speaking books in two other *major* respects: situational and integrative. The former stresses our concern for the millions of people who regularly and without notice deliver public speeches: Policemen giving briefings, foremen explaining projects, salespersons outlining strategies, quarterbacks calling signals, and even little girls and boys selling lemonade are giving public speeches. Unlike most current books, which either recycle student speeches given to other students in classroom situations or present "great models" of giants in history, *Stand Up, Speak Out* addresses *all* speakers in *all* situations.

The second major difference between our approach and most others is the integrative approach we take in presenting our principles of effective speaking. We believe that classical purposes of speaking (i.e., speaking to inform, persuade, entertain) create unnecessarily restrictive boundaries for speakers in determining why they should speak. We believe that traditional injunctions—such as "Analyze your audience *before* you select your topic," "Don't mix your purposes of speaking," "Tell jokes to hostile audiences"—ignore the interdependent nature of human communication. We speak for many purposes, all of which interrelate and overlap, and such injunctions may often stifle student creativity. Our book presents an integrative approach throughout. While presenting the principles we think will enhance your effectiveness as a public speaker, we caution that there are really *no* hard and firm rules governing human public speaking behavior (including this one).

*Stand Up, Speak Out* is a practical public speaking book which combines time-tested principles with real-life examples of Americans speaking in public, at their homes, schools, jobs, clubs, and special events. Chapter 1 begins by tracing the life of a woman from the early 1930s to the present, showing how public speaking is a part of everyone's life. We follow this woman through a period that includes three wars, through the joys of marriage and the sorrows of death. We see her at work, at school, and in the midst of violent protest. We discover that speaking and listening skills are necessary tools for day-to-day existence.

In Chapter 2 we talk about *preparing for the event* by preparing yourself, preparing for the audience, and preparing for the environment. We discuss the selection of a purpose as an interdependent phenomenon; that is, we speak for *several* purposes which all interrelate to one another. This chapter also includes some "self-brainstorming techniques" and gives detailed steps to help reduce stage fright that are based on current principles of assertiveness training.

Chapter 3 includes an eight-step process for *doing research,* which includes using ourselves, others, libraries, and current technologies as valuable information sources. This chapter presents practical material on how to enhance your perceptual and memory skills, gives a sample letter for seeking help from others, gives details on group brainstorming, and presents an overview of the latest technologies available to speakers.

Chapter 4 attacks the problems inherent in *developing the message* ethically, emotionally, and logically. While addressing ourselves to each area, we continue to stress how emotions and reason interrelate. We discuss the ways a speaker can build an image. The language of emotions and the responses of listeners to emotional appeals are presented with examples from everyday occurrences. Inductive reasoning, deductive reasoning, and reasoning from cause and from analogy are clarified so the reader understands how to develop the message logically.

Chapter 5 explores the many and interesting ways of *supporting the message verbally and visually.* Besides presenting practical illustrations to support our central idea that speeches are situational, we instruct the speaker on ways of constructing the visual aid.

Chapter 6 presents basics of *organizing the message* with many lively, entertaining examples of current interest to students and other readers. A five-step process for organizing a speech is detailed and sample outlines are included.

Chapter 7 deals with *starting and stopping* your speech. It clearly identifies the purposes of introductions and conclusions and presents a case for the limited or no introduction or conclusion. Clear and relevant examples illustrate the functions of introductions and conclusions.

Chapter 8 explains the differences between oral and written styles *in wording the speech.* It explores the multiple meanings of words with lively illustrations from current events. A section called "The human touch" approaches the problem of putting warmth into a speech in a unique manner. Liveliness, simplicity, and appropriateness are all handled in clear terms.

Chapter 9 explains what the audience sees and hears when a speaker is *delivering the message.* Guidelines for interpreting the messages your body sends to an audience are practical and easy to follow. Information on gestures and clothing and a chart on the symbolism of color make this chapter highly readable and informative. Down-to-earth explanations of phonation, resonance, pitch, rate, volume, and quality take the mystery out of the science of how voice is produced. A special section on dialects and accents is a practical addition. Detailed instructions about delivering the message on television and radio, an explanation of the styles of delivery, and some pointers on rehearsing round out the chapter.

Chapter 10 explores the problems a speaker faces when *speaking in groups*—as one of many speakers on a panel, in a symposium, or in private group discussions. It discusses the types of group presentations, the types of goals, the roles people assume in groups, the concept of leadership, problem-solving and decision-making in groups, and delivery in group situations.

Chapter 11 presents a unique approach to the question: *is anybody listening?* It suggests that both speaker and audience have two responsibilities in every public speaking situation—the responsibilities of *speaking and listening at the same time.* In other words, every speaker and every listener participates in the communicative act simultaneously, thus listening on the highest level. This chapter also explains the various levels of listening and presents some lively stories about those levels.

Chapter 12 talks about these occasions that are almost certain to occur, when you suddenly realize that *"Speaker, you've got a problem."* It is a chapter about the problems we all face at one time or another in our speaking careers, relating real-life situations in which speakers have documented their speaker-related, audience-related, and environment-related problems in often humorous ways.

Chapter 13 puts the listener into the role of critic, suggesting that when we hear someone—even ourselves—*stand up and speak out*, we are all critics. This chapter is designed to help the speaker analyze his or her own performance, as well as the performance of others, for the purpose of becoming a better speaker. We present analyses of the Mondale/Dole debate and the Carter/Ford debates together with excerpts and analyses of several other speeches.

In the last section of this chapter, we present the entire speech of a young student who received his master's degree in Speech Communication and whose message to a city council supports our theme that people not only *do* speak out many times during a lifetime, but *should* speak out in a democratic society.

As with any book, we owe much to those who supported us physically and emotionally! Tom Zannes, whose original photographic artwork has greatly enhanced the visual pleasure of this book; our reviewers, whose comments kept us conceptually in touch with the field; Richard Bronson, Susan Dandler, Timothy Zannes, and Ellen Sklarz, who taped many of the speeches appearing in the book; and our families, Tim, Tom, and Maria Zannes, and Mara and Michelle Goldhaber, whose feedback as people who regularly stand up and speak out, gave us valuable practical insights. To all of you we are forever grateful. The book is stronger for your input.

*Albuquerque, New Mexico*                                                  E.Z.
*Buffalo, New York*                                                              G.G.
*October 1977*

# CONTENTS

# STAND UP, SPEAK OUT

# 1 THE LAVINIA STORY: A LIFETIME OF PUBLIC SPEAKING

**Like everybody else, Lavinia began "public speaking" at an early age.**

On September 7, 1932, Lavinia Adams stood in front of her home in Brooklyn, New York, and in a loud, high voice called: "C'mon and get your lemonade. It's good and it's cold and it's only a penny. C'mon and twy it."

The twins and their brother, who lived next door, snickered. They didn't have any pennies but they bartered a marble and a bottle cap for a taste. Since they were Lavinia's only customers, she shared the rest of the lemonade with them.

Later that day Lavinia entertained her family with a rendition of Franklin Roosevelt's campaign theme song, which she had learned while listening to the radio:

*Come on and row, row, row with Roosevelt*
*On the good ship U.S.A.*

*Sail with Franklin D. to victory*
*And to real prosperity.*

*He's honest, he's strong, and he's steady,*
*A chip off the one that gave us Teddy.*

*Come on and row row row with Roosevelt*
*On the good ship U.S.A.* [1]

Lavinia, however, couldn't quite manage the r's and she "wode" more than she "rowed."

Her family believed in Roosevelt. They too were "pulling" for him. They saw the bread lines and the bank runs. Church was about the only place they could afford to go. Lavinia's mother always said that "Prosperity is out and about, poverty stays home."

Roosevelt won the presidential race and on March 4, 1933 he told a radio audience:

*I am certain that my fellow Americans expect that on my induction into the Presidency, I will address them with a candor and a decision which the present situation of our Nation impels. This is preeminently the time to speak the truth, the whole truth, frankly and boldly. Nor need we shrink from honestly facing conditions in our country today. This great Nation will endure as it has endured, will revive and will prosper.*

*So, first of all, let me assert my firm belief that the only thing we have to fear is fear itself—nameless, unreasoning, unjustified terror which paralyzes needed efforts to convert retreat into advance.*

By 1934 people were divided about the great experiment. Roosevelt had created a controversial administration, but production and employment were up and folks kept reminding themselves that "the only thing we have to fear is fear itself."

New York City, where Lavinia lived, got a new mayor. Fiorello LaGuardia spoke on the radio and although Lavinia was made to listen (and be quiet), she didn't understand much of what he said:

*Yes, I have the proof that my kind of city government is the kind of city government the people of our city want. Isn't that grand? There isn't a single solitary county chairman of either party who is in favor of my administration. To use the phrase that Al Smith liked to use in his days, "I can run on a laundry ticket and beat these political bums anytime."*

In spite of the fact that this high-spirited, barrel chested, rumpled, short, intense man became mayor, the Adams' did not prosper in New York City. With the help of a brother-in-law, Mr. Adams found a job in Cleveland at the Union Terminal.

Lavinia attended school in Cleveland, where a speech therapist worked with her on her r's and l's. Her classmates in school gathered around to listen to her "funny talk." She wasn't aware of it but her New York accent made her very popular. She soon started imitating her best friend, who came from Poland, and then the speech therapist corrected her th's, which had become d's.

During the next few years, the National Recovery Act was declared unconstitutional, the Dionne quintuplets became internationally famous, and Lavinia gave a few more speeches.

**We begin public speaking in a formal sense earlier than we realize.**

In the second grade she spoke about the "Boy Hero of Harlem." Her Harlem was in Holland, and the boy hero gained his fame by thrusting his arm in the dike. In the fourth grade she chose radio as her subject and gave a demonstration speech. She showed the class how to build a receiver out of an oatmeal box and two tungsten wires. She called the wires "cat's whiskers."

Though Lavinia missed New York, her family seemed to find life a little more prosperous and tranquil in Ohio. Unemployment in the United States, though still very high, was gradually decreasing. Though there was much turmoil in the world, it was mostly in Europe. In 1939, Hitler's attack on Poland began World War II.

In June of 1940, Mussolini declared war on France, and President Roosevelt said, "The hand that held the dagger has struck it into the back of its neighbor."

While German soldiers marched across Europe, Americans
marched to "America First" rallies. General Hugh Johnson warned
against ". . . reckless shooting craps with destiny for the sake of democracy." Charles Lindbergh cautioned that "If we enter fighting for
America abroad, we may lose it at home." Winston Churchill offered
his countrymen ". . . blood, toil, tears, and sweat," and asked of the
United States, "Give us the tools and we shall do the job."

In late 1940, Lavinia's brother registered for the peacetime
draft—and was among one of the first groups called. As Lavinia
waved goodbye to him, the radio was playing a newly popular song,
"Goodbye, dear, I'll be back in a year." And in the weeks that followed, while thousands of young men were learning to right-shoulder
arms, Lavinia and about fifteen million other movie-goers were paying twelve cents to see Charlie Chaplin play *The Great Dictator* at the
Saturday matinee.

At 10:15 on the morning of December 7, 1941, Secretary of
State Cordell Hull went to his office to send a message to Japan. By
early afternoon the Japanese ambassador was delivering a reply
while other Japanese at their embassy were destroying diplomatic
papers and yet others, 5000 miles away, were trying to destroy Pearl
Harbor. On December 8, 1941, President Roosevelt told the Congress and the people of the United States, "Yesterday, December
seventh, 1941—a day that will live in infamy—the United States of
America was suddenly and deliberately attacked by naval and air
forces of the Empire of Japan."

Ways of life changed rapidly. The one-year draftees realized that
their term of service had been extended indefinitely. A week or so
after the attack on Pearl Harbor, Lavinia stood before her current
events class and read a letter from her brother.

*Dear Lavinia* (it went), *Well, it looks like I won't be back in a year. I
guess it was only natural for us to hope, to shut our eyes against the
painful truth, to listen to all the America-First songs, until we were no
longer sensitive to the world around us. We know now that there is
no hope of peace with our enemies. If we want to be free, if we wish
to preserve those rights and privileges we have talked about for so
long, I guess we have to fight. You know me, I've never been aggressive but we're in this now all the way. Remember to write. That'll
sure help pass the time, and remember I love you.*

Lavinia then made a passionate appeal for letters and said she
could get names of soldiers for those who wished to send letters or
cookies or something. All the girls in the class volunteered.

During the next few years Lavinia followed the war very closely.
She especially liked Ernie Pyle's columns. She suffered with Pyle as
he wrote of the front-line soldiers who lived ". . . in a way that is in-
conceivable to anyone who hasn't experienced it. They walked and
fought all night without sleep."[2]

**3    The Lavinia Story**

Roosevelt

Lavinia and her schoolmates

Lavinia singing
Row Row Row with
Roosevelt

Truman

Lavinia & Gregory

CONVAIR/ASTRONAUTICS

Missile Countdown

Lavinia as a Bride

Korean War

UNATIONS (From U.S. Navy)

Rosalynn Carter

McGovern

On April 12, 1945, President Roosevelt died of a cerebral hemorrhage at Warm Springs, Georgia. Lavinia did not leave her chair near the radio all day. She stayed home on the day of the funeral and listened as Arthur Godfrey described the funeral procession: "The drums are muffled. The pace of the musicians is sooo slow. I can see the horses drawing the caisson." He spoke of the new president upon whose shoulders fell the burden of responsibilities. Godfrey solemnly stated, "God bless him, President Truman."

Lavinia wept.

Then, 2172 days after it had begun, the war ended and Lavinia's brother came home.

A new era was upon the earth, an era that would usher in the atomic age and the iron curtain, that would bring vast social and political changes, and would see the first human being set foot on the moon.

By the time the American soldiers returned home Lavinia had finished high school, worked as a car hop, attended secretarial school, and had her first interview for a full-time job. For the interview, Lavinia put away her bobby socks, borrowed her mother's silk stockings, and bought a hat. Her mother gave her a pair of white gloves. She was so excited that she kept smiling and saying "yessir." Her interviewer asked, "How are you with figures?" "Great," she replied. He gave her a problem dealing with fractions and she finished solving it before he did. She got the job.

She had been working for three years when she was faced with delivering the most important speech of her life. Although the speech had been written generations before, she insisted on adapting it to the occasion and to her beliefs. She deleted the word "obey" and substituted "cherish." Her mother was a little upset and her father was amused:

The eyes of every person in that audience were upon Lavinia when on February 5, 1950, Lavinia Adams, 22, married Mark Lavdas, 32, a Naval air pilot stationed in Pensacola, Florida. He was a friend of her brother's.

After the wedding, Mark and Lavinia settled in an apartment in Pensacola, Florida, where Mark was stationed. They had been married for almost five months when certain far-off events occurred that were to shape their destinies.

On June 25, 1950, without warning, the North Korean army forces struck across the 28th parallel into South Korea. Two days later, President Truman ordered a naval blockade of the Korean coast, and on July 1st, Mark was on his way to Korea. Mark's departure was made no easier for the couple by the recent discovery that they were to become parents.

In 1951, while Red China swarmed into Korea, the Giants were on their way to winning the Pennant, and Lavinia was busy taking care of a baby son, Gregory, born in February of that year. In 1951,

***A public speech can be deeply personal.***

too, she bought her first television set, sewed new curtains for her apartment, and settled down to watch the news on television and to wait.

On April 19, 1951, General Douglas MacArthur appeared on the screen. He told Congress and the nation that "Old soldiers never die, they just fade away."

Fascinated, Lavinia listened to General MacArthur. She really liked the way he *dressed*, but all the while she was listening to his speech her mind kept saying, "Oh yes, old soldiers never die—but the young ones do." She kept thinking of Mark and sat down to write another letter.

Though the new television set was exciting, Lavinia was not ready to give up her daytime radio shows. She especially liked "Valiant Lady," a story of a brave woman and her brilliant, but unstable, husband; "Life Can be Beautiful," "One Man's Family," "The Guiding Light," "Young Dr. Malone," and particularly "The Right to Happiness." She was irritated at all the loud music that was finding its way onto radio.

By July, 1953, four battleships, eight cruisers and approximately 80 destroyers had participated in the Korean War. By the end of July, 1953, Navy and Marine aricraft had flown more than 225,000 missions, not without casualties. One casualty was Mark Lavdas, age 35. His aircraft was shot down over Wonsan, Korea.

When Lavinia received the news of her husband's death, her first instinct was to run and clutch her baby to her bosom. Then she wept. Then she was angry. She insisted upon writing the eulogy, but when the time came she could not deliver it. The Chaplain at Pensacola read it at the memorial service:

*I stand helpless before the fact of death.*
*My disbelief has given way to sorrow and anger, and words*
*cannot express the anguish in my heart.*
*Still I must speak out.*
*I knew him for such a short time,*
*because he was on earth for such a short time.*
*We honor him as a defender of a cause,*
*but I cannot help thinking how much more he could have done*
*had he only the chance to live.*
*I cry for him and myself and his son and*
*the country—because his death is a loss to us all.*

During the rest of the 1950s, Lavinia isolated herself from the outside world. She concentrated on her son's upbringing, took him to the beach, to the zoo, to the amusement park. She used Mark's insurance money to live, occasionally augmenting her income with typing, which she did at home. She seldom hired a baby sitter for Gregory, for she greatly enjoyed being with him herself.

Outside, the '50s were years of change, when cities were loaded with explosive ingredients attached to very short fuses. Prison riots swept the country, fear of ideologies prompted the McCarthy hearings, and racial unrest was beginning to shake America.

Though many blacks had been moving to the North before the second World War to work in factories, it was during the beginning of the 1960s that the great emigration of blacks from the south occurred.

Lavinia also moved north in the early '60s. When her father died, she went to stay with her mother during her mother's bereavement. Lavinia had become restless in Florida and thought Cleveland meant security, familiar things, perhaps peace.

Instead of a calm refuge, she found a city rocked with dissension. Remarkable changes had taken place, but the biggest change was demographic. From 1950 to 1965 the population declined, as over two-hundred thousand white residents left the city. During that period, black residents in Cleveland rose from 16.1 to 34.4 percent of the city's population, while 43 percent of the residents were from foreign stock—mainly Germans, Poles, Czechs, Hungarians, and Italians. A reporter described the city, for all its cosmopolitan ingredients, as a kind of witches' cauldron: "Essentially a group of juxtaposed tribes more or less at war with one another. . . She is a melting pot that has never melted but continues to boil, casting up hard racial lumps in indigestible form."[3]

Nonetheless, Lavinia felt alive and needed. Her mother's pension was small, and Lavinia realized she herself was ill equipped to make the money she would require to help her mother and support her son. She went to work and, at the age of 33, she enrolled in the evening program of a community college in an attempt to develop new skills. She was one of the oldest students in any of her classes.

In September 1961, after almost 30 years of giving speeches (she had started at four) Lavinia took her first speech class. She gave her first consciously organized speech about Franklin Delano Roosevelt and the 1932 campaign; a topic with which she was familiar. She did all her research at home. Her mother had kept copies of all of Roosevelt's speeches, as well as campaign posters. In addition, Lavinia probed her own memory. Her most vivid memory was when her mother had taken her downtown during one of Roosevelt's visits to the city. An American Legionnaire had lifted her on his shoulders and she had seen the President ride by, a long cigarette holder clutched in his teeth. She decided to start her speech with her own experience. She said: "I'll never forget the first time I saw Franklin Delano Roosevelt. It was on Superior Avenue in downtown Cleveland. I had heard about him for four years and to me he was some kind of hero. Well, President Roosevelt's motorcade came toward me. I was trying hard to see. My mother tried to lift me up and while she was struggling a man in a uniform swung me up on his shoul-

**Our own experience is a rich source of speech topics.**

ders. And there *he* was. His hat had a jaunty tilt to it, his cigarette holder pointed upward—in fact, he looked just like his pictures. He waved and I waved and almost fell off the man's shoulders.

"That was F.D.R., the super campaigner. That was 1936, but he hadn't changed his habits. He was just as aggressive against the Republican party then as he had been in 1932. Roosevelt did two things: He traveled a lot, and he hit hard.

"He said it was time for common sense and truth, but he did not hesitate to claim that the Republican party was the culprit that had brought the country to its present state of chaos." Without looking at her notes, Lavinia listed Roosevelt's arguments against the Republicans and offered some statistics about the number of speeches he gave. She concluded by saying that his aggressive method of speaking was instrumental in securing him the presidency of the United States.

Lavinia's classmates enjoyed her speech, although most of them said they didn't remember Roosevelt at all (most of them had not been born until after he had died). Many of her classmates were from the east side of Cleveland and were black. They spoke about unemployment and poor housing. A representative from an organization called CORE visited the class one day and spoke about "The Congress of Racial Equality."

After that Lavinia began speaking about "black people" and corrected her son when he said "Negro." Her mother thought she was getting "radical."

Both the nation and Lavinia survived the 1960s. In 1969, Lavinia, after eight years of night classes, finally obtained her degree. She had been active in Vietnam protest marches, city elections, and PTA meetings. She was asked to speak at the commencement, along with several other members of her class. She had gone from the community college to a state university which was located in the center of town. Most of her classmates came from lower- and middle-income families. At her graduation, before two thousand people, Lavinia made the following comments: "The passion play that began in the sixties has lasted these many years. It began with an awakening, moved to the mountains where we crucified our heroes, burned our cities, and cried out in protest at what we had done. But we survived.

"The nation's journalists are now busy reviewing the horrors of our own making, but are also predicting a new and better life in the seventies. We cannot sit back and hope they are right. We must make it happen."

The campaign work Lavinia had done in city elections paid off, and in 1970, degree in hand, she got a job as a bailiff in domestic court. From nine to five she listened to divorce cases.

When her mother urged her to consider remarriage, she laughed and told her mother stories of the domestic battles she heard in court. Lavinia's mother surprised everyone by finding a "gentleman caller," who took her to Tarpon Springs, Florida. There the elderly couple decided to share an apartment. Lavinia's mother tried to explain that she would lose her dead husband's railroad pension if she remarried.

Lavinia had mixed feelings about the arrangement, but her son Gregory thought it was "cool." Gregory was a student at Kent State University and was actively involved in the movement to protest the Viet Nam War. He told his mother that grandma was just one of the many women who suffered under the "system." He said Lavinia should be more concerned with her rights.

Lavinia was intrigued with another movement, the one to give women equal rights. She began reading *The Feminine Mystique* between court cases.

On May 4, 1970, a volley of gunfire from the ranks of frightened young National Guardsmen left four young people dead and nine others wounded at Kent State University. Lavinia heard the news at court. Frantic, she left the courtroom and drove the 20 miles to the University to find her son.

She wandered among the terror and chaos all night, and the next day she put on a black armband and joined her son in a protest rally. She found herself speaking out against the Guardsmens' actions. She urged nonviolent and vigorous protest of President Nixon's Cambodia policy and an end to the bombing and burning of North Vietnamese villages. She appealed to the students for total involvement for peace and said: "Let the violence stay with those who are violent." Before she could finish her speech, a student took over the platform and urged a strike and boycott of classes as a protest against the killings.

Gregory joined the boycott but Lavinia had to return to work. She needed the money to ensure her son's education, *whenever* it resumed.

The period of perpetual protest in America reached its peak in 1970 with 1800 demonstrations on America's campuses.

In 1971, while the turmoil over the Vietnam war continued, President Richard Nixon and Senator George McGovern took to the campaign trail with promises of ending the war if elected.

Lavinia's son urged her to become a delegate and fight for a place for women on the Democratic Platform. She did so, and campaigned energetically, but both Lavinia and McGovern lost their elections.

In the process, however, Lavinia found added excitement in the women's fight for equal rights. She found that the movement offered her an opportunity for discussion and reevaluation of her own role in society. While she knew she had been lucky to obtain the bailiff's job, with some envy she now watched the attorneys that came into her court.

*Many (but not all) speeches call for action from the audience.*

In the winter of 1973, Gregory graduated from the journalism department at Kent State University. Because his favorite sport was skiing, Lavinia decided his graduation present would be a ski trip to the most difficult mountain in America, situated in the Taos Ski Valley, New Mexico. Gregory loved the southwest. He skied and went hang-gliding—and decided to stay in the area and write for a small independent newspaper.

Restless and alone, Lavinia decided there were more ways of growing than just growing old. She took her LSAT tests and scored very high. She applied to Case Western Reserve Law School, and, at her son's insistence, to the University of New Mexico Law School.

Case Western Reserve thought Lavinia was too old, but she was accepted at the University of New Mexico. Delighted at her acceptance at UNM, Gregory wrote, "Come on out right away Mom. There's so much room to grow here."

When Lavinia arrived at the Albuquerque airport, Gregory met her, took out his reporter's pad, and said, "What are your thoughts as you embark on a new career, counselor?"

Lavinia smiled confidently and addressed her son and the passers-by:

"Unaccustomed as I am to speaking publicly, let me just say, 'This is not the end, but the beginning.' "

## YOU AND LAVINIA

On finishing the Lavinia story, you might be ready to agree with Emerson that "Every man is an orator, how long soever he may have been a mute." You will understand Socrates, who referred to himself as "... a pining man who was frantic to hear speeches," and you will concur with Aristotle that "All men attempt to discuss statements and to maintain them, to defend themselves and to attack others."

Public speaking is a part of everyone's life—Lavinia's, yours, ours. We are the speakers. We are the critics. We have more arenas from which to speak than did the Roman or Greek citizens in the 4th Century, BC. Most public speaking took place then in the legislative assembly, in a court of law, and in some kind of ceremonial setting. Speaking today takes place in the home, at school, at church, in government buildings, at places of business, in factories, airplanes, on the street, in front of cameras, microphones, and even on the moon. The occasions are many and varied and the subject matter different, but the arguments still arise from our desire to exhort or dissuade, to accuse and defend, to praise and to blame; that much we still have in common with the Athenians.

Like Athenians, when we listen we are still the spectators or the judges. We still judge things either past or to come, or sometimes we are mere spectators considering the ability of the speakers. It is not necessary that we hold high office to do these things; we can applaud at the local Kiwanis luncheon or, with a mere flick of the wrist, remove a speaker from our television screen. We can rise and protest our local zoning ordinance at city council and we can still rally around a candidate.

*One of the great and universal needs of human beings is to communicate.*

We are both speakers and consumers of messages, and what happens around us affects our public statements. Sometimes we harbor a thought for years until the occasion arises that seems appropriate for its utterance. Sometimes, like Lavinia, we listen and don't understand a word. And, like Lavinia, we absorb the attitudes and beliefs of our parents and store information for later use. When Lavinia gave her first speech in class on Franklin D. Roosevelt, she was summoning up from her memory a decade and a half of information. She wrote a eulogy because she felt compelled to do so, just as she felt compelled in later years to protest injustice. Because of her temperament, her background, her love of justice, her readiness to praise and to blame, she naturally found a fascination in the study of law. She was mindful that her listeners were to be judges of things past.

Quite informally, Lavinia went through stages of development in both her speaking and listening skills. When she was four she listened to and repeated, "Row, Row, Row with Roosevelt." She had memorized the speech, but she was not aware of the message. She was listening on a nonparticipatory level and it was natural for her to substitute an easy phoneme for a difficult one because of her limited ability at that age to imitate sounds. Later on, she listened on a level that said, "I hear, I repeat back, and I obey." But she still was not participating entirely in the events because she was busy thinking of next week's movies, or of the latest Sinatra record. Her most active listening took place when she listened to the sounds around her in a changing city; when she listened to the speaker who came to the class and spoke about inequality. She was *ready* for that experience after almost a decade of shutting out certain sounds that demanded her involvement. In the 1970s she was ready for new ideas, confident of her speaking abilities, anxious to voice her opinions.

*We are born with the ability to make and hear sounds, but learning to speak and listen effectively takes years.*

Surely our speaking and listening skills depend very much on our view of the world around us. Subconsciously we may feel things aren't worth our attention, but it is impossible to retire from the world forever and still be a public speaker and a public consumer of messages. Withdrawal and participation are just not compatible.

Fortunately, judging from the number of public speeches given in America every day, there is little chance that silence will prevail for any period of time. Even the quiet times are literally blasts of silence interspersed with oral arguments.

More than any other time in history Americans seem to be endowed with the knack of talking. In Greece and ancient Rome, speechmaking in government reigned supreme. Through the middle ages speechmaking was an instrument for converting nonbelievers to Christianity. In Britain, and during the Renaissance, the art of rhetoric became an intellectual pursuit.

In the United States there are no boundaries. Speechmaking survives in spite of the technological methods of disseminating information. It survives on all levels. There are those highly specialized formal speaking occasions in which few of us are ever involved: a nationally televised campaign speech, addressing 2,000 members at a convention, announcing a football game to 80,000 screaming fans. There are also those situations that call for public speeches in front of small audiences of from five to 100 people. How many of the following situations have you considered to be platforms for public speeches?

- Accepting the best athlete award at the junior high sports banquet.
- Giving an oral book report to the eighth grade English class.
- Welcoming the family at the annual reunion.
- Giving the fund-raising report to the CYO (AZA, BBG, etc.) youth group.
- Giving your "gang" its pep talk before the next "rumble."

- Running for office in college.
- Giving the weekly project report to your club (sorority).
- Giving your fund-raising report to the Kiwanis, Rotary, Lions, Optimist, etc., club.
- Accepting the winning bowling league trophy.
- Saying a special "grace" before a meal at the family outing.
- Giving a report to the PTA group on low standards in classes.
- Addressing your homeowners' association on declining property values.
- Telling your church or synagogue group about a coming project.
- Explaining a new product line to the workers.
- Presenting the blueprints for the new building to the board of directors.
- Giving the annual report to the stockholders.
- Giving a speech to the community as a member of your organization's speakers' bureau (academic, business, military).
- Telling the 15 kids playing in your neighborhood to keep quiet so you can sleep.

What do the following jobs have in common?

- Quarterbacks
- Politicians
- Clergy
- Teachers
- Trainers
- Entertainers
- Business leaders
- Military officers
- Stadium announcers
- Radio/TV announcers
- Tour guides
- Coaches
- Policemen
- Firemen
- Sports instructors
- Theatre directors
- Union leaders
- Airline hosts, hostesses, pilots
- Fashion show announcers

- Journalists/authors
- Public relations and advertising specialists

You are right if you answered "public speaking."

When you examine the number of persons holding such jobs in America today, when you include the millions of persons who, in their daily lives, give similar speeches to those mentioned above, it is plain to see that public speaking is a lifetime experience.

While we cover the techniques that are useful for those formal occasions we mentioned, this book is especially geared to all those varied and seemingly insignificant occasions when we stand up and speak out, when we seek to reveal by speech our own feelings, thoughts, and values in order to persuade others to believe and feel with us and to act upon our recommendations.

This book is for that person who spends a lifetime standing up and speaking out and feels it's time to find out what it's all about.

## SUMMARY QUESTIONS

- What were some of the major events in Lavinia's life which resulted in her giving public speeches?
- Why was it so easy for Lavinia to deliver her first classroom speech in 1961?
- What public speeches do you think are typically given by:
  a) students?
  b) business leaders?
  c) quarterbacks?

## EXERCISE

Trace your own life to discover the many times you stood up and spoke out: at a family gathering, at church, school, clubs, in a job, at a meeting in the park, etc. Then try to remember those times when someone's speaking impressed you, whether the speaker was a national figure or the grade-school teacher. Write your own "Lavinia" story. Remember to consider public speaking as *any* event when you spoke to *any* audience, *no matter what the size,* in a *public* situation.

## REFERENCES

1  *Row, Row, Row With Roosevelt,* by Eddie Dowling and Fred Coots. Copyright © 1932, 1959 by Sam Fox Publishing Co.
2  Ernie Pyle, *Here is Your War* (New York: Holt, 1944).
3  W. Abbott, "Cleveland: A City Collapses," *Forum Magazine,* Sept. 1938, pp. 99–103.

# 2 PREPARING FOR THE EVENT

Maria knew she'd be called upon today to give her report. After all, it had been three weeks since the club president had asked how the garage sale to benefit the Chilean earthquake victims was coming. That's why she had taken the time yesterday to call a meeting of her committee and to later put the summary of their plans on a note card. She knew the president was sometimes tricky and would call on committee members when they least expected. Maria guessed right.

As she spoke to the forty people in the small meeting room, Maria stood in front of them, but taking advantage of the intimate surroundings, she felt free to speak in a low voice and look almost all of them in the eye. She also knew better than to let her report go beyond five minutes, with questions, since her listeners were all getting ready to go home. As Maria sat down, her friend Nancy smiled and congratulated her on a nice report. "Thanks," said Maria as she gave a big sigh, "I was ready, but I was scared to death!"

Inexperienced as she was in public speaking, Maria had managed to prepare herself by getting her information collected, organized and noted. She had little choice in what she would say. Because she was head of the garage sale committee, it was only natural that her club would ask her for specific information on the committee's plans. Contributing to her preparation was her knowledge of her audience: about forty middle-aged women members of the Women's Activist Society many of whom she had known and loved for several years. She knew generally what they liked and disliked, especially about community matters. By adapting her delivery to the physical setting and time of day, Maria further demonstrated both her preparation and flexibility. She was able to do all this in spite of her completely normal feelings of nervousness and apprehension.

Whether you soon will speak to your civic club, your church, your office staff, your construction crew, your class, your PTA, or your family reunion, adequate preparation of what you will say and how you will say it can only improve your effectiveness. Preparation generally requires that you give some thought to yourself, your audience, and your environment.

## PREPARING YOURSELF

Among the factors you should consider in preparing yourself for your speech are your subject, your purpose, and your attitude toward yourself and your speech. Also important is your ability to locate needed materials, organize them meaningfully, select a style appropriate for the audience and occasion, and deliver the speech at the scheduled time and place. Since we will devote later chapters to most of these factors, our primary concern now will be the first three: subject, purpose, and attitude.

### Subject

Unless you are a professional public speaker, toastmaster, or speech student, you will rarely select the *general* subject of your speech. Most of us are not in a position to choose among a wide variety of possible subjects and topics. More typically, we are thrust into a speaking situation as Maria was, with our subject predetermined or influenced by our own expertise and reputation, our jobs or assignments, our travels and hobbies, our audience's goals, or the needs of the occasion and the times. On some occasions, however, we will not select our topic until *after* we have completed our analysis of the audience's needs and expectations. It's important to realize that whether we select our topic first or analyze our audience first depends on several factors related to the *specific* speech we have to deliver.

*You will choose your topic far less than it will choose you.*

The drill sergeant has learned from experience exactly what to say to new recruits when they get off the bus, and he also knows *how* to say it. The training director has as little latitude in preparing the content of training modules as has the third grade teacher in preparing lesson plans. Prior to the game in which his team is a 35-point underdog, the football coach is confident that the best he can tell his players is to survive and not to look too foolish. (In fact, one coach once said this to his team before they played Ohio State.) Returning from a tour of the Far East, Doug knew exactly what his Rotary Club wanted him to say. Since it was his turn to address his stamp club, Alan's freedom to speak was limited to which "presidential plate blocks" he demonstrated. Police captain Walters was aware of the crime wave hitting the city, but as he stood before the morning shift in the briefing room, he couldn't afford the time to say more than a few words and then give out the day's assignments. Speaking at her AA meeting, Ruth was very sensitive to their personal need to hear her say, "I am an alcoholic, and here's my story . . ."

Although you will choose your topic far less than it will choose you, your responsibility to the subject of your speech does not end with its selection. You still must determine which aspect of your general subject you will speak about. In other words, you must narrow down your topic so that it is appropriate for the audience and manageable within the given time constraints. For example, our traveler Doug could speak about the different foods he sampled in Japan, Hong Kong, and the Philippines. Or, should he desire, he could discuss the politics, the climate, the clothing, the customs, the sports, the economy, etc. Even if he chose to discuss the sports, he would still need to considerably limit his talk, since the Rotarians could only spare 20 minutes before having to leave for work. Influenced by his time limit, his personal interest in baseball, his knowledge that his club had sponsored a Little League team (and the availability of the 97 slides he had had developed), Doug decided to speak on the differences between Japanese and American baseball games.

*Often your speaking time will be limited.*

Sometimes you may be lucky (or unlucky) enough to have complete choice over both your general subject area and specific speech topic. Now what do you do? What will you talk about? How will you decide? Although many inexperienced speakers may feel frustrated and say, "I just don't know what I can talk about; I haven't anything to say," the problem is more often one of selecting one of the *several hundred* topics you can speak about. That's right, we said several hundred. To illustrate the enormous availability of topics to you, we would like to share with you the thoughts of this chapter's writer as he sat in his motel room thinking about this chapter. Note the myriad of possible speech topics generated from a little self-brainstorming in just one environment:

**The problem is often to select one of many possible topics.**

Well, here I am again. My typewriter is awaiting me. I wonder if it needs to be cleaned? If so, how is it done? (1. The proper care and cleaning of your typewriter.) I see the blue walls, blue ceiling and blue rug in this room. Someone likes blue. Why do motels choose such bland colors and ugly paintings? This mural on the wall above my bed is a classic case—a picture of a swamp. (2. Colors and moods: the effect of motel decorations.) Do they get these at auctions? For that matter, they must get all their furniture at the same auction. (3. Motel auctions: bargains and junk collections.) The managers of this place must be really affected by the recession. I can see that my TV is locked to the dresser. Crime must be a problem in this city. (4. Crime problems in motels: precautionary measures.) I wonder how much my bill is affected by crime and vandalism here. (5. Motel bills: the effect of the criminal and vandal.) The speaker on the wall plays good listening music. It helps me relax as I write. But I wish I could change the station occasionally. I don't understand why they don't give us radio dials. (6. Motel comforts: the choice of radio moods.) My room is on the second floor and I have the curtains drawn open so that the sunlight will come in. It's so clear that I can see the mountains in Grants over 60 miles away. They still have snow on their peaks. The sky here is blue and unpolluted; the air is so clean and fresh. (7. Climate conditions in the "land of enchantment.") I can see why solar energy is popular in this state. (8. Solar energy fur the future: implications for the homeowner.) An old lady just walked by carrying a small bag of groceries. I wonder if she gets all the food she needs on her fixed income from social security? (9. Fixed income in bad recessions: the plight of social security recipients.) It's relatively quiet outside. I'm glad because I don't concentrate with noise pollution. (10. Sanity and noise pollution: what can be done by the citizen?) I'm looking in the mirror and I can see that although I shaved, my face still has lots of stubble on it. I just changed blades too. That entire industry probably needs some regulation. (11. Cuts and bruises: the regulation of the shaving industry.) As I write, I keep thinking of the meal we had last night in the French restaurant. I asked the chef for his recipe but he politely refused. I wonder how many chefs keep their recipes a secret. (12. Culinary success and kitchen secrecy: profits from gourmet cooking.)

**Let one thought trigger another.**

During this process of brainstorming, random thoughts would sometimes trigger other thoughts, ideas, plans, or feelings. Some of these would be incidental and fade away as quickly as they arrived. Still, others would connect with a particular feeling—anger, frustration, happiness, or sadness. Those thoughts or topics which generate feelings inside you may be the kind you care about or have some interest in. Such topics may be good starting points for your selection of a worthwhile speech subject.

Whether your task is to choose a general or specific subject, you can greatly simplify this job by using the accompanying checklist. The more checkmarks you can honestly make on this list, the more appropriate will be your subject and the more effective your speech.

---

**SUBJECT CHECKLIST**

___ Are you knowledgeable about your subject? (through readings, experiences, research, occupations, travel, etc.)

___ Are you interested in your subject?

___ Do you know your subject well enough to handle questions?

___ Is your audience interested in your subject?

___ Is your subject appropriate for your audience?

___ Is your subject appropriate for the occasion?

___ Is your subject timely or significant?

___ Have you narrowed down your subject sufficiently for the time limit?

___ Is your subject appropriate for your purpose?

___ Is your subject suitable for the physical setting of the speech?

---

*The best communicators are those who can closely identify with and relate to their listeners.*

The best communicators are those who can closely identify with and relate to their listeners. Thus, your speech subject should definitely be one which follows a thorough analysis of who your listeners are, what they expect from the speech, and why they're coming to hear you. Later we will discuss how you can adequately prepare for your audience, but for now keep in mind that sometimes a speaker thinks the subject is just perfect for the audience only to later be greatly disappointed. One teacher of speech, when confronted by her fourth speech on abortion (by a male student) proclaimed, "If I hear one more speech on abortion, I'm going to start wondering why you're all so interested in it."

Traditionally, politicians choose speech subjects and issues which they think hold great interest for their audiences. Despite their use of surveys and polls, politicians sometimes make mistakes about what will be important and interesting to the electorate. During the 1972 presidential campaign, Edmund Muskie's wife told an off-color story overheard by some reporters. When word reached the powerful New Hampshire publisher, William Loeb, he attacked both Muskie and his wife for their bad taste and "unpresidential-like" conduct. Believing that the electorate would sympathize with his position, Muskie went to New Hampshire and, although Loeb wasn't in his office at the time, delivered a highly emotional speech attacking Loeb and his

"yellow journalistic techniques." So touched was Muskie, so angry was he at the attacks upon his wife, that during the speech he broke down and openly cried. The reaction was swift and cruel—for Muskie! Although he won the New Hampshire primary, he was soundly attacked throughout the American editorial pages for allowing himself, a presidential candidate, to show emotion, to cry.

A similar fate almost befell Jimmy Carter in the 1976 presidential campaign when he gave his famous *Playboy* interview in which he openly discussed his occasional "mental lusting" for women other than his wife.

## Purpose

Closely related to *what* you say in your speech is *why* you are saying it. Subject and purpose are influenced by similar factors. When you refer to your purpose, you are talking about your goals, your objectives, your desired outcomes. You are talking about your reason for speaking. Just as you typically have little control over your subject matter, so is your purpose often dictated to you by your own reputation and expertise, by the audience's needs and interests, and by such environmental limits as time, occasion, job duties and requirements. For example, after your listeners have finished a satisfying meal, they are hardly in the mood for a serious talk on the evolution of man, the causes of lung cancer, or the pros and cons of mercy killing. Your purpose in this instance will be dictated by your audience's need for a relaxing, entertaining, light speech, to coincide with their currently jovial mood. When Doug was invited to tell the Rotary Club about the Far East, it was because the members wanted some facts about his travels in specific countries. This doesn't mean that Doug must restrict himself to presenting straightforward information. In fact, he will, as most speakers do, give his audience some information, make them feel good (by telling some jokes), and perhaps even persuade a few Rotarians to call their local travel agents.

*You may have more than one reason for speaking.*

In other words, you may have more than one reason for speaking; you may have several reasons that all interrelate. Occasionally, they may conflict with one another. A politician may desire to give his listeners information about "the mess in Washington" and find that his speech also results in creating audience bad will for him, since he was one of the politicians who helped contribute to that mess.

The key to determining what the purpose or purposes of your speech will be lies in answering the questions, "What do I want to happen as a result of my speaking?" and "What do I want the audience to know, believe, feel, or do?"

Do you want to increase their knowledge and processing of information? Do you want to teach, educate, or enlighten them on certain facts, principles, ideas, or concepts? If so, then you may be giving a report as a student does to his English class about a book he's just read, or as a company president does to her stockholders on the company's current assets and liabilities, or as a sales manager does to his sales force about the applications of transactional analysis to sales situations. If you want your audience to understand you and your ideas, then you may be giving lectures as millions of teachers and professional speakers have done over the years. If you want your listeners to acquire new information, then you may be giving them directions, as a foreman may do to his construction crew on how to handle heavy equipment without endangering their lives, and as a coach does to his football team by showing them how to run the next pass play.

Do you want your audience to accept you, your beliefs and behaviors? Do you seek to influence them in some way? If so, then you may be advertising or selling a product, or promoting an institution or its name, as the oil companies' public relations spokesmen are now doing. Do you seek to convince or persuade your audience? If so, then you may be seeking their money (as do fundraisers), their time (as do civic clubs), their verdicts (as do attorneys).

**What are you trying to accomplish?**

Are you trying to improve your audience's feelings or relationships? Are you trying to get them to relax and enjoy themselves? If you seek good times for them and you, then you give after-dinner speeches on such things as (for example) the sexual stereotypes found in our language or a speech of welcome at the annual family reunion. Do you want your audience to increase its liking and respect for a person, idea, or event? If so, then you want what hundreds of commencement speakers every year desire, what thousands of clergy seek every week. Are you trying to inspire your listeners? If so, then your objective is similar to the coach whose Sunday pep talks with his football players are legendary, to every keynoter or nominator at a political convention, and even to the protesters and rioters seeking to disrupt our institutions. Thus, we have shown that although you may have several purposes in mind when you begin to speak, you typically will be giving your audience information, seeking to influence their opinions or beliefs, or improving their feelings and relationships.

**Central idea**   Whatever the goals, whatever the outcomes, both your purpose and your subject can be treated generally or specifically. Your purpose can be limited by using the same criteria you use to narrow your subject. In fact, the two will probably be done simultaneously. When you can clearly and succinctly state (in one sentence) exactly what you want to say to and get from your audience, then you have succeeded in phrasing both your specific subject and your purpose. Sometimes this one-sentence statement of the main point of your speech is called the *central idea*.

Note the thought processes in this example of a speaker narrowing his speech subject from the general to the specific, starting with a broad subject and ending with a detailed central idea. "Sports are definitely becoming more of a big business today than they used to be. Owners of sports franchises are constantly raising ticket prices, players are demanding higher salaries, and even concession stands are bilking the public. Football players seem to be getting the most money today, especially quarterbacks and running backs. Neil Anderthal just signed a multi-million dollar contract making him one of the highest paid professional football players. I will tell my class about the details of his contract and let them decide if they think he was worth all that money." Thus, his central idea is: Neil Anderthal may not be worth the money he's being paid. In giving the audience information about the player's contract and asking them to form an opinion on his worth, this speaker is trying to both inform and persuade his audience.

**What's your central idea?**

Thus, among your first tasks as a speaker are the selection and narrowing of both your subject and your purpose. Stating the essence of both in your central idea will help synthesize your thinking and make your later research and organizing tasks a lot simpler.

## Attitude

You start to sweat under your arms and in the palms of your hands. Your hands, legs, and knees begin to tremble. Your heart beats faster and you become short of breath. Your mouth is dry, your throat tremoring and your stomach queasy. If you are like many Americans, you are probably about to either board an airplane or give a public speech. A 1973 survey of 2500 adults showed that almost 41 percent feared giving a speech before a group more than doing anything else.[1] This speech fear or apprehension is sometimes called "stage fright" and refers to the anxiety associated with either real or anticipated public speaking. Speaking about stage fright, Harry Truman once remarked:

*I heard a fellow tell a story about how he felt when he had to make speeches. He said when he has to make a speech, he felt like the fellow who was at the funeral of his wife, and the undertaker had asked him if he would ride down to the cemetery in the same car with his mother-in-law. He said, "Well, I can do it, but it's just going to spoil the whole day for me."*[2]

Some degree of stage fright is very normal, and most speakers seem to experience this. The remarks that follow are primarily addressed to those of you with similar reactions.

An analysis of normal stage fright shows the following syndrome: Certain *physiological symptoms* (increase in blood pressure, heartbeat, burning of more blood sugar, increase in the flow of adrenaline) result from *anxiety and fear* associated with giving public speeches; this anxiety is typically associated with the *insecurity* many speakers tend to feel as a result of their *lack of control* over the speaking situation.

Perhaps we build up a speech's importance to the point where we think we can be personally or emotionally damaged should we fail in the speech. Perhaps we are insecure because of our lack of experience either as speakers, or with a particular audience. Perhaps we are insecure because while we know we need the positive reinforcements available from successful speaking (applause, laughter, heads nodding), we fear not being able to get these rewards. In other words, our real fears may stem from the doubts we have about how the audience will respond to us as speakers and people. To illustrate: A vice president of a large multinational corporation once asked his speech trainer to accompany him to New York City, where he had to give a speech to an audience of security analysts. While flattered, the speech trainer replied, "I've done all I can for you now. The rest is up to you." The vice president came back, "But I need you in the audience. You know when to applaud and laugh, and the rest of the audience may not."

The reverse of this analysis of stage fright is the assumption that if only we could control our audience and our environment, we would then supposedly feel more secure, less anxious, and that we would ultimately experience fewer physiological symptoms of fright. *This assumption is the myth of stage fright!* We *perceive* that we don't have control over our situation (and thus our feelings) because of certain unknowns associated with the audience and the environment. We *perceive* that if we can control our audience and environment we can reduce our stage fright. The *myth* is that *we don't* already have control over our feelings. The *reality* is that *we do*, whether or not we increase our control over the audience and environment. The *reality* is that, while it is obviously to your advantage to have as much information about your audience as possible, the final decision about how this control or lack of control affects your feelings is yours and yours alone.

Among the typical long-range solutions to stage fright are: Build a positive attitude or get more experience. Among the short-range solutions are: Do a thorough audience analysis (to give you information to reduce your uncertainty and increase your control); be well prepared (know your speech, rehearse it, etc.); take several deep breaths (immediately before speaking); place your speech in its proper perspective (how important is it really going to be to your career and welfare?); use up some of your excess energy (by exercise, jogging).

*Some degree of stage fright is normal—but we can control our feelings.*

Some, or all, of these short- and long-range solutions may work for some of you some of the time. Given the complexities of human nature, the differences among situations and audiences, the unpredictability of people, you may still never cover all contingencies. Furthermore, given that most of these solutions are grounded in the *myth* that fright exists because of our lack of control over others and our environment, we would like to offer an alternative approach to handling stage fright, based on the principles of assertiveness training.

*Behavior can be changed before attitudes.*

**Assertiveness training for stage fright**[3] Assertiveness training is grounded in the belief that behavior can be changed before attitudes. Assertiveness is neither putting yourself down ("I can't speak, I don't know what to say," or "I can't speak, I'm not ready.") nor putting the audience down ("I can speak, I'm better than they are. They're just people."). Assertiveness is feeling confident that you've prepared your speech as best you can, accepting the fact that you don't exercise ultimate control over your audience and their behavior, accepting the concurrent fact that you can and will control your own behavior in the speech, and recognizing that you are likely to win (accomplish your purpose). The key to assertiveness in public speaking is to practice new behavior patterns based upon valid information about existing patterns.

The common nonassertive pattern in public speaking goes like this: "I'm afraid to speak because I'll lose control and my behavior will be bad (e.g., I'll forget my speech), and the audience will not like me and give me bad feedback (e.g., they may boo). This booing will then reinforce my bad feelings about speaking." The assertive pattern in speaking calls for the cycle to be broken by getting information about your nonassertive behaviors, changing them in practice situations, and receiving positive reinforcement for the new behavior.

The following thirteen steps are suggested as a method for applying the principles of assertiveness training to the public speaking situation where stage fright is a mediating factor. We offer them as a behavioral outline for implementing traditional suggestions for reducing stage fright, such as "get in the proper frame of mind," "get lots of experience," "be prepared." We make no guarantees, but firmly believe that following all the steps may help remove some of the stage fright you now experience when you give public speeches.

Step 1    *Observe your own public speaking* (by audio or video tapes or personal feedback). Are you speaking adequately? Are you satisfied with your effectiveness in public speaking? If you are ineffective, is your apprehension and fright contributing to this ineffectiveness? How?

Step 2    *Keep track of your stage fright.* Make a diary of those public speeches where you think you failed because of stage fright, or where you avoided speaking for similar reasons.

**Step 3**   *Concentrate on a particular speech where you had stage fright.* Imagine yourself delivering a speech where you are highly nervous and apprehensive. Think about the details and your feelings during and after the speech.

**Step 4**   *Review your speaking behaviors in this speech.* Write down your verbal and nonverbal behaviors in this stage fright situation. In what ways were you behaving confidently? Apprehensively? Note the differences; e.g., when you were *apprehensive,* did you speak faster, did you avoid looking at the audience, did you hide behind a podium, did you forget your speech? When you were confident, did you look directly at the audience, did you gesture naturally, did you speak in a level, well modulated voice, did you speak slowly and deliberately?

**Step 5**   *Observe an effective public speaking model.* Watch a speaker who handles a similar speaking situation effectively. Observe particularly such nonverbal behaviors as voice, facial expressions, gestures, movement, and articulation. If the speaker is a friend, talk to him or her about his or her speaking approach.

**Step 6**   *Consider different speaking behaviors.* What other speaking behaviors and techniques could you have used? Would your responses have been more effective? For example, maintain good eye contact with listeners, face the audience directly, lean toward them, avoid artificial or contrived gestures by using only those that are natural to you and congruent with your message, maintain facial expressions consistent with the emotions you are expressing, avoid whispering or shouting by maintaining a level, well-modulated voice, avoid articulation errors by speaking slowly and deliberately.

**Step 7**   *Imagine yourself speaking in that situation.* Close your eyes and imagine yourself speaking effectively in the situation. You could behave as the effective speaker described above or differently. Be natural and assertive. Keep imagining this until you imagine a comfortable speaking style for yourself (using some or all of the above-mentioned behaviors) which is successful and effective.

**Step 8**   *Rehearse the speech.* Try out the speech either alone (perhaps in front of a mirror) or in front of friends, family, or colleagues, using the new behaviors you imagined above. Carefully log your behaviors (using paper or tape).

**Step 9**   *Get feedback from your listeners.* Ask your friends for honest feedback on your strengths (which you should note to repeat) and weaknesses (which you should replace with different behaviors, as discussed in Step 6).

**Step 10** *Re-rehearse the speech.* Based upon the feedback and the changes you have made, rehearse again (and again) until you feel comfortable and natural with the different behaviors.

**Step 11** *Deliver your speech.* Now you are ready to deliver the speech to the real audience. Your delivery (since you have prepared so well and practiced nonapprehensive assertive behaviors) should be almost automatic. If you doubt this, you need more rehearsing.

**Step 12** *Repeat the above process for future speeches.* You may feel that after speaking, you need more practice to develop the new behaviors to your satisfaction so they minimize stage fright.

**Step 13** *Develop reinforcements for effective speaking.* You will be able to give yourself reinforcement by connecting the "high feeling" after speaking to the actual speech. Think about that feeling and how it resulted from your control over your behavior. Also, your audience's responses (applause, nodding, laughter, etc.) will reinforce you and provide you with the security you seek from speaking.

As Lavinia sat waiting to address the state political convention, she remembered those thirteen simple steps and how they had helped her to get to that podium. Even though she experienced stage fright, Lavinia really liked public speaking and knew that it was important to her success in politics. Thus she always made a habit of tape-recording her speeches and logging those times when she was particularly ineffective due to speech anxiety. While listening to these speeches, she noted that she would speak much faster than her normal rate, would slur several words and often lack appropriate emphasis in her tone of voice. She realized that other politicians whom she regularly listened to on the campaign circuit rarely did these things. They typically spoke at a moderate rate with clear diction and appropriate vocal variety in their tones to increase the dramatic impact of their speeches.

She knew she could be as effective as they were and often imagined herself speaking with such a well-modulated voice. Fantasy became reality as Lavinia began to rehearse these three new voice-related behaviors. Long hours would pass as she would address her tape recorder, practicing her new rate, diction and tone. Occasionally she would let her son Gregory listen to one of her tapes. Gregory told her that although she seemed to be slowing down and speaking more clearly, she still was talking in a flat monotone.

More rehearsals and more sessions with Gregory finally corrected this last problem. As Lavinia began to address the convention, speaking deliberately, clearly, and dramatically, she began to feel genuinely relaxed and confident that her newly developed behaviors would help make her speech a success. In future visits to the political podium, she would often remember this surge of confidence coupled with the exhilaration provided by the loud audience applause. She knew these responses resulted from her ability to identify and correct previously ineffective behaviors.

## PREPARING FOR YOUR AUDIENCE

Bob stood before his class of two hundred New-Mexican students and began his lecture on intercultural communication by discussing the differences in nonverbal cues between "Anglos and Spanish Americans." Immediately almost half of his class began to shift uncomfortably in their seats and several visibly frowned. After his third reference to "Spanish Americans," five students actually got up and left the class.

Tom began his talk to the Advertising Club by discussing ads with propoganda techniques used by clients seeking sensationalism. Tom had determined that this would be a topic of high interest and Importance to his immediate audience. Tom presented lots of examples of border-line propaganda techniques used recently by an anti-Cable-TV group of advertisers. As he drew to a conclusion, he seemed perplexed and somewhat frustrated when only *one* person in the audience (the head of the Cable-TV organization) applauded.

## Why Analyze Audiences?

Both Bob and Tom could have avoided the negative reactions they received with some advance preparation and additional information. Bob needed to know that in New Mexico, most young students of Spanish descent prefer to be called "Chicanos." He could have found this out quite easily by asking any of his colleagues or students *before* he gave his lecture. Tom on the other hand, needed only to know that the designers of the very ads he was criticizing would be in the audience when he spoke. Although he might have kept his topic, he could have used a more friendly approach.

Unfortunately, most speakers (and people) probably behave much as Bob and Tom did, from an egocentric position which subordinates the audience's needs in favor of the speaker's ego and desire to talk *at* someone. Sales personnel have known for years that successful communicators find out first what their audiences want and need, and then proceed to give it to them. It's good business and good communication to identify yourself with your audience, since the goal of public speaking is to get something from an audience (understanding of ideas, acceptance of you or your beliefs and behaviors, appreciation of the feelings of yourself and others). The greater the similarity between senders and receivers of messages, the greater the chance of communicating effectively. If you view communication as a process in which senders and receivers mutually influence each other by sending each other messages, you will strive to involve your audience before, during, and after you interact with them—despite your egocentric tendencies to talk *at* instead of *with* others. Furthermore, as you have just seen, information obtained about your audiences prior to your speaking can reduce your uncertainty about how they may react to your speeches. This information may reduce the stage fright you feel before and during your speech.

As we present some information about the *what* and *how* of audience analysis, remember that control of the audience is not yours as a speaker. Each audience is composed of individuals, each with feelings, attitudes, and relationships formed prior to coming to your speech. Each one will understand you to the extent that he or she perceives your use of language (verbal and nonverbal) to communicate ideas and feelings approaching his or her own. Your audience will accept you and your ideas to the extent that it sees a need to do so. In other words, you must fulfill a need for it. Analyzing your audience can give you information which can expand your opportunity to accomplish your purposes, to make you more flexible as a speaker by adapting to it and its needs.

*Find out what your audience wants or needs.*

## What to Analyze

The basic rule to follow in conducting an audience analysis is to get as much information as you can to help you accomplish your purpose. What information about your audience can you use which will enhance your chances of getting across to it, of gaining its understanding, acceptance, or behavior change? This information typically relates to important logistics about the audience, demographics describing the audience, and attitudes held by the audience, individually or collectively.

**Logistics**  The size of the audience can give you some useful data. Larger audiences tend to differ in composition; this makes it more difficult for you to find similarities in background with which to identify. Emotional appeals tend to work better in larger audiences because an aroused audience member may find it easy to "hide in the crowd" and avoid being identified. If you doubt this, witness the behavior of your "unassuming" next door neighbor at the next professional football game you attend. Larger audiences also affect your delivery—for them you probably will need a microphone and a PA system, will be less able to use visual aids, will have to use more dramatic gestures, and will be unable to maintain eye contact with more than a few audience members (depending on the lighting arrangements). Larger audiences are more formal and prevent physical closeness between you and them. Information about the size of the audience is also useful if you plan to give any handouts during your speech.

Another important logistical consideration is the reason the audience has assembled. Were they invited? Are they there voluntarily or have they been required to attend your speech? If the latter (forced by a boss, team, teacher, etc.), they may be hostile toward you at first. Sometimes they have assembled just because their club or organization meets regularly. In this case, knowing the goals of the club will be most useful to you as a speaker, because you can aim your speech toward their expectations or adapt to their reactions.

*Knowing the audience's size, reason for attending, average age, educational background—all can help you get your point across.*

**Demographics**  Demographics are characteristics of audiences, such as age levels, educational differences, or sexual makeup. Although audiences are made up of several individuals, sometimes you may be able to draw inferences about audience preferences if you have sufficient numbers representing a particular demographic characteristic. For example, knowing the *age* of most of your audience members may clue you in to the best style and language: in any society older persons tend to be more conservative (many live on a fixed income and are quite conscious of fiscal matters), while younger audiences tend to be more idealistic and subject to emotional appeals.

Although we live in a liberated age today, some research seems to indicate that women tend to be more persuasible than men.[4] Thus, especially when you seek acceptance of your ideas, knowing the *sex* of your audience may give you a slight edge in framing your arguments. We also know that women are more easily persuaded by men and men more easily persuaded by women.[5] Some audiences are exclusively one sex or the other, such as the League of Women Voters or the Kiwanis Club. Recognizing that some of our language is inherently sexist in usage and interpretation may help a speaker avoid offending members of the audience.

The way you use language and examples, the way you frame main points and illustrate them, will all be affected by such demographic characteristics as *education, occupation* and *socio-economic* status. The more educated audiences will tend to understand your facts and also tend to be more critical of them. Given the state of the economy these days it is hard to predict differences in attitudes between the rich and the not so rich, but richer people tend to be more conservative (hold on to what they've got) than those who are financially less fortunate.

Information about the religion of audience members may be useful when one is speaking on certain emotional issues (abortion, liquor, gambling, birth control, mercy killing, etc.). For example, knowing that Mormons don't drink liquor, coffee and tea may help you avoid embarrassing examples in your speech.

Additional demographic data about *cultural/ethnic* breakdowns (to help you avoid using stereotypes and inappropriate racial jokes), *political affiliation* (to steer you away from inflammatory issues—such as Watergate for some Republicans), and *group membership* (American Legion, B'nai B'rith, AAUP, NAACP, etc., all have widely known goals) can also be of value to your preparation. For example, your audience analysis might cause you to vary the introduction to a speech on race relations for the American Legion and the NAACP in the following ways:

American Legion: ". . . *and I hope to show you tonight that just as men of all races fought and died together in our last world war, so should they work together now to combat today's hated enemies— recession and inflation.*"

NAACP: ". . . *and I hope to show you tonight that those businessmen who discriminate in their employment practices are to be condemned for their unlawful behavior.*"

**Audience attitudes**  Besides logistical and demographic data about your audience, information about their feelings toward you, your speech, the occasion, your purpose, etc. can directly affect your chances for success. In addition to knowing their attitudes, you should attempt to find out how strongly they are committed to those attitudes. If you disagree on issues, those who are more strongly committed (ego involved) to their attitudes will be much harder to persuade. If you agree with your audience, your purpose will probably be to reinforce their beliefs.

*Knowing your audience's attitude toward you and/or your topic should influence your approach.*

Audiences may be predisposed toward you, because of information circulated through a newsletter, your reputation as an expert in your field, or even personal contacts and friendships. Sometimes their attitudes toward you are formed when you arrive or are introduced; your pre-speech conversations, your physical appearance and dress all will contribute to these attitudes.* Your delivery during the speech will also influence the audience. Generally, the less they know about you, the more neutral they will probably be. The more information they have about you, the more favorable (or unfavorable) they will probably be toward you. Similarly, audiences may form attitudes about the occasion or other aspects of the environment, such as the ventilation system in the room. Finally, they will have attitudes toward your speech subject. The more timely, significant, controversial, or important the topic, the less neutral they may likely be toward it. If they don't perceive your topic as one of high interest to them, they will probably be quite apathetic toward it and you.

When confronted with a neutral audience, you should be objective and open-minded as you present straightforward reasoning and simple facts: "In the last five years, several of our nation's top corporations were involved in unethical and illegal practices. I would like to share some of the following statistics and examples with you."

*Neutral, friendly, apathetic, and hostile audiences all require different approaches by the speaker.*

With friendly audiences, you may be able to use more emotional appeals: "No matter how you try to gloss it over or cover it up, the corruption and scandal coming out of America's boardrooms in the last five years has been disgraceful!"

Apathetic audiences may need to be aroused and interested in your subject before you can deal with your major message. Telling short stories or appropriate jokes may help: "I see I'm going to have my work cut out for me. The situation reminds me of the two skeletons who were hanging in a closet at a medical school. One said to the other, 'How long you been in this place?' 'Dunno,' replied the second skeleton, 'But if I had any guts I'd get out of here.' "

Hostile audiences may require your finding some points of agreement before beginning to seek their acceptance of other ideas: "Now I'm sure that all of us corporate leaders assembled here today would agree that bad publicity is bad business. What I want to talk to you about is both of the above."

Sometimes humor at your own expense can be most helpful when confronted with extreme hostility.

If hostility results in heckling, you may decide to switch the direc-

---

*
The New York State Court of Appeals ruled unanimously that when tried for prison crimes, prison inmates must be allowed to wear street clothing rather than prison uniforms. The court opinion stated, "clothing sends a continuing visual communicant to the judge and jury." Clothing expert John Molloy insists that clothing sends messages and recommends wearing clothes in the following color combinations which tend to please almost everybody: blue, white and maroon; blue and beige; and gray and blue without patterns.[6]

tion of your humor, as did one speaker when a loud heckler constantly disrupted his message, "Sir, the last time I saw a mouth like yours, there was a hook in it!" Milton Berle once confronted a loud female heckler with the following gem, "Madame, didn't you heckle me here ten years ago also? I never forget a dress!" Sometimes, you may perceive hostility when it isn't really there. For example, when a speaker addressing the local Lions Club on inflation suddenly saw five members get up and walk out, he became quite nervous and stopped his speech to ask the audience if he had done anything wrong or said anything offensive. The chairman promptly pointed out to him that those five members had to get back to work early.

## How to Analyze the Audience

The effective speaker tries to gather audience data before, during, and even after the speech. Before a speech your best sources will be the host or arranger of the program (if one exists); prior experience with or knowledge about the audience; readings from organizational literature, pamphlets, and newsletters; published newspaper stories; libraries and other available data banks (Chamber of Commerce, private agencies); other audience members or club members; casual contacts in airports, parks, hotels, stores, and restaurants. Usually these sources are contacted personally, although sometimes telephone or written surveys can be conducted. At other times, simply reading available literature may give you some clues about your audience.

During a speech, your best source of data will be the nonverbal (and sometimes verbal) cues given by the audience—which you should monitor carefully. Do they get up and leave? Do they cough a lot? Do they close their books and shuffle their feet? Do they start whispering or talking? Do they laugh at appropriate times? Do they look at you and attempt to maintain eye contact? Do they applaud or cheer when they should or do they boo or shout instead? Do they sit there in stonefaced silence? Do they frown? Do they smile? Do their bodies shift uneasily in their chairs? Do they start to heckle you? Do they throw things at you?

*Remember that you can still gather audience data after the speech.*

After a speech you sometimes can remain a few minutes and ask audience members how they liked it. You can do informal surveys by asking the chairperson for some feedback. Or, should the situation (e.g., political campaign) warrant, you may seek formal feedback by means of such tools as surveys or interviews.

The accompanying checklist summarizes much of what we have said about audience analysis. The more checkmarks you can make, the better prepared you will be and the more success you will likely enjoy. However, as you will see in Chapter 10, (Speaker, You Have a Problem), this success is not always guaranteed.

## AUDIENCE ANALYSIS CHECKLIST

— Do you know how large your audience will be?

— Have you made plans for such things as visuals, PA, microphone, lighting, as a result of the audience's size?

— Do you know the circumstances under which the audience will be assembled?

— If so, have you made plans for the different contingencies (required, voluntary, group members, etc.)?

— Do you know the age distribution of your audience?

— Do you know the sex distribution of your audience?

— Do you know the educational level of your audience?

— Do you know the occupations represented by your audience?

— Do you know the socio-economic status of your audience?

— Do you know the religions of your audience?

— Do you know the cultural or ethnic composition of your audience?

— Do you know the political affiliations of your audience?

— Do you know what groups your audience belongs to?

— Have you made any plans based on your demographic inputs?

— Do you know your audience's attitudes toward you?

— Do you know your audience's attitudes toward the occasion?

— Do you know your audience's attitudes toward your subject?

— In general, do you know if your audience will be neutral, friendly, hostile, or apathetic?

— Have you made any plans to deal with their attitudes?

— Do you have a systematic plan for gathering data about your audience before you speak?

— Do you have a plan for observing your audience's reactions during your speech?

— Do you have a plan for gathering any reactions from your audience after your speech?

## PREPARING FOR THE ENVIRONMENT

When we speak, we do so in an environment whose composition may influence what we say and how we say it. It is to our advantage to be familiar with the speaking environment—the nature, time, and program of the occasion, and any factors relating to the physical setting of the speech. With sufficient lead time to gather needed information, we may avoid or minimize potential problems.

## Occasion

What is the main reason for the audience's presence? Is it a regular meeting of a group or organization? Is it part of their job? Is it an informal gathering of friends, family, or acquaintances? Or is it a more formal, special occasion, such as a commencement, holiday, banquet, or a commemoration honoring a person, event, or date? Is the occasion known to all the audience? Is it important to them? The occasion will definitely influence the subject and purpose of your speech. Sometimes you will have to take special steps; a speaker at an academic conference in Mexico, where consecutive translation was used to help the audience, was forced to speak much more slowly and deliberately than he normally did.

## Time

The season of the year may have some impact upon your speech and audience. For example, in colder regions of the country it is often necessary to cancel many speaking events because of bad weather conditions. During warmer times of the year, room facilities, such as air conditioning, may become more important. Of more immediate concern to you, however, should be the time of day or night that you are scheduled to speak, and the amount of time allotted for the speech.

If you are scheduled in early morning (e.g., at a breakfast meeting), the audience may still be tired and may need to be roused; often this is also the case in late afternoon speeches, when many are tired from work. A meal served before the speech, as discussed earlier, influences the mood of the audience. Speakers should adapt the type and length of their speech to the time of day they are scheduled. In 1972, George McGovern committed a classic mistake in timing when he delivered his nomination acceptance speech at 2:30 A.M., eastern time, when most Americans were either asleep or exhausted from the previous oratory.

The amount of time allotted for your speech will, of course, determine what and how much you can say. Your subject and purpose must be narrowed sufficiently to meet time constraints. If you are scheduled first on the program, you probably will have few problems imposed on you by limited time. However, if you are scheduled later in a program (if there are other speakers or reports), you may find the audience tired or disinterested (or leaving). You may, therefore, have to make some last minute adjustments in your speaking plans—as did the speaker who found herself with only five minutes left to deliver her twenty minute speech on oil spills: "After that lengthy introduction, I was beginning to wonder who was going to give the speech. I find myself with only a few minutes left. Had I more time you would have heard the following. . .''

## Program

If there are other speakers on the program, or if there is a theme, you should have this information. Consider exactly how you fit in with both the theme and the other speakers. Knowing their topics can give you some useful insights which you may relate to your own speech. On the other hand, this can work against you at times. One speaker who sat numbly listening to a previous speaker giving most of the speech that he himself had intended to deliver suddenly developed severe stomach cramps and was forced to leave immediately. Other speakers have been known, when this happens, to inhale deeply and deliver a short impromptu talk.

## Setting

Will the speech be indoors or outside? Different settings provide unique considerations of facilities and distractions.

**Indoors**  If you are speaking in a hall, auditorium, conference room, or classroom, you should get advance information about the room's size and facilities. The larger the room, the more formal the speech. Your movements, visuals, and voice will all be affected. You will need a PA system, use fewer visuals, need to exaggerate your movements, and use fewer gestures in larger rooms. In a smaller room, you have more freedom to become spatially intimate with your listeners, you can use vocal variety, sometimes even whispers, to enhance the dramatic impact of your speech. The shape of the room is also important. Is the room round? Can all listeners see you? Will your back be turned to some?

The room's facilities may affect your speech. Are there *seats*? If so, are they hard or soft? The former may cause your audience some discomfort and limit the amount of time they will listen to you. Are there enough seats or do some people have to stand? Is there a *platform*? Can you be seen without one? Recognize that although a platform may enable some audience members to better see you, it does formalize the situation and physically places more space between you and your listeners. During question periods some speakers choose to move down off the platform right into the audience. Johnny Carson and Carol Burnett regularly do this on their TV programs. Will you use a lectern or podium? If so, how big is it? Will it hide you from the audience? Does it have a light? Is there room for a glass of water? Is the microphone attached to the podium? If so, can it be adjusted for your height? Can you control the projectors or equipment from the podium?

Other facilities include a *PA system*. Is the microphone adjustable? Can you wear it round your neck? If you go into the audience, is the microphone cord long enough? You may find, if you take the

IS THERE A PLATFORM?

*The impact of a speech can be affected by many factors other than the speech content and the speaker's delivery.*

time to test the acoustics, that you don't need a PA system. This will make your speech less formal. When testing for acoustics, check out any dead spots or echoes in the room. As a rule it is probably better to avoid using a microphone unless you find yourself straining your voice to be heard.

If you are using any *equipment* or audiovisual aids, can the room be darkened? Will the equipment be delivered or do you have to bring it? Will there be a projectionist or will you have to run the equipment? If the latter, this will affect where you stand during the speech. If the former, you will need to rehearse with the projectionist so he or she knows exactly when to do what. Have you checked out the *lighting* in the room? Avoid spots and footlights, if you can, because they prevent eye contact with your listeners. Ideally, you should have the house lights turned on and some bright illumination over your head, to help you be seen. A word about *ventilation*: As a general rule it's better to be too cold than too hot because in the latter case your audience may tend to doze off. If you're in a large room, see if the temperature can be set at about 65 degrees; smaller rooms may call for warmer temperatures (68 to 70 degrees) because fewer people will be warming the room with body heat.

Finally, indoor settings are sometimes plagued by noise *distractions.* Other people may be whispering or talking, laughing or coughing. Waiters may be clearing tables, guests may be coming or going, fans may be humming. Sometimes you can wait a minute or two before beginning to allow for most distractions to disappear. Occasionally, you may need to make a frank appeal for attention. More often, effective and dynamic speaking on your part will call attention to itself. One speaker, annoyed by the distraction caused by several audience members stated, "If you stop listening before I stop speaking, raise your hand."

**Outdoors** Many of the concerns affecting the indoor speaker also influence those who speak outside in such places as stadiums, arenas, streets, or even on the grass in a park. However, due to the possibility of more distractions (noise from cars, airplanes, construction, people walking by), the outside speaker will usually require a PA system. Since sound tends to diffuse more widely outside than within a confined room, speakers should probably speak a little more slowly and distinctly when they are outdoors. Finally, such natural factors as the weather and the sun must now be accounted for. Have you made arrangements for inclement weather? Will you move inside or cancel? Also, bright sunlight can get in the eyes of the speaker or audience. Sometimes, arranging the platform away from the direct impact of the sun can minimize this problem.

Much of what we have said may at first appear to overwhelm you as you get ready for your speech, but effective speakers have long known that preparing themselves and their attitudes, and accounting for audience and environmental factors *in advance* of the speech, will most likely improve their chances for getting the results they want from their opportunity to stand up and speak out.

## SUMMARY QUESTIONS

- What three factors affect speech preparation?
- What are several reasons for giving a speech?
- What are several methods used to control anxiety or stage fright?
- Why should a speaker analyze his or her audience?
- How does a speaker analyze his or her audience?
- What environmental factors must be taken into consideration when speaking?

## EXERCISES

1 Select a room in your house and look around carefully. Then do some self-brainstorming and see how many topics you can generate from the objects around you.

2 Visit city council meeting, a university lecture hall, and a luncheon at which someone is speaking. Note how the environment affects the speaker's presentation.

3 Think of three instances in which politicians chose improper subjects for their audiences.

4 Choose a subject, then choose a purpose to fit it. Choose a purpose, then choose a subject to fit it. Note your ability to mold the mood for the speech in either case.

5 Choose a purpose, then think of an audience known to you and list its characteristics, molding your purpose around the audience.

## REFERENCES

1 "What Are Americans Afraid of?" *The Bruskin Report,* 1973, no. 53.

2 George Caldwell (ed.), *Good Old Harry* (New York: Hawthorn Books, 1966), p. 84.

3 This analysis and the 13 steps were adopted from R. Alberti and M. Emmons, *Stand Up, Speak Out, Talk Back!* (New York: Pocket Books, 1975), pp. 85-92.

4 Irving L. Janis and Peter B. Field, "Sex Differences and Personality Factors Related to Persuasibility," in *Personality and Persuasibility,* Carl I. Hovland and Irving L. Janis (eds.) (New Haven, Conn.: Yale University Press, 1959), pp. 55-68.

5 *Ibid.*

6 John T. Molloy, *Dress for Success* (New York: Warner Books, 1975), pp. 49-51, 164-165, 180-182, 230.

# DOING RESEARCH

As Julius walked to the school podium to tell the 300 alumni and administrators how to raise the $650,000 for their new building, he remembered the advice of his mother, now dead for 15 years, "When you start something, finish it and finish it well!" He knew this advice would be part of what he told this school audience, now frustrated by three previously unsuccessful campaigns. Julius appreciated failure. His own career as a fundraiser had been marked with many dismal experiences. He had also known success in the 23 years he'd studied and practiced his art. As he spoke to the group, he remembered the campaign in Athens, Ohio, where he had helped a woman's club of small membership to raise $47,000 in just one week by knocking on doors to solicit funds. He remembered the hospital staff in Ottawa whom he had persuaded to drive "bloodmobiles" into local neighborhoods, resulting in 1437 new blood donors. And how could he forget the Boston church rebuilt in just six months after he persuaded the church board to hold a telethon?

But Julius had never worked with a school before. During his speech, he remembered the hours he'd spent in the library going through newspaper stories of other school campaigns. He remembered the interview with the tax consultant to find out about the loopholes in tax laws that protect schools. He remembered the two visits he'd paid to schools in neighboring towns who'd made and lost money during similar campaigns. During the question period, he was glad he'd taken the time to copy some financial data from the almanac. As he sat down, he felt relieved. He had been able to answer all of the questions the audience had put to him, and was confident that he would be asked to direct their campaign.

*Before you speak, know what you're talking about.*

Before Julius could speak to this group, he had to gather information, to investigate the entire phenomenon of school fundraising. This investigation phenomenon is known as "doing research" and includes an instructor's memories of his five years of exercising before talking to his exercise group, and Lavinia's reading of several of Roosevelt's speeches prior to making her first appearance before her speech class.

## THE RESEARCH PROCESS

The research process can be summarized by the following steps:

**Step 1**  Assess your current knowledge (based upon memories, personal experiences, files, clippings, previous educational experiences).

**Step 2**  Determine the limits of your knowledge (by memory probes, conversations with others, skim reading).

**Step 3**  If adequate knowledge exists, proceed with your speech.

**Step 4**  If inadequate knowledge exists, seek additional data (by reading, interviewing, writing, observing, telephoning, etc.).

**Step 5**  Develop an initial structure for organizing the information.

**Step 6**  Record (by notetaking, taping, etc.) the data according to initial organizational structure.

**Step 7**  Evaluate information and structure (by talking to others, probing memories, continuing to read).

**Step 8**  Finalize structural pattern and inclusion of valuable data.

Although this research process is and must be initially time-consuming and extensive, you will actually be saving time and money by guaranteeing the accuracy of your data and, ultimately, a high quality product. In order to follow this process, you need to know *where* to go to get your information and *how* to get it once you're there. Today we have four major sources of information open to all of us: ourselves, others, libraries, and technologies. While it may appear that a successful speaker simply starts talking, the fact is that many hours have been devoted to obtaining information from these four major sources. You see and hear the product of the labor but not the labor itself.

*You need to know **where and** how **to get your information.***

Perhaps you will better appreciate and understand how Julius used his memories, personal experiences, talks with and observations of others, readings and on-site visitations to prepare for his speech if we tell you how two colleagues prepared for their book on transactional analysis. They began with their present knowledge and memories about how people relate to one another. They talked to each other, jarred each other's memories, fed on each other's ideas and responses, and took notes on these transactions. Next, they skimmed the indexes, tables of contents, prefaces, and main headings of books dealing with this subject. Once they saw what was there, they chose what they felt was most appropriate for their purposes. Then they read, took notes, and discussed the notes with each other and other experts whose opinion they valued. As they recorded their notes and synthesized their discussions, they began to formulate a structural pattern to the information they were collecting. This made their task of gathering information a little easier because they could now start to code the data into meaningful categories. They knew this would make their retrieval job a lot easier when they sat down to write. As they continued to read, take notes, and discuss, they were able to discriminate among the data and evaluate their actual worth to the book. They also were able to jar additional personal memories and examples. These examples were supplemented with phone calls to known transactional analysis experts (for additional examples), visits to transactional analysis workshops (for observations and taping), and informal talks with family and friends. Finally, after discarding the useless and organizing the pertinent, they formalized an outline, inserted the examples, did a final check with each other, and began to write.

## OURSELVES

You may be your own best source of information. Your travels, work, reading, observing, listening, studies, and play all contribute to your lifetime of personal experience. Tragically, this vast and rich source of data may go unused if you are unaware of its existence or if you lack the skills to tap into your memory banks. You may never have gone to Europe, led a gang, sold beer, run for office, taught an exercise class, or raised money for a school. However, you *are* a rich source of experiences, stories, and images. Everyone is, only some have never learned to perceive, to be aware, to remember. To effectively use yourselves as resources, you must increase your perceptual and memory skills.

### Increasing Your Perceptual Skills

You may have recently sold soft drinks or beer at a football game but not been *aware* of all the stimuli which interacted with you during the experience. Or you may have been aware but failed to attach significance or meaning. The first case is a problem of perception, the second, of communication. Failure to attach meaning to stimuli means that you have filed a piece of information in your data bank without giving it any message value. You can only use as messages those stimuli to which you have attached meaning.

**Awareness**  Consider these examples of perceptual gaps: You may not have seen the competition selling beer across the field; you may have had a stuffy nose and so not smelled the foul aroma emanating from the garbage bags next to your stand; you may not have noticed that your own beer had become flat; you may not have heard the referee's whistle signalling the end of the game. All of these were real experiences which escaped your perception.

*Remember, you may be your own best source of information.*

Heightening your sensitivity to experiences means "listening with a third ear" and "reading between the lines." Sharpening your powers of observation means paying close attention to such details as sizes, shapes, colors, objects, events, smells, tastes, sounds, textures. When you sit in a bus terminal waiting room, stand in line in a crowded theater lobby, dodge traffic on busy streets, or leisurely bike in your open parks, you need to apply all your senses and take in as much as you can. As you become aware of more stimuli, you build the size of your data banks with potentially useful information which can help both your communication and your memory skills.

**Meaning**  What is the use of the information you gather if you fail to attach any significance or meaning to it? This failure is a communication problem, because if information has no meaning, you can't use it either in your current communications or in triggering past memories. You may see a friend selling beer in the next row of the stadium and not link his presence with a drop in your sales. You may smell the garbage next to your stand but fail to connect the foul aroma with the lack of customers. You may taste your beer but not associate its flat taste with your friend selling his faster than you are selling yours. You may hear the referee's whistle but not realize that the game has ended. When you attach meaning to information, you can use it in your daily communication, you can form messages which will allow you to interact with others. As you will see later, the degree of success you have with others will be, to some degree, a function of how closely the meanings you attach to stimuli correspond with the meanings attached by other people. But this will all be in vain if you fail to attach meaning and relevance to the stimuli you perceive. Sometimes, discussing an experience, including all the details, with other people may help you to attach meanings. For example, if your boss reads your automobile sales report, tells you it's awful, and tells you why, you may begin to attach some meaning to its inadequacies. Sometimes reading will help you to attach meaning to stimuli. After you have read books on the importance of writing brief, clear, and substantive reports, you may attach meaning to the boss' comments or the drop in sales. Without meanings, later recall of information may be difficult, if not impossible.

## Increasing Your Memory Skills

Plato said, "knowledge is to remember." You may have had the experience of standing in the unemployment line—and you may have attached meaning to it. But over the years you may forget the experience, and so lose the ability to use it in your messages. A computer, with its memory core, is able to store large volumes of data. Humans put the information in the computer and maintain records of

what and where it is; by using the right program, humans can get it back out. (Although at times highly specialized, this process is basically routine.)

With human memory, however, the process is much more random. Like the computer, you have the data in memory banks. And like the computer, you use programs to get it out. Unlike the computer, however, your programs are often random or serendipitous, seldom written with any structure. Typical of the way human memory works is the story told by Thomas Harris in his best-selling book, *I'm OK—You're OK:*

*A forty-year-old female patient reported she was walking down the street one morning and, as she passed a music store, she heard a strain of music that produced an overwhelming melancholy. She felt herself in the grip of a sadness she could not understand, the intensity of which was "almost unbearable." Nothing in her conscious thought could explain this. After she described the feeling to me, I asked her if there was anything in her early life that this song reminded her of. She said she could not make any connection between the song and her sadness. Later in the week she phoned to tell me that, as she continued to hum the song over and over, she suddenly had a flash of recollection in which she "saw her mother sitting at the piano and heard her playing this song." The mother had died when the patient was five years old. At that time the mother's death had produced a severe depression, which had persisted over an extended period of time, despite all the efforts of the family to help her transfer her affection to an aunt who had assumed the mother role. She had never recalled hearing this song or remembering her mother's playing it until the day she walked by the music store.*[1]

Had this forty-year-old never heard the song when she was four, or had she heard it but attached no meaning ot it (when the mother died), no feelings of depression would have haunted her in the present. The more stimuli you perceive and the more information you attach meaning to, the greater will be your chances to trigger past memories when you communicate in the present.

If you are to maximize your potential as a source of information, it is to your advantage to:

1  Increase your world of experiences.

2  Increase your ability to perceive information during these experiences.

3  Increase your ability to attach meanings to these perceived data by finding relations between the objects of thought.

4  Increase your ability to recall meaningful data.

By following these steps, you will be using all your past memories to enrich your communication in the present and future.

## OTHERS

As the cabbie drove him into the city for his speech to the weight watchers' meeting, Marty talked with the driver about dieting. She volunteered, "You know, the biggest headache I've got now is paying for my husband's new wardrobe." Marty smiled and immediately jotted down the cabbie's comments, perhaps to use in his speech later.

Other people, sometimes formally and sometimes quite casually, can be a rich source of information for you as you do research. You may be chatting with a colleague over coffee, engaged in a heated family discussion over dinner, having a bull session with friends, watching two people in an airport terminal, writing to your congressman, or interviewing a fellow student. All afford you the opportunity to review your own thinking process, check out your ideas, probe your own memory banks, and get the opinions and reactions of others.

For his debut at the sales meeting, a new sales manager sought expert advice from previous sales managers before he spoke on effective sales techniques to the new recruits. A gym teacher wrote to three exercise teachers for new routines before she spoke to her class. Patrick, a gourmet, watched three chefs make shrimp and crab chantilly before he attempted to teach it to his gourmet club. And an office-seeker polled a sample of all the voters in her district before announcing her candidacy.

While friends, family and co-workers can provide you with a casual sounding board for testing your ideas, experts and authorities can give you hard data to solidify your messages. Attending formal lectures, classes, or workshops sponsored by high schools, colleges, and businesses exposes you to such expert opinion. Usually businessmen and -women are more than willing to give you their expert advice on photography, stereophonic equipment, travel, and clothing. They may even tell you the names of others to see for additional information. Patrick, the gourmet, seldom missed an opportunity to go back to the kitchen and talk with the chef who prepared a meal he enjoyed. Sometimes he even "discussed" not-so-hot meals.

Whomever you seek for clarifying old information or giving you new, you usually rely on your skills of writing, observing, talking, and listening to collect these reactions and data.

**Research your topic; get other opinions.**

---

## Writing

Congressional representatives, business executives, college professors, and community leaders may have staffs to process your requests for information. Many organizations willingly provide reports, books, pamphlets, and newsletters. Much of this data is not in libraries because of the limitations of space, money, and time. For example, the American Medical Association provides pamphlets on health care in general and many diseases in particular, and many of these pamphlets you regularly find in your own doctor's waiting room. The *World Almanac* lists the addresses of "Associations and Societies in the U.S." to whom you may write for relevant information for your speech. *Government Reports Announcements and Index* combines references and abstracts for all technical reports typically subcontracted by the federal government to universities and industries. Reports in such varied fields as aeronautics, agriculture, astronomy, behavioral and social sciences, biological and medical sciences, chemistry, physics, and space technology can be ordered, once identified, from the National Technical Information Service of the U.S. Department of Commerce. The *Index to Publications of U.S. Congress* includes everything ever published by Congress, including all testimony to all committee hearings. To use this index, you need only know, for example, the name of the person who provided testimony to a congressional committee, and by writing to the U.S. Government Printing Office, you can receive a copy of his or her testimony.

Whomever you write to, you should address your letter to a specific person (as opposed to such nonentities as "Dear Sir," "Dear Madam," "To Whom It May Concern") and be clear, precise, and concise in your request. The sample letter below illustrates three qualities. Occasionally, you may have time to survey several people at once by using a questionnaire. Mail questionnaires typically bring from 8 to 12 percent return rates. However, you can improve your chances of getting valid responses. Sending out about ten times the number you need back, drawing a sample either totally at random or purposefully according to some valid criteria (e.g., surveying all doctors in your neighborhood), enclosing a self-addressed stamped envelope, promising a copy of the results, structuring your questionnaire with previously tested questions, leaving space for comments, and using very few questions all may help increase your return rate.

## Observing

Infants one month old can perceive and attach meanings to a variety of aural and visual stimuli. In fact, infants are much like video recorders, scanning and zooming, panning and dollying as they detect, record, and store a multitude of data in full-channel stereo and living color, to be replayed with feeling much later in life.

A REQUEST LETTER

Dr. Gary Richetto                                    May 18, 1977
The Williams Companies
Williams Center
Tulsa, OK 74136

Dear Dr. Richetto:

Please send me one (1) copy of your recent report,
"The Nation's Fading Energy Supply," which you
released in March 1977. I would like to use the
information in the report for my graduate class.
Your attention to this request would be most
appreciated. Thank you.

Sincerely,

Lavinia Adams

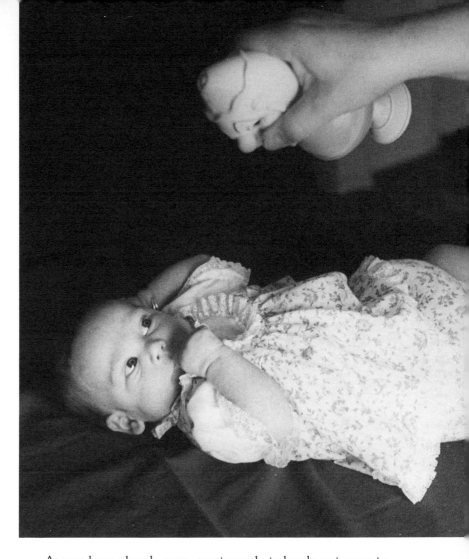

As you have already seen, most people today do not seem to possess the observation skills of little infants. Increasing your ability to perceive and record what you see others do will not only provide illustrative material for your speeches, but also facilitate your own recall of similar episodes. In addition to heightening your sensitivity to environmental cues, you can also improve your observation by being unobtrusive, recording on a note pad, or audio or video recorder, and comparing your observations with those of others who share the same experiences. Even these precautions may not result in truly valid data, as many of you may know from trying to piece together an accident story from the eyewitness observers.

## Talking and Listening

In doing research for your speech you may talk and listen to others during formal face-to-face interviews, telephone calls, or brainstorming sessions.

**Interviews** Interviewing authorities, like writing to them, takes much careful planning. Following a few basics of courtesy and process can help you to accomplish your purpose. First, you should plan to interview only those who can give you the answers to your questions. Avoid wasting the time of those who may not have what you need. If several people can help you, use sampling techniques to select your interviewees. Second, you should phone for an appointment and, once it has been arranged, follow-up with a written note reminding the interviewee of your coming. Finally, prepare an interview guide with sufficient probes (e.g., "why") written out in advance. The interview questions may be highly structured and closed-ended, calling for specific answers in a specific order, or they may be more flexible, allowing you to adapt the language and sequence of questions to the immediate needs of your interviewee. Note the difference between these two sets of questions asked of an oil company executive. The first set has specific, highly structured, closed questions; the second has open-ended questions.

*Closed questions*

Are you familiar with the causes of the recent oil spills off the New England coast?

Should there be tighter regulations in international shipping lanes to prevent such spills?

Should companies such as your own be responsible for financial losses suffered by fishermen affected by such spills?

Could you give me the figures on your own company's record with oil spills?

*Open-ended questions*

What is your opinion of the recent oil spills off the New England coast?

Tell me about your company's involvement with oil spills.

What recommendations do you have to prevent such spills?

*When interviewing, make sure that the interviewee understands the questions.*

Regardless of which approach to questioning you select, you should be aware that personal references or opinions, loaded or leading questions may have undesirable effects. However, do include sufficient probes and checks on the interviewee's understanding and responses (e.g., "In other words, you are saying . . ."). Remember, since you are using the interviewee's time, never take more than one hour of it without his or her explicit permission.

**Telephone calls**   Telephone calls may serve the same purpose as interviews and questionnaires, but may cost less in time and money while providing a higher return than most surveys. Since using the phone has some built-in problems—unlisted numbers, people without phones, lack of cooperation, busy signals, no answers—you may end up spending considerable time on the phone. Nevertheless, for extremely short questionnaires, the telephone may give you the largest return in the shortest period of time for the cheapest cost. Some tips to help you in using the phone include:

1   Select about five names for *every* one you hope to reach.

2   Write out your questions in advance.

3   Call after meals.

4   Immediately identify yourself and explain your purpose.

5   Be brief and to the point.

6   Thank your party after you finish.

**Brainstorming**   Sometimes speakers want a lot of ideas in a short period of time. Brainstorming is a technique designed specifically for this purpose. The idea behind brainstorming is to use ideas to trigger other ideas, to have people's memories and imaginations jarred by multiple stimulation from a variety of sources.

In order to work most effectively, you should follow a few basic rules: assemble a minimum of five people; set a time limit (ten minutes to one hour); designate one person to record all ideas (on a pad, blackboard, easel, tape recorder); generate as many ideas as possible during the time limit (quantity is the goal—far-out ideas may trigger others, more useful); and avoid any evaluation, criticism or judgment (good or bad) until after the session.

## LIBRARIES

Before Julius could give his speech on fund raising to the school audience, he had to pay a visit to his local library to collect some news-story information about school campaigns. Before the gourmet, whose name was Patrick, could give his talk to his gourmet club, he too was in the library using the card catalog to locate a relevant book on gourmet dieting. Before Marty could address his weight-watchers group, he consulted the *Reader's Guide* to locate a popular magazine story to gain the interest of his listeners. The library is probably the most used—and possibly the most abused—source of information open to speakers. Although libraries are readily accessible to most any American, how many of you have taken the time to talk with your librarian? How many of you have taken a guided tour of your library? How many have read your library's literature on "How to Use the Library"? By taking a few minutes to familiarize yourselves with your library and its resources, you will save hours when you use it or them. Most libraries have books, periodicals, newspapers, government documents and other references which can provide speakers enough data so that they may speak on just about any topic. The basic problem facing most library users is what to do once you're inside the doors. Where do you go to get the information you want?

We strongly encourage you to take advantage of your library's free service of giving you a guided tour of the libarry and its resources. In the next few pages we provide you with the basics for using most libraries, but you can complete your understanding only by being thoroughly familiar with the actual building and contents of your own library.

### Books

The *Card Catalog* of your library lists all books (and usually phonodiscs, tapes, microforms, archives) by author, title, and subject. The cards for author and title are in one catalog and those for subject in another. All cards are filed alphabetically and each gives the following information: call number; author's name; title of book (and edition, if any); place and date of publication; name of publisher; number of pages, illustrations, portraits, diagrams, maps; size of book; presence of bibliography; subjects on the book (for cross-references). For example, while Patrick was doing research for a speech on cooking

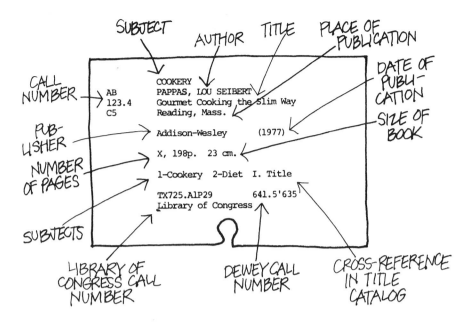

shrimp and crab chantilly, he discovered a card in the subject catalog like that shown above.

If you want to find a book and you know the author, look in the Author/Title Catalog under his or her last name; if you know the book title, look in the same catalog under the first letter of the title, excluding the articles "A," "An," and "The." If you want to know what books the library has in your subject area, look in the Subject Catalog.

*Bibliographies and footnotes are great sources of additional information on your topic.*

After you have identified the book you want, copy its call number and either get it from the stacks or seek the asistance of your librarian. *When you get the book, consult the bibliography and footnotes for additional leads in your subject area.* Since most libraries use either the Dewey Decimal or Library of Congress Classification systems to designate their call numbers, we include both categories for your information. (See next page.)

In addition to the Card Catalog, many libraries stock the *Cumulative Book Index* (formerly the U.S. Catalog) which, like the *Readers' Guide*, lists published books by title, author, and subject.

## Periodicals

Most libraries carry both popular and scholarly periodicals and journals. Over 160 of the former are indexed in the *Readers' Guide*, a cumulative author and subject index published monthly about four weeks later than the material itself is published. Each entry in the *Guide* contains: title of article; author's name, if known; description of

| *Dewey Decimal System* | 000 | General works | 500 | Pure science |
|---|---|---|---|---|
| | 100 | Philosophy | 600 | Technology |
| | 200 | Religion | 700 | The arts |
| | 300 | Social sciences | 800 | Literature |
| | 400 | Language | 900 | History |

| *Library of Congress System* | A | General works—polygraphy | L | Education |
|---|---|---|---|---|
| | B | Philosophy—religion | M | Music |
| | C | History—auxiliary sciences | N | Fine arts |
| | D | History and topography (ex. America) | P | Language and literature |
| | | | Q | Science |
| | E | America | R | Medicine |
| | F | America | S | Agriculture—plant and animal |
| | G | Geography—anthropology, industry | T | Technology |
| | | | U | Military science |
| | H | Social science | V | Naval science |
| | J | Political science | Z | Bibliography and library science |
| | K | Law | | |

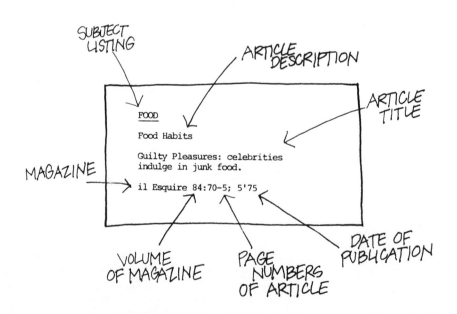

the article; name of the magazine in which the article was published; volume number of the magazine; pages of the article; date of publication; and cross-listings ("*See,*" or "*See also*").

For his speech to his weight-watchers' club, Marty located the listing shown on the preceding page in the November 10, 1975, issue of the *Guide*:

After you have copied down all relevant bibliographical information, you get your article by going to the stacks where journals and magazines are stored, to the microfiche or microfilm storage areas (if your library has placed its periodicals on microform), or to the librarian for assistance.

Some of the more popularly used magazines indexed in the *Guide* are:

| | |
|---|---|
| American Heritage | Madamoiselle |
| American Home | Modern Photography |
| Art News | Nation |
| Atlantic Monthly | National Geographic |
| Business Week | National Review |
| Car and Driver | Natural History |
| Commonweal | New Republic |
| Consumer Reports | Newsweek |
| Dun's Review | N. Y. Times Magazine |
| Esquire | New Yorker |
| Forbes | The Observer |
| Fortune | Physics Today |
| Good Housekeeping | Psychology Today |
| Harper's | Readers Digest |
| House Beautiful | Science |
| McCall's | Scientific American |

If you cannot find your periodical in the stacks or on microform, it may still be in the periodical room unbound (due to its recency).

Scholarly publications and journals are also located in either stacks or on microform. Handy indexes for most professional fields make the job of locating a particular article or author somewhat routine. Some of these indexes, listed according to their field, are:

*There are indexes for most professional fields that can help you locate information.*

| *Field* | *Index* |
|---|---|
| Agriculture | Agricultural Index |
| Art | Art Index |
| Business | Business Index: The Bulletin of Public Affairs Information Service |
| Education | Education Index |
| Engineering | Engineering Index |
| Government | The Bulletin of Public Affairs Information Service |

| Humanities and Social Sciences | Social Sciences and Humanities Index |
| Music | Music Index |
| Psychology | Psychology Index |
| Science | Applied Science and Technology Index |
| Sociology | The Bulletin of Public Affairs Information Service |

## Newspapers

Many libraries carry the following newspaper publications and indexes:

1 *Alternative Press Index:* subject index of all alternative and underground publications, published irregularly.

2 *Asian Recorder:* weekly publication of major news events of Asia, listed alphabetically by country, with a quarterly index.

3 *Austrailian Public Affairs Information Service:* monthly classification of public, socio-economic, and cultural affairs of all English-speaking countries; also indexes some social science and humanities journals.

4 *Congressional Quarterly:* published quarterly, contains the major news events relating to national politics and the federal government.

5 *Current Digest of the Soviet Press:* weekly publication translating into English many Soviet press publications, including *Izvestia* and *Pravda.*

6 *Facts on File:* weekly classification of world news.

7 *Index to the Christian Science Monitor:* monthly subject index, including London and the U.S.

8 *Keesings Contemporary File:* weekly diary of important world events, indexed from official and unofficial publications of the U.K. and other countries.

9 *Latin America Index:* quarterly subject guide to Latin American countries (from 1973)

10 *Newspaper Index:* monthly index of the *Chicago Tribune, Los Angeles Times, New Orleans Times-Picayune, Washington Post.*

11 *New York Times Index:* bimonthly index of the daily issue.

12 *Public Affairs Information Service* (PAIS): weekly summary of factual and statistical information from English-speaking countries.

**13** *Times, London. Index to the Times:* quarterly, dictionary index of the *London Times.*

**14** *Update (Urban News File):* monthly categorization of the news in 10 major subjects, summarizing news reported in over 150 metropolitan newspapers.

Once you have located the news story you think will help you, its date will help you locate similar stories in other newspapers. In addition to those papers mentioned above, some others with good reputations are: *Wall Street Journal, Washington Star, St. Louis Post-Dispatch, Manchester Guardian, Atlanta Constitution,* and the *L.A. Times.*

## Government Documents

The Monthly Catalog of U.S. Government Publications lists all publications put out by every department, agency, and bureau of the government. The Catalog is published by the Superintendent of Documents with a subject index in each issue, and a cumulative index at the end of the year. For every document, it lists the title, publishing department, number of pages, price (if any), and the classification number (Sudoc number). If your library does not have the documents you desire, you may order them directly from the U.S. Government Printing Office, Washington, D.C.

Additional government references are: *Commerce Yearbook; Congressional Record;* STAR (the index of NASA); *American Statistics Index* (statistical data of the U.S. Government); and *Nuclear Science Abstracts* (index of the Energy Research Development Administration—formerly the Atomic Energy Commission).

## Other References

In addition to the books, periodicals, newspapers and government publications, most libraries have several reference books at your disposal. Among them are atlases *(Rand McNally Commercial Atlas), Encyclopaedia Britannica World Atlas),* biographies *(Who's Who in America, Current Biography, The Directory of American Scholars, International Who's Who, American Authors, Who was Who in America, Dictionary of National Biography, Biography Index),* almanacs *(Information Please Almanac, The Statesman's Yearbook, World Almanac, Statistical Abstract of the U.S.),* encyclopedias *(Encylcopaedia Britannica, Encyclopedia Americana),* and quotation handbooks *(Bartlett's Quotations, A New Dictionary of Quotations).*

Libraries even have a bibliography on bibliographies, the *Bibliographic Index.*

## TECHNOLOGIES

Marshal McLuhan has stated that we are now in the age of the non-print media. Judging by the opportunities available to do research without reading, he would appear to be right. You can dial an expert in San Francisco, place his voice on your tele-lecture system, and have him give a speech live to 2000 people assembled in Boston. You can do research on a war (as many did with Vietnam) by simply turning on your TV; in some homes, you can even videotape a program while you go out to the movies. You can even let computers do your literature searches, saving hundreds of hours of card catalog drudgery of the past. Major technologies affecting your researching for speeches include: mass media, telephone systems, microforms, and computers.

### Mass Media

The gourmet mentioned earlier, Patrick, can easily watch one of several cooking shows on television, enjoying the close-ups as he prepares his own speech on shrimp and crab chantilly. There are ample television news shows, documentaries, and specials to give you access to sources not found in libraries or with other people. Additionally, radio, movies, educational films, home videotape systems, and home movies (available on film discs, similar to phonograph discs) provide data you can receive without leaving your homes.

### Telephone Systems

In addition to the conference call, enabling several persons in various parts of the country to simultaneously discuss a subject on the telephone, today you can connect a speaker from one part of the country to a loudspeaker system in another part of the country by using a tele-lecture system. Many communities also have dial-access tape libraries, providing callers with taped messages about medicine, drugs, social problems, etc.

### Microforms

With most libraries running out of space to store books, magazines, journals, and documents, the advent of microforms has greatly helped the librarian store information. Four types of microform exist: microfilm, microfiche, microprint, and microcards. All require special mechanical readers, and all allow for storage of large amounts of information. For example, microfiche is a four-by-six-inch sheet of photographic film which prints up to 98 microimages a sheet. Special readers project the image to full page size on a small screen. Readers are usually located throughout your library.

## Computers

Today, individual computers do the work of several people and save hundreds of hours. Since about 1965, literature searches by computer have been a common activity in most large libraries, usually at minimal cost or even none. If your library cannot perform this function, speak to your librarian about the possibility of acquiring computer search facilities.

**Making a computer search**  To conduct a computer search you must first make up a list of descriptor words which you would expect to appear in the titles or headings of books, articles, documents, etc. about your topic. (For example, for a speech on exercise you might list "exercise," "jogging," "physical fitness,""calisthenics," "gymnastics," and so on.) You submit your list, usually on a special form provided by the library, to your librarian for access to a major computer data bank such as ERIC (Educational Resources Information Center), DOD (Department of Defense); N.Y. Times Index, or Psychological Abstracts. When you collect your computer printout (usually the next day) you will find a list of bibliographic data for entries all keyed to your descriptions. Then you proceed to locate the books, articles, or documents as you would normally after a manual literature search.

Naturally, a computer search is only as good as the entries filed and the identifiable descriptors used.

## RECORDING YOUR INFORMATION

If you are conducting a computer search, you still must locate the books or articles and read them; computers can't do that for you. If you interview someone, you still must record the information from the interview. When your questionnaires return, you must tabulate and analyze them. After completing an observation, you had best record your sights and sounds. Even after probing your memory, you should immediately record what you recall, lest it be in vain.

Various methods exist for recording your information. Many interviews can be tape recorded and later transcribed. Some observations can be videotaped for later content analysis. Questionnaire data can be computer analyzed, if you have the right programs and skills. Memory probes can also be audiotaped for the record. Despite all our technological advances, the most common method still in use today seems to be taking notes by hand on pads or cards. *Cards are usually better since they allow you to shift them around as you begin to classify and develop organizational structures for your information.* Whenever you take notes from a library source, you should be sure you record all necessary bibliographical data (source, date, pages, publishers), all key facts, and optionally, a quick summary of the reference (opposite, above). This last one can be coded, using numerical categories, if you have enough entries on a given topic.

*Record your information correctly the first time—and you won't need to do it a second time.*

We cannot overly emphasize the importance of carefully recording the information gained from yourself, others, libraries, or technologies. Without such efforts, your previous work may be wasted, necessitating return trips to libraries or for additional interviews.

We hope that in this chapter we have dispelled the myths that good speakers simply get up and begin talking. They do not. Much time is needed in researching ourselves, others, libraries, and modern technologies before we can feel that we'll be speaking with authority.

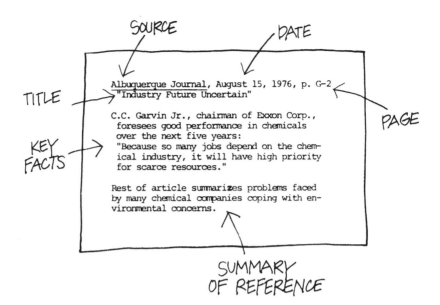

SOURCE DATE

TITLE

KEY FACTS

Albuquerque Journal, August 15, 1976, p. G-2
"Industry Future Uncertain"

C.C. Garvin Jr., chairman of Exxon Corp.,
foresees good performance in chemicals
over the next five years:
"Because so many jobs depend on the chemical industry, it will have high priority
for scarce resources."

Rest of article summarizes problems faced
by many chemical companies coping with environmental concerns.

PAGE

SUMMARY
OF REFERENCE

## SUMMARY QUESTIONS

- What are the eight steps in the research process?
- How do you assess and determine the limits of your knowledge?
- If self-knowledge is inadequate, what different methods may be employed to expand the existing knowledge?
- What are the different ways of getting information from others?
- What are some of the first steps in using the library as an information source?

## EXERCISES

**1** Select a topic of interest to you and talk it over with a friend. Then visit the library and look up three books on the topic.

**2** Conduct two interviews on the same subject. Use open-ended questions in one and closed questions in the other.

**3** Write to Washington for a pamphlet on a topic you have selected to speak about.

## REFERENCE

**1** T. Harris, *I'm OK—You're OK* (New York: Avon, 1973), p. 28.

# DEVELOPING THE MESSAGE

Now that you have prepared yourself for the speaking event and researched your topic, you are ready to develop your speech. You will very often find it difficult to isolate the concepts of persuading, informing, and entertaining, because while it is entertaining, a speech may both inform and persuade. Realizing that these purposes are not necessarily mutually exclusive, you may wish to explore the purpose of your speech as it may appear in the model below. The model on the next page can also be used with organizational patterns. It may prepare you to make some decisions prior to selecting the pattern that will best serve you. (A more in-depth explanation of organizational methods and patterns is presented in Chapter 5.)

The methods of reasoning you use to develop your speech depend in a large measure on your purpose. But no matter what your decision in this regard, as a public speaker you must consider the *ethics* of your presentation and attempt to present yourself as an honest and intelligent person.

You must try to establish a *rapport* with your audience by your words and actions and support your ideas with a variety of materials.

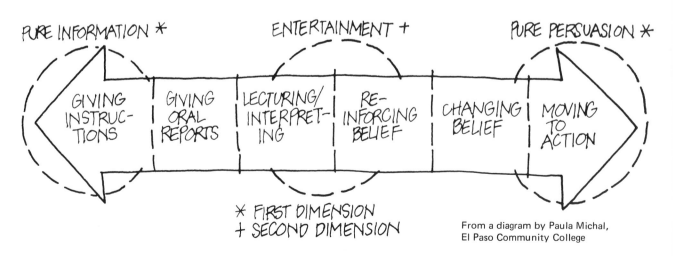

From a diagram by Paula Michal,
El Paso Community College

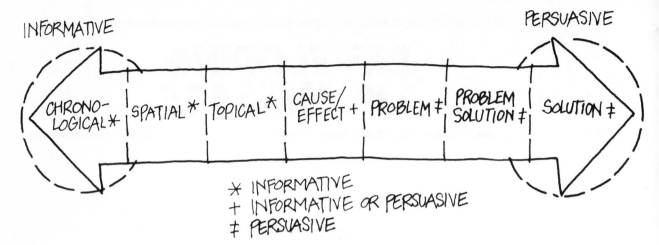

* INFORMATIVE
+ INFORMATIVE OR PERSUASIVE
‡ PERSUASIVE

When developing your message consider both emotional and logical appeals and inform, entertain, persuade, or combine all three, by using correct reasoning and valid thought.

It is important to note that while we separate ethics and emotion and reasoning, we do so solely for the sake of clarifying each area. *Practically speaking,* human responses do not isolate the logic from the emotions but unify them, and suggest that feeling is not devoid of reason, nor reason devoid of feeling.

With this thought firmly in mind, in this chapter we discuss the ethical, emotional, and logical development of a message and the application of ethics, emotion, and logic to a persuasive speaking situation.

## DEVELOPING THE MESSAGE ETHICALLY

One warm May afternoon, in a small town in Arizona, a young Navajo girl named Wendy addressed a graduating class of seniors and their parents. She was the only native American in the class. Her speech was not what the audience expected to hear. Instead of speaking about the education she had received and what the future holds for the graduating senior, she chose to relate the ways in which she had been discriminated against by her foster parents, her teachers, and her fellow students. She talked about how it felt to be the only Navajo in the school and the many subtle ways she had been made to feel "different" and "inferior." She spoke about her culture and her heritage and the pitiful manner in which her people had been treated through the years. She spoke softly, slowly, and with great sincerity.

After the speech was over, her foster parents, several of the students and their parents, and one of her teachers all told her that they were upset over her speech and did not think she should have taken that opportunity to talk about discrimination against the native American.

Though her audience did not care to hear what Wendy had to say, they were, nonetheless, greatly moved by her words.

Wendy told them that she assumed full responsibility for what she said and had thought about the consequences of her speech while she was preparing it.

While mindful of her audience's predispositions and the fact that her accusations would disturb them, she felt she had to tell the truth as she had experienced it. The standards she had set for herself as a Navajo took precedence over the attitudes of the audience. She knew her image as a student was at stake, but she felt that her ethical responsibility as a speaker was a part of that image.

Many rhetoricians, most particularly those in Roman times, used the words ethos and ethics interchangeably. "Ethos" then meant what the speaker chose to do. Today we define ethos as the *image* the speaker projects. To communication scholars, "image" also means credibility. Aristotle suggested that the three constituents of what he called "ethical proof" are character, sagacity, and goodwill. He felt audiences are persuaded by "ethical proof," or what a speaker chooses to do; he explored the sources of credibility and analyzed the ways in which the speaker achieved that intangible quality. Cicero took the orator's point of view and asked what *ought* a speaker to be or seem. Quintilian tried to define the "oughts" of credibility. St. Augustine thought that if a speaker possessed virtue it would shine through.

A speaker who seeks to build his or her ethos or credibility assumes some ethical responsibilities. "Ethics" is often defined as "the principle of morality, including both the science of the good and the nature of the right." Since in rhetorical situations we deal with human choice, someone's "good" or "right" or someone's "bad" or "wrong" is always at issue.

*Every speaker has an ethical responsibility toward his or her audience.*

Although we accept the fact that ethos and ethics are often viewed as interchangeable, we believe it is impossible to standardize ethics. We cannot make a list of ethical responsibilities because ethical standards are relative. To concentrate on a single standard might lead to dismissing social effects and diminishing the value of rhetorical skills. Therefore, while we feel that a speaker should consider his or her ethical responsibilities when attempting to establish an ethos (or image), we cannot say *exactly* what those responsibilities are. However, several ancient and modern rhetoricians have advocated the following ethical considerations:

1 *Don't mislead out of ignorance.* Are you quoting a medical report you do not fully understand? Before you present information, be sure that you comprehend the meaning of it. Repeating a story that has not been verified can mislead the audience.

2 *Examine all sides.* Though you may wish to present one side of an issue, you must explore all sides in order to arrive at an intel-

ligent decision. We like to hear evidence that supports our point of view, but you have the responsibility to your audience to be well informed on the topic.

3 *Weigh the validity of the source.* Is the medical "fact" printed in a tabloid or sex magazine as valid as an interview with the doctor who performed a heart transplant? Ask yourself how valid is a source that is out of date, not credible to your audience, or difficult to verify.

4 *Test the validity of reasoning.* Are you arriving at a conclusion because you do not understand the evidence and have heard someone else put it together in like manner? In your own mind, do you honestly believe you have arrived at the solution in a reasonable manner?

5 *Don't suppress vital information.* The Watergate affair has made it very important that a speaker be honest about disclosing vital and accurate information.

6 *Accept full responsibility for what you say.* If, like Wendy, you feel you must speak out and know that your audience will disagree with you, prepare yourself to accept the consequences and to stand by your convictions.

## Building an Image

Once you have decided what you want to say, and recognized your ethical responsibilities to yourself and to your audience, you are prepared to establish your credibility and build an image that will be instrumental in persuading your audience to listen to and accept your message.

Aristotle stated that the speaker's character is the most important means of persuasion. Character and credibility, he felt, went hand in hand. Whereas Aristotle claimed a speaker should establish his or her credibility *during* the speech, modern rhetoricians consider the credibility of a speaker *prior to, during, and at the completion of* a communicative act.

*Prior* ethos is a powerful factor in any type of speech, be it entertaining or persuasive. An audience that is aware of a speaker's personal characteristics, background, and appearance has formed a mental picture of him or her. Consider the ovation awarded to Congresswoman Barbara Jordan at the 1976 Democratic Convention.

*Your image is important—to you and to your message.*

The image of this brilliant woman was so positive that she received the first standing ovation of the Convention. Her reputation as a public speaker, although probably few of the audience had heard her in person, heightened their expectations. She did not disappoint them.

She built her ethos *during* her speech. During a speech the speaker has control. The speaker can alter a prior image or reinforce it. The speaker *produces* an image which comes from the impact of the message, the effect of the circumstances in which the communication takes place, and the delivery of the message.

At this point, the speaker who is aware of the predispositions, attitudes, and beliefs of his or her audience, who is sensitive to the communicative act as it takes place, and who can feel the impact of the verbal and nonverbal clues the audience is sending and react to them on the spot, is the speaker who is most likely to secure his or her credibility.

**Your image can change as your speech progresses.**

Ethos at the end of a speech is the product of the interaction of the prior ethos and the produced ethos. The image or ethos of the speaker may become *more* favorable at the end of a speech or it may become *less* favorable. To illustrate, let's consider the plight of a young white police officer in a midwestern city:

In 1968 a group of militant blacks ambushed two tow truck operators who were dressed in dark blue uniforms. It was speculated that the militants thought they were police officers. When the police responded to the call there had already been much shooting. By the time the evening was over, eleven deaths and fifteen injuries were reported—half of them police officers. Burning of buildings and looting resulted from the shoot-out. For some time the mayor would not allow white police to go into the area. For months there was dissension between the black and white communities, particularly between the police and the black community. Finally a young black councilman thought it was time to get the police and members of his community together, but he knew he had to go slowly.

He arranged for members of the community to come together and discuss their problems with him and with a communications consultant. Then at one meeting he suggested they invite an officer that patrolled in their area. Many of the members agreed, although they expressed doubts about the character of the officers.

When the officer appeared he was warm and friendly—and black. He made a few jokes, but the body of his speech was directed toward persuading the audience that they should support their local police, that the militants should be punished, and that only with understanding and cooperation could they hope to reduce the crime in their area. The audience appeared receptive. They minimized the uniform and maximized the fact that he was black and might understand.

The officer acted with tact and moderation. He said "This is my home too. I want my children to be safe. I've read the statistics, and the largest number of *victims* in this country are young and black. I've got a sixteen year old son and he's young and black. I want him to have protection." In making that remark, he revealed a familiarity with the interests of the day, and showed that he possessed integrity and wisdom.

Then the officer asked if he could bring his partner into the meeting. The audience agreed. He radioed his request to headquarters and soon his partner arrived. The partner was a young white officer.

When he came in, the young white officer used restraint when a member of the audience cited an act of police brutality that had occurred during the shoot-out. "White policemen were knocking heads. I saw one of them pull one brother into a warehouse and beat him up and he was just walking by the area."

"Was that white policeman built like me? Did he have red hair, blue eyes?" The Officer pulled off his hat and everyone laughed. "I know that I'm a part of the force but that doesn't mean I'm *that* policeman, or that I believe in what *he* did. Don't judge us all by what you saw that day."

The officers were attempting to remove or minimize unfavorable impressions of themselves or their cause previously established by their opponents (who happened to be the entire community). They did so by using common sense. The black officer was right to come into the meeting first and establish a commonality of interest between himself and the audience. The white officer tried to reveal as honestly as possible his personable qualities as a messenger of the truth. He did so by disassociating himself with what he and his audience believed was unjust.

Though the meeting was not without accusative and defensive rhetoric, the audience listened and responded and agreed to invite the Safety Director and police in their area to the next meeting.

**Some rules of character, sound judgment, and good-will were set down by Aristotle centuries ago.**

Some of the methods that the young officers employed to establish their credibility can be found in very traditional rules set down by Aristotle centuries ago. For example, to improve your image (ethos), consider the following:

*Character*
- Associate yourself with what is virtuous and elevated.
- With proper humility, praise yourself, your cause, or your client.
- Remove or minimize unfavorable impressions of yourself or your cause that have been previously established by either your opponent or well-meaning but misguided individuals.

*Sound judgment*
- Use common sense.
- Act with tact and moderation.
- Display a sense of good taste.
- Be familiar with what is happening in your city, state, nation, the world, but particularly in your immediate area.
- Handle your speech materials in a manner that reveals your intelligence, integrity, and wisdom.

*Good will*
- Don't praise your audience too much, or too little.
- Identify yourself with your audience and their problems.
- Be candid and straightforward.
- If you must rebuke the audience, be considerate.
- Remove any suspicion from the audience's mind that there is personal gain for you.
- Remember—you are a messenger of the truth.

## DEVELOPING THE MESSAGE EMOTIONALLY

You should consider the ethics of the situation *before* deciding whether to use arguments that bring about emotional responses from the audience.

The power to sway others, to evoke strong feelings in them, to affect their deepest emotions, should be used with the utmost respect and never abused.

History is filled with stories of orators who used excessive emotionalism and caused their listeners to make decisions on unreasonable grounds. For centuries speakers have elevated minor points to undue importance and given more attention to irrelevancies than to sound reasoning. We all know people who hide the facts in flowery language, concentrate on emotional issues and highlight trivia. Sometimes we are moved, in spite of knowing better, by the pure charisma of the speaker.

Understanding the nature of human feelings was of prime importance to Aristotle, who sadly observed that people were indeed swayed by emotions. He tried to interpret and understand the social psychology of Athenians. The Romans were concerned with how the *speaker* put emotions into a speech. Modern rhetoricians are more concerned with studying the readiness of the *listener* to accept the feelings and intellect of the speaker.

Whichever approach is taken, it is necessary for you to pay attention to *the language employed to arouse emotions,* to *the ethics of those choices of language,* and to *responses of the listeners to those emotional appeals.* Ultimately every speaker's task is to link the truth to the audience's emotional nature.

### Language of emotions

Sometimes the very *subjects* you select and the *words* you use to tell about those subjects affect audiences emotionally. If your audience is composed of persons who have been unemployed for some time, talking about creating new jobs or mentioning the breadlines of the 1930s will touch them personally. In a southwestern city, a speaker chose to speak on the subject of child abuse. He did so the day after a little nine-month old boy was found dead of head injuries inflicted by the father. Even though the speaker attempted to "give the facts," the audience was very upset by the speech.

Some of the most emotional language is used in political campaigns. In an eastern city, a mayor ran for reelection by talking about food. He attended 98-cent chicken dinners given on his behalf. At every dinner he would say "Where else can you get chicken like this for 98 cents?" Then he'd ask for a show of hands, "Are you enjoying the dinner?" The people would raise their chicken legs and shout, "Yeh!" There was no attempt at these dinners to appeal to reasons why he should be elected. He just talked about food and how great the women were who donated their time to cooking for everyone.

Appealing to emotions is very important in political campaigns, where it is often not at all necessary to support propositions logically and where the appeal is sometimes made simultaneously to a variety of audiences by means of the electronic media. The main task of the politician in a campaign is to establish credibility (image) and build rapport (emotional appeal). If we use politics in the manner that Aristotle used it in the ancient Greek concept of polis (a man as part of his social environment), then we are all politicians every time we attempt to influence someone or to support our causes. Though Aristotle stated that a speech was composed of the speaker, subject, and audience, he also stated that it was the audience that determined a speech's end or object, and stressed *adaptation,* or adjustment to the variables of human behavior, in any specific group.

Adapting, of course, does not imply that the speaker forgo the ethics of his or her presentation or the integrity of his or her ideas. However, having some foresight about the emotional makeup of an audience is simply being practical.

## Ethics of the Choice of Language

According to psychologist Abraham Maslow, human needs fall into five categories. Starting with the most basic, they are: physiological needs, safety needs, belongingness and love needs, esteem needs, and self-actualization needs. Audiences respond to messages that meet these needs. The question the speaker must ask is: "What responsibility do I assume when I seek to arouse strong emotions?"

For example, people like to be safe and they fear having their security taken from them. Joseph McCarthy and Adolph Hitler aroused those fears to great levels with frightening consequences. However, the speaker who says "One out of every four people in this room will die of lung cancer," also arouses fears. We fear ill health, bad breath, and a lot of other things, both significant and insignificant. The speaker who desires to arouse emotions must keep in mind the following consequences:

1 He or she can use words that are too strong, too terrifying. Audiences may just quit listening.

2 Fear appeals may lead the audience to become irritated with the speaker. When Joseph McCarthy pushed his rhetoric of fear too far, his listener said: "Have you no sense of decency?"

3 If appeals are too strong, listeners may choose to ignore the speaker and minimize the danger.

The speaker who is *sensitive* about venturing into personal experiences concerning fears, hopes, failures, or ideals of the audience

*You, too, should establish credibility . . .*

often succeeds in reaching that audience, particularly if its members *sense* the speaker's deep concern for them. We often relax our guard and become involved when we *trust the speaker's intentions.*

Some speeches, such as inspirational talks, ceremonial talks, and after-dinner speeches, are just naturally more emotional than others, giving priority to our emotional needs. But *all* speeches have some degree of emotionalism, and it is important for the speaker to understand how to build rapport with the audience.

*. . . and build rapport.*

People get involved when they *contribute* to the message. A device used by advertising agencies to build rapport with their audiences is one that calls for the audience to *supply* some of the message. For example, Pepsi Cola once ran an add that began like this:

Test Yourself.
She's in the _____ Generation.

_____ Cola grew up with her
MATCHED HER TASTES AND HER PACE.

No wonder _____ is the official drink
of her generation.

Yours too.

Come alive!

You're in the _____ Generation.

This technique of involving the audience can be used successfully by the public speaker. Recently a lecturer at a university in the east spoke about the merits of speed reading. He talked about speed reading and then passed out some material and invited the audience to read the material and note the time it took to read two paragraphs. He advised them that within fifteen minutes he could cut that reading time in half. The audience listened intently for the next fifteen minutes. He appealed to their love of gamesmanship and used emotional phrases like, "You look like a pretty smart class." He also explained the process in a very reasonable manner, thereby mixing the emotional and rational appeals. A good speaker realizes that the skillful interweaving of the rational with the emotional is like finding the right frame for the right picture, for our reasoning influences our feelings and our feelings influence our reasoning.

## Response of Listeners to Emotional Appeals

In January of 1977 over 130 Americans saw on television the stirring story of an American family, a drama by Alex Haley called *Roots.* It was an emotional experience for both black and white viewers. For weeks afterwards researchers asked viewers how they felt while watching this moving drama, which began centuries before with the capture of a young African who was sold into slavery.

The response of the millions of Americans was that their feelings were positive, and that they felt a stronger desire to move forward toward better relations between blacks and whites. The drama spanned the gamut of emotions, illustrating fear, hate, love, suffering, hostility, vengeance, and cruelty. In an interview after the phenomenal success of the program, Haley said that there was a message about *responsibility* in the drama that all of us could relate to.

*Try to learn as much as you can about your listeners' motives, goals, and attitudes.*

A listener's values, that is motives, goals, and attitudes, will always elicit some degree of emotional response. Of course there are various degrees of emotional response which any statement can arouse. For Haley, as for all of us, emotions exist in relationship to our past experiences, our attitudes at the moment, and our future hopes and fears.

Several years before the television showing of *Roots,* Haley addressed a group of faculty and students at Cleveland State University. During his speech a bomb scare was announced. The audience followed Haley to another room but would not leave the building until he had finished his long narrative. Their desire to hear this story minimized their fear of a bomb.

Haley was relating, in highly emotional language, his reaction to a story teller in Africa. He said:

"We were now entering the next phase of unbelievability for me. There is a saying that a person can have a peak experience, that which no other experience transcends. And I was to have it that day."

He then related how the entire village of seventy-five people came to hear the village's oral historian tell tale after tale of the history of the village. Haley said:

"It was mesmerizing. He talked about three and a half hours . . . (he told) about the time that the King's soldiers came and the eldest of the four sons, Kunta, was away chopping wood and he disappeared. And the family searched and searched and searched and they could never find him, and they assumed that toubob had gotten him . . . and he went on with his story. I sat there. It was goosepimple time all over."

Haley said he felt like he was "carved in rock" as he sat in that little village listening to an African tell a story that was exactly like the story he had heard many times from his grandmother when he was a little boy.

Later the villagers responded to Haley's story by forming a circle around him and thrusting their babies into his arms. He said he held about a dozen babies and later learned that this was a ritual known as the "laying of the hands," and meant that he was one of them.[1]

Response of listeners to emotional appeals can vary from the "unbelievable" experience that Haley describes to a very small feeling of relief from fear, or a pleasant feeling of enjoyment. The hearer's estimate of the speaker's intent, as well as the speaker's knowledge of the listener's motives, goals, and attitudes, is a vital element in the building of a strong rapport.

While we should never minimize the importance of emotional proof and fully realize that emotion plays an important part in speech, we should keep the words of A. L. Hollingsworth in mind: "The instincts do not always lead men aright, and . . . the emotions are by no means infallible guides to truth."[2]

With that in mind we shall move on to what Aristotle believed to be the most important part of a speech—the reinforcement of ideas through logical means.

## DEVELOPING THE MESSAGE LOGICALLY

Aristotle believed that the most important ingredient of a speech is rational demonstration through severe argumentation. He believed that man is a thinker, a seeker of knowledge, and that the ability to communicate meaning and thought is at the center of discourse. The term logic, from the Greek "logos," denotes "correct reasoning or valid thought." A speaker who uses logic is able to analyze the subject matter, to weigh it and understand it, and then to see and draw connections from idea to idea and from idea to conclusion.

There are several ways of arranging ideas and drawing conclusions. Some of the more popular ways are reasoning from *induction*, reasoning from *deduction*, reasoning from *sign*, reasoning from *cause*, reasoning from *analogy*, and reasoning by *comparison*. We shall discuss each one of these methods and see how they apply to public speaking.

### Inductive Reasoning

Angelo decided to give a speech about health foods, but he really didn't know what he would find when he began his research. He visited the local supermarkets and looked at the fruit departments. He decided fruit was a health food, but he still didn't know what he would find out about the fruit. He decided he could do a number of things: (1) he could sample each piece of fruit; (2) he could, with the help of friends, sample many different kinds of fruit; or (3) he could sample a few fruit at random. Depending on which method he chose, he might find out that: (1) all the fruit is sweet and fresh; (2) all the fruit is *probably* sweet and fresh; (3) *some* of the fruit is sweet and fresh.

What Angelo was doing to arrive at a conclusion was reasoning from the *specific* to the *general* by *induction*. However, in two of the three instances he was reasoning by generalization. Since he decided he could not sample *all* the fruit, he decided on the third option, sampling at random.

The first option, sampling *all* the fruit, is the most reliable but difficult to do; the second option is fairly reliable, although a conclusion can be altered; and the third option has an opportunity for error (you may miss the apples with the worms and so still come to the conclusion that the fruit is sweet and fresh). However, if you must generalize, like Angelo, be sure that: (1) the examples are fair, and typical of the whole; (2) there is a sufficient number of examples to justify your conclusion; (3) there are no exceptions to the examples that are not accounted for in the conclusion.

## Deductive Reasoning

It is easier to support something the audience generally believes is true than something they do not believe. Moving from an accepted truth to a particular judgment is something we do every day of our lives. We say, "Janie Smitherson is an equal member of our society." The implication is that *all* members of our society are equal, and, since she is a member of our society, Janie is equal. We just don't bother to go through the whole procedure of deductive reasoning out loud. Our audiences would get bored. So we just shorten the process.

You may reason in your mind that all your office buddies are really helpful and Sally works in the office, so Sally is helpful. You may say, "Sally's one of the gang, she's helpful," and your audience may supply the missing premise—which is that you *all* are helpful. Practically speaking, you do most of the reasoning in your head. It is neither necessary nor customary to get up before an audience and spell out an entire categorical syllogism* such as the classic one:

All men are mortal.
Socrates is a man.
Socrates is mortal.

You would just say Socrates is a mortal because he is a man.

There are a few ways of reasoning from the general to the specific that we can explore. The first way is by *classification,* such as we just did with Socrates.

All good students get high grades.
Lavinia is a good student.
Lavinia gets high grades.

The major premise of the first line is "All good students" (group includes *all* the students). The major term is "get high grades." The minor premise of the second line is "Lavinia" and the middle term is

---

*
A syllogism is a formal pattern of logic by which, from two known or accepted statements, we can arrive at a third statement, or conclusion. A categorical syllogism, which usually begins with the word "all," involves two statements that are generally accepted as universal; that is, they do not need to be qualified.

"is a good student." The conclusion is that: "Lavinia" (minor term) "gets high grades" (major term).

To judge whether your syllogism is valid you should ask: Does the syllogism contain a major premise, minor premise, and conclusion? Does it contain a major, middle, and minor term? Is the middle term distributed; that is, used in a universal sense, meaning *all* or *every,* in at least one of the premises? If the middle term is distributed in the conclusion, then it must also be distributed in one of the premises.

We can also reason from the general to the specific by *elimination* or *alternative.* Suppose we can discover two possibilities with the condition that if one is true, the other must be false. For example: Either Lavinia is blond or she is brunette. She is blond. Therefore she is not a brunette. This type of reasoning states that there are only two possibilities and they cannot exist together.

We can also reason from the hypothetical, to the consequent. We state that "if" something happens, "then" something else will occur. For example: "If" we get an A, "then" we will be on the honor roll. "If" is the antecedent and "then" is the consequent.

## Reasoning from Cause

Cause relationships are those in which one factor causes another, or, conversely, one factor is the effect of the other.

For example, we can say that one of the effects of flu is a weakness in the legs. We might be more specific and say "He was suffering from the flu and his legs felt weak." The cause was flu; the effect was weakness of the legs.

Or we might list a number of circumstances that lead to a predictable effect or set of effects. For example, we might say:

Lavinia studied hard for the LSAT exams.
Lavinia is a bright woman.
Lavinia really wanted to make a high score.

Those are the facts of the case, and because of all of those facts—that intelligence, study, and desire are causes of or result in high scores—we conclude that Lavinia did extremely well on the LSAT exams.

## Reasoning from Sign

Reasoning from sign also includes a causal relationship, but the reverse of reasoning from cause. For example, your legs feel weak because you have the flu, but your weak legs did not *cause* the flu; they are just a *sign* that you have it.

## Reasoning from Analogy or Comparison

When Chief Ten Bears said "I feel glad, as the ponies do when the fresh grass starts in the beginning of the year," he was making a *figurative comparison,* that is, comparing *unlike* objects. A *figurative* comparison is very effective because it mixes two images and your audience is doubly aroused. A *literal* comparison, such as "The students of my day weren't any different from the students of today," compares *like* objects or ideas of the same class—such as cities to cities, or thermometers to thermometers.

Literal comparisons can serve as a form of reasoning, of logical proof. They can be used to make things clearer, or to make the unknown into a known quality. *Figurative* comparisons are not generally used as logical proof, but are often used as emotional proof.

Reasoning from *comparisons* can be valid when you remember that: (1) the greater the similarity between the two examples, the more accurate your conclusions may be; and (2) the similarities are more significant and greater than the dissimilarities.

In reasoning from *analogy* you go further, and try to show that similar circumstances produce similar conclusions. For example, when a fund raiser was addressing a group of volunteer workers for the March of Dimes, he talked about the previous year's drive and told a story of a worker who had trudged in the snow for hours collecting pennies and dimes from people. He also told of some of the ways the workers worked hard this year. His conclusion was that because people worked as hard *this* year as they had *last* year, the results would be the same—victory.

What the fund raiser was saying is that "what is true or will work in one set of circumstances is true or will work in another comparable set of circumstances."

When reasoning from analogy you must remember that the subjects being compared should be similar in important ways. If their dissimilarities outweigh their similarities, then conclusions drawn from the comparisons will not be valid.

## Fallacious Reasoning

Keep in mind that it is easy to use fallacious reasoning. Basing judgments or generalizations on insufficient evidence or experience is one way. Walter Van Tilburg Clark's book (and film), *The Ox-Bow Incident,* clearly shows an example of fallacious reasoning—and its results. In this story, set in the West in the late 1800s, a group of men hang two others whom they believe to be cattle rustlers—even though the evidence is inconclusive. Soon after the act they find that they were wrong, that the two men were not rustlers.

You may also assign a false cause to a certain happening or effect. When Hitler said the Jews were the cause of all the problems in Germany, he was assigning a false cause to certain conditions to suit his own purposes.

Evading an issue, using irrelevant arguments, or appealing to the audience's passions or prejudices are all examples of fallacious reasoning.

Exploitation of ignorance can occur when the speaker knows that his or her audience does not have access to certain information. For example, many recent land frauds have been perpetrated by people who know that their audiences know nothing about the area under discussion or the real estate laws pertaining to it.

Trying to impress an audience with oratory that is unfamiliar to them should also be avoided.

But because we are all human and we wish to impress or sway an audience, we may at one time or another in our lives be tempted to use such devices.

Fight the temptation.

## APPLYING ETHICS, EMOTIONS, AND LOGIC TO THE PERSUASIVE SPEECH

Though we have stressed repeatedly that speeches are seldom purely persuasive or purely entertaining or informative—and that it is impossible to isolate those concepts—there are times when the speaker clearly *intends* to put a little persuasion into his or her speech. Though a little humor might creep into the speech as well, the speaker specifically wishes to reinforce a belief, or change one, or move an audience to act. For example, a salesman may tell a joke, but he or she clearly wishes to sell you a car.

Fully realizing that the intent to persuade doesn't exclude the possibility that a speech can also entertain or inform, we realistically present some guidelines for the speaker who sets out to persuade and wishes to apply some of the principles mentioned in this chapter.

*Three elements need to be successfully combined.*

Whether the audience is friendly or hostile, it is important that the speaker consider the *ethics* of the choice of the topic, the *emotions* of the audience, and the *logic* of the reasoning. Only when all *three* elements are interwoven successfully can a persuasive speaker feel confident of his or her message.

Therefore, before you embark on the persuasive speech, there are several questions you should consider.

1 Does the audience trust you?
2 Does the audience need or desire a change?
3 Is your statement of purpose close to the audience's focus of belief?
4 Can you show logical reasons for change?
5 Will the language you plan to use motivate the audience?
6 Is your purpose ethical?

You will notice that *all* of these questions are directly related to the concepts mentioned when we discussed developing the message: *ethics, emotional appeals, and logical appeals.* Furthermore, they are linked with those things the speaker does to persuade people: He or she presents information, causes the audience to like him or her, reasons logically, uses appropriate language, and meets the audience's needs.

If you can answer yes to the questions we asked and have seriously considered and understand the things that persuade people, then your next step is to plan a purpose statement or proposition. You may start with a proposition of policy, a proposition of fact, or a proposition of value.

## Propositions of Policy

A proposition is like a purpose statement—it immediately lets your audience know what your intentions are. There are several types of propositions of *policy.* One type suggests that some change come about, that the status quo is no longer advantageous. For example, a young man running for mayor of a midwestern city said the existing government was unproductive, unhealthy, and bogged down with a political dynasty that had lasted for twenty years. His proposition was one of policy: "Our city needs a new mayor." Such propositions call for overt action. Politicians often urge people to vote, salesmen urge people to buy.

Another type of proposition of policy is one that calls for an endorsement, or acceptance of a certain policy. For example: "The citizens of River's Edge should support their local police force." That's all one needs to say: "Please support the local police."

Other propositions of policy call for indictments while not actually asking for change in the status quo. For example, "Our president should be censured for being late to three meetings."

There are also propositions that affirm or deny:

1  The existence of things.
2  The occurrence of acts.
3  The classification of objects.
4  The connection of events.

## Propositions of Fact

Propositions of fact simply ask whether something is true. There is no suggestion that a change is in order, only that the audience consider the question put before them. These propositions of fact can be mild statements such as: "Lexington, Kentucky, is an independent municipality." Or propositions of fact can suggest the desirability or undesirability of certain policies, such as: "The present city government is detrimental to all citizens." Propositions of fact can also affirm or deny:

1  The existence of things. (There is a shoe store in the area.)
2  The occurrence of acts. (Neighbor Potter shot the intruder.)
3  The classification of objects. (The cat is a four-legged creature.)
4  The connection of events. (The water boiled before the eggs were dropped in.)

## Propositions of Value

Propositions of value simply present a value judgement: Phyllis is a super organizer. America is beautiful.

Sometimes you know exactly what your proposition is going to be. Other times you have to think about it for a while.

## How to State your Proposition

In a formal speech you may say, "We resolve that capital punishment should be abolished," but in an informal speech you may just say, "I don't think we should use capital punishment under any circumstances.'' Or you may state the proposition in the form of a question, "Should murderers be executed?''

Sometimes you make propositions in a speech without being aware that you are doing so. A young man at a luncheon meeting said he was going to tell a couple of stories, that's all. "I'm not going to give a speech," he said, then added, "I'm just going to let you know that the fishing is good at Gulf Creek." Then he proceeded to tell some funny stories, illustrations, both factual and hypothetical. He didn't intend to do so, but he was persuading an audience that it was time to get out their fishing poles and head for Gulf Creek.

No matter how you decide what your proposition will be or how you will state it, when you start a persuasive speech, you should observe the following recommendations:

*In stating your proposition, there are certain things to keep in mind.*

1 *Use one central idea.* Don't confuse your audience. If you wish to argue that a street light be installed at 4th and Maple, that's sufficient. Don't add that the road should be changed to a four lane highway and the bike lanes eliminated. Some speeches have two or three propositions, however, and if you decide on more than one, try to relate one to the other.

2 *Keep it simple.* Avoid ambiguous terms. The proposition beginning: "Resolved that the United States should guarantee higher education to all its citizens," has several ambiguous terms. Does "guarantee" mean that food, clothing, tuition must be provided, or just the opportunity to seek them? Does "higher" mean university, trade school, graduate school?

3 *Try to avoid prejudicial terms of adjectives.* Don't say "the infamous Senator McFillie should be removed from office." That's what you're trying to prove—that he is infamous.

4 *Don't hurry.* Phrasing a proposition, finding out whether it is valid, whether it can be adapted to the occasion and to the audience, should be a thoughtful process which determines the purpose of your persuasive act.

Remember—the proposal is desirable to the audience if it agrees with their values, is associated with sound values and the arguments you present are consistent with their standards of what is true and desirable.

The next step is to show the relationship of your proposition to sound reasoning, based on methods previously explained in this chapter: i.e., cause–effect, induction, deduction, analogies, etc.

## The Persuasive Speech

Now that you have (1) decided that you wish to persuade, (2) designed your proposition, and (3) stated your case by showing the relationship of your proposition and your reasoning, you are ready to organize your persuasive speech. Chapter 5 will help you understand the types of supporting materials you have to work with and Chapter 6 will help you understand various organizational methods.

Most persuasive speeches usually deal with problems and solutions: (1) There is a problem that requires change; (2) your proposal offers a solution; (3) your proposal is the best solution.

You can always offer an alternative course of action, but you will still wish to prove that your proposal is superior. Therefore think it through.

In Chapter 6, "Organizing the Message," we will clarify the problem–solution organizational pattern you will most often use when deciding to persuade an audience. If you will recall the chart at the beginning of this chapter, you will remember that we speak for many purposes, all of which interrelate and overlap. Though we have discussed persuasive speaking, remember that you need not restrict your speech to persuasion alone. Tell a joke and give the audience a little information at the same time.

## SUMMARY QUESTIONS

- What are some ethical considerations that a speaker should think about before selecting a topic?
- What does "prior image" mean?
- What are some of the dangers in using highly emotional terms?
- What methods of reasoning are mentioned in this chapter? What are the differences between two of the methods?
- What types of reasoning are generally applied to a persuasive speech?

## EXERCISES

**1**  Attend a lecture by a visiting speaker in your school or place of business. Make a note of the image that was projected in the advertisement of the event. Then record all the specific statements the speaker used to establish his or her credibility, such as: "As an author of three books," "I researched this topic for five years," etc.
Did the speaker fulfill the image of his or her prior publicity?
Did the speaker establish a new image in your mind?

**2**  Give the same speech to two different audiences. To one audience, explain in detail your background and your knowledge of the subject. In speaking to the other audience, refrain from any mention of yourself. Could you sense any change in acceptance?

**3**  Give a speech on a favorite topic to two audiences and change the method of reasoning. Which method worked best? Why?

# REFERENCES

1 Alex Haley, "Virus of Violence," a speech given to the faculty and students of Cleveland State University, spring semester, 1970.

2 H. L. Hollingworth, *The Psychology of the Audience* (New York: American Book Co., 1935) pp. 110.

# 5 SUPPORTING THE MESSAGE VERBALLY AND VISUALLY

Dr. Evelyn Lasser set up her flip chart on the right side of the podium. She arranged her paper so that she could find the quote from *TV Guide* easily and went over quickly in her mind the manner in which she intended to present the evidence she had gathered. She had spent weeks developing her message for this occasion. She began with a question:

"How many of you here today believe—truly believe—that discrimination does not exist in American television?"

As she paused and looked at the men and women in the audience, she was glad she had the facts.

Whether, like Evelyn, you are dealing with a controversial subject, or whether your purpose is to entertain the crowd at the Convention Center, you need *support*. You need some facts or observations; you need to verify those facts, and you need to make some inferences about those facts.

Your first step is to find out just what supporting materials are available and how you can make the best use of them. Like Evelyn, you may wish to support your speech both *verbally* and with *visual aids*.

From the previous chapters you have begun to lay a foundation for your speech. You have prepared yourself for the speaking event, selected and researched your topic, and considered seriously your ethical responsibility and the manner in which you will attempt to build rapport with your audience. You have also started to think about how you will move your speech from idea to idea and from idea to conclusion.

**As a speaker, you're in the building business. You build speeches.**

You are now ready to consider the various materials needed to put all these things together. Just as a fence builder uses wood, nails, iron hinges, and paint to construct a fence, so the public speaker uses illustrations or examples, statistics, testimony, analogies or comparisons, and visual materials to construct a speech.

Neither the builder nor the speaker haphazardly places one material upon the other without regard to design. A house builder may wish to build a house by placing one adobe brick on top of the

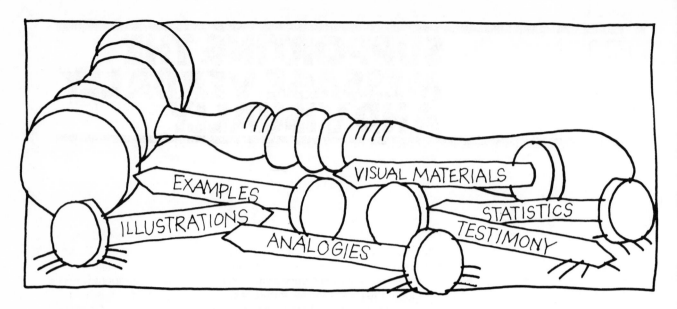

other until a design is evident to the onlookers, or may start with a wood frame and then fill it in with more wood, plaster, and other materials. In much the same way you may decide to present one supporting material after the other until the audience sees the argument or heading it amplifies and is slowly made aware of the design of the speech. On the basis of what you have learned in Chapter 4, you will recognize that method as inductive. On the other hand, you may wish to forthrightly state the heading under consideration and then present supporting material and show how that evidence helped develop the point in mind. This procedure, as you know, is referred to as the deductive method. Or you may wish to move from cause to effect, or reason by comparison. Whatever your choice, the following supporting materials will help you.

## SUPPORTING THE MESSAGE VERBALLY

### Example or Illustration

Homer was a story teller. He survived the ages because everyone loves a story teller. The earliest documents we have of the history of man are filled with narratives. Aristotle felt that every important point in a speech should be followed by an example.

The words "illustration" and "example" are used here interchangeably and both refer to the narration of an incident that helps to clear up the point you wish your audience to understand or consider. There are three types of illustrations: (1) detailed, (2) short (or the example), and (3) hypothetical.

**When and why may detailed illustrations be useful?**

When do you use the detailed illustration? If you feel the audience is not easily convinced and you wish to increase your own credibility, the detailed illustration can be effective. It is used to create interest, clarify a point, and supply persuasive evidence. It also adds vividness to your speech.

For example, a student in a political-campaign class reported to the class that he had just returned from Atlanta. "I was personally invited by Chip Carter," he said. The professor asked him to relate his experience, so he rose and, realizing that everyone in the class did not immediately believe his statement, he said:

"About a year before the election, when Jimmy was still 'Jimmy Who?,' I was invited to a party. When I arrived in my leisure suit, I found everyone very dressed up and very few people my age there. I looked around and saw this young kid in casual attire so I decided to talk to him. We hit it off pretty well and after he left we corresponded. Well, his name was Chip Carter. Last week I got a telephone call and, when I answered, a voice said 'Hi, this is Chip Carter,' and I said 'You bet.' But then he kept talking and I thought 'Hey, maybe it *is* Chip Carter.' Well, he invited me to a special party *he* was giving for all the people he had met around the country while he was campaigning for his father. Everything was paid for, my room and board, except for the airfare. Well, I didn't have the money, but my aunt raised it and I spent two great days in Atlanta."

The student went on to tell in detail what was served and who attended. Everyone in the class knew he had worked for the Carter campaign in New Mexico and they enjoyed the detailed and factual story. The narration took fifteen minutes of class time.

**Short stories can be useful, too.**

You may not wish to devote that much time to an illustration. Or you may wish to tell several short stories to persuade people to join a campaign or to buy a product. Short illustrations take less time and can swiftly and vividly make a point.

When Muhammad Ali was asked to give a speech at the Bobby Foster Awards Dinner in Albuquerque, New Mexico in 1974, he chose to give several vivid examples to support his contention that he was the greatest fighter on the platform. On the platform with him were Ed Norton, George Foreman, Joe Frazier, and Bobby Foster. Although many of the examples were similar, the audience enjoyed hearing him tell several stories about his fights.

*A short illustration or example* can be as simple as the one a skier used to explain the many aspects of being on a ski patrol. He talked about the search for the body of a friend after an avalanche.

*I had a long pole and I kept probing at the snow. Heck, I didn't even know what a body was supposed to feel like. I kept worrying that I'd miss it. One of the other skiers laid down in the snow and said, "Go ahead and poke me. See what it feels like." I did and then I was haunted by the thought that maybe somewhere on the hill I had touched him without knowing it and every minute was precious.*

*A short example* can also merely be a statement like: "Don't forget the incident at Kent State, when innocent students were shot down."

*Short illustrations* are often condensed, undetailed, and contain only the essential elements.

*Hypothetical illustrations* can often be used when you do not have a suitable factual example at your disposal. Hypothetical illustrations can also be adapted to the particular moment and audience. They can also be used to explain a complicated process. For example, a professor of law used a hypothetical example as a teaching aid. He said:

*Assume for the sake of an example that a small boy has fallen into a pit in the back of a house, in a construction area partially filled with broken terrazzo, and has suffered severe cuts and bruises over much of his body. Assume that the attorney knows that the testimony of the defendant's witness shows that this is customary procedure in the construction business for disposing of terrazzo. Surely one of the themes you are going to develop should be that the industry is negligent.*

**Like the other elements in a speech, illustrations also have rules.**

When using illustrations or examples, keep in mind the following points:

1 *Illustrations must be relevant.* The attorney gave an example that dealt with the point of law he was making.

2 *The relationship of the heading and the subheading must be clear.* Muhammad Ali said he could beat *all* the fighters at the dinner (heading). He told a story about how he beat Foreman (subheading), then one about how he would beat Norton and Frazier (subheading).

3 *Use detail and be vivid but don't crowd the point with frills.* The attorney used detail but did not go to unnecessary lengths about the manner in which the boy's eyes were affected.

4 *Develop the example in an orderly sequence.* It is difficult to follow a rambling story. Use the same technique to illustrate a point as you do to organize a speech; that is, give the story a beginning, body, and conclusion.

5 *Be accurate.* People love to repeat stories. If your example is hypothetical, be *sure* to tell your audience that such is the case. Try to relate the facts of a real happening as truthfully as you can.

6 *Use a number and variety of illustrations.* Several short illustrations will make your speech vivid and exciting. If you tell a long story, make the remainder of your illustrations short and clear.

**Statistics**

A 1973 survey by the R. H. Bruskin Associates involving 2543 male and female adults indicated that 40.6 percent of the respondents feared speaking before a group. They were asked to pick the items from a list of the following: speaking before a group, height, insects, financial problems, deep water, sickness, death, flying, and loneliness. Some 40.6 percent were afraid of speaking before a group; 32.0 said they were afraid of height, 22.1 of insects, 21.5 of deep water, 18.8 of sickness, 18.7 of death, 18.3 of flying, 13.6 of loneliness, and 11.2 of dogs.

What do these statistics mean? That folks are more afraid of deep water than of dying? Or maybe it means that some people are afraid of insects and some are afraid of dying—but a lot are afraid of speaking before a group.

Can you remember all those figures? Do you believe them? You may want to ask who the group of male and females were. The study didn't indicate that.

*Build your statistics ve-e-ry carefully.*

People are apt to throw a lot of figures around because others are generally impressed by them. But there are a few rules for using statistics in speeches that you may wish to consider:

1 When using statistics in comparisons, make sure each item has the same base. Know also the sample size upon which percentages are based, otherwise comparisons using statistics are invalid. And invalid statistics can be very misleading. For example, last year at School X, student participation in intramural activities increased 100%; at School Y it increased 25%. By percentages, School X did better than School Y in that area. But numerically it looks different: Participants at School X went from 50 students to 100, while the participants at School Y increased from 4000 to 5000. So is School Y doing better than School X? Maybe. But School X has a registration of 400 students and School Y has 20,000—which means that at *each* school, 25% of the students participated in intramural activities. As we can see, it is very important to use only those statistics that are valid for the point being made.

2 Comparative statistics must also use the same units of measurement. In distances and speeds, for example, 100 miles and 100 kilometers aren't even nearly the same.

3 Statistics should support the point or heading they are intended to reinforce, not something else.

4 If exact figures are relevant to your point, then go ahead and say "It will cost 312,916 dollars." But your audience will find it much easier to remember "over 300,000 dollars," and in most cases that is sufficiently precise, too.

5 Use statistics that are easy for the mind to grasp. It is accurate to say that "In 1965, motor vehicles were involved in 49,000 fatalities in this country." It is equally accurate, and easier to comprehend, to say that "In 1965, motor vehicles in this country were involved in a fatality every 11 minutes."

6 Attribute the statistics to a reliable source, unless, of course, *you* are the president of the company.

7 Be prepared to defend your statistics.

It's a good idea to check out the manner in which the data was gathered. For years crime reports based upon FBI information were not questioned. Cities were considered no. 1 in crime, or no. 10, on the basis of how many felonies, homicides, and other crimes were reported. Lately evidence shows that not all police chiefs report every item. Furthermore, for various reasons, not everyone who is burglarized, for example, reports the burglary to the police. Unless we consider all the factors that go into the collection of our data, it is difficult to come to a valid conclusion.

However, whether or not you have access to this information, it is well to be aware of the values and beliefs of your audience, as well as their attitude toward both the use and the source of your statistics.

## Authority and/or Testimony

In public speaking, testimony mainly means proof by authority. That is why, when we speak of World War II, for example, we often quote Roosevelt, Churchill, Stalin, and Hitler.

Every day of our lives we quote or paraphrase someone whose testimony we respect. A mother says, "My son, the doctor, says there is no cure for the common cold." We quote the bus driver who knows the city streets, a reporter on an evening paper, our sister, our dentist, or even the President of the United States. We use such testimony because it is so *easy* to obtain.

There are several weaknesses to the use of testimony to support our propositions. One is that such evidence really doesn't prove anything. All it says is that a certain person possesses certain beliefs which you feel are worth quoting. And you feel they are worth quoting because you believe that the audience will accept their beliefs as valid.

In spite of all that's said, testimony can be effective, especially if:

1 It is relevant and appropriate.

2 It is accurate and you have some kind of written proof to back it up.

3 The meaning is not altered when the testimony is taken out of context.

**4** When paraphrasing, the audience is informed of what you are doing.

**5** It is short enough to follow and long enough to make the point.

**6** The source of the quote is acceptable to the audience.

**7** The recency of the quotation is relevant to the subject.

No special rule tells us when to use an example and when to use a statistic. Aristotle favored using examples whenever possible; he urged speakers to follow every statement with an example. Today, however, audiences are interested in statistics and are often swayed by testimony. A speaker must present those materials that are persuasive to the particular audience. Using a *number and variety* of materials strengthens your statements of purpose and adds zest to your speech.

## SUPPORTING THE MESSAGE VISUALLY

A form of supporting material relatively new to the public speaker is the visual aid, which can be useful in presenting the materials just discussed. When considering using the visual aid, ask yourself what your purpose is in doing so. Do you wish to simplify your oral message with visuals because it is complex? Do your visuals present more accurate sensory images than your oral message? If you are satisfied that visual aids will contribute substantially to your message, then design them so that they will do one or more of the following: Add new understanding to your speech, catch the attention of your listeners, aid in the retention of information, and generally improve your presentation.

It would be impossible to list all the many ways of presenting information visually, especially since new ways are created as new ideas are born. Since the arrival of Phineas Taylor Barnum, Americans have applauded imaginative visual methods of gaining their attention.

Let's explore situations in which you might use visuals as supportive material and to gain attention. We will consider the use of visual materials in a television appearance, in the instructional or informational message, and in the persuasive speech.

### Planning the Television Graphic

In advocating the passage of legislation to eliminate billboards in your city you have aroused so much interest that the manager of the local television station has asked you to present your views on that station's facilities. The subject is important to you, so you agree to appear on TV. At other appearances you have made, you've passed

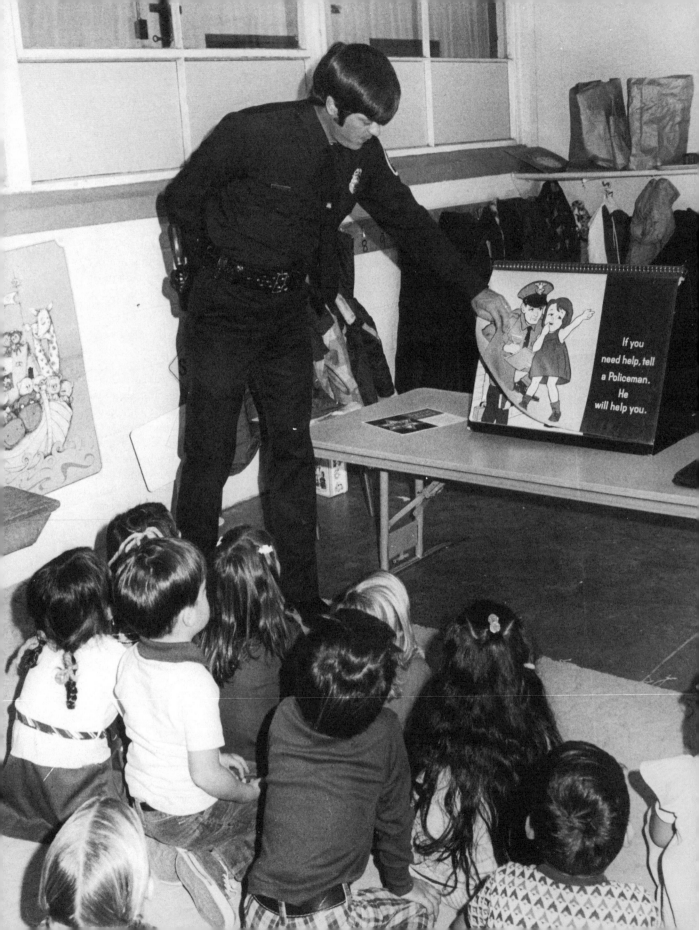

around pictures of the countryside as it was years before without billboards, then shown some color slides of the existing billboards. You want to present these visual materials on television.

Most of your slides are acceptable to the station's producer. They were shot horizontally and the composition is good. The billboards are situated in the central part of each slide and are colorful. Some of the slides show many billboards and signs. All your vertical slides were rejected.

Your photographs are black and white and are not as dramatic as the slides. However, because they show the before-and-after aspects of the situation and contain much needed information, the producer wants to use some of them. Those used have had a 3 × 4 ratio and are mounted on colored cardboard backgrounds of the same proportions.

The key considerations in planning television graphics are: (1) picture ratio; (2) system limitations (black and white or color); (3) major types of visuals; and (4) basic lettering systems.

**Picture ratio**  The ratio of the television picture is three units in height by four units in width. The size of the television image is called the camera field. The picture you see on your monitor is smaller than the camera field. Therefore, when you use a picture you have not prepared especially for television, be prepared to lose some of the outer edges of it. For television, all graphic materials must appear in what is called the critical area.

For example, a television title card should be 14 × 17 inches overall. The working space should be 9 × 12 inches and centered on

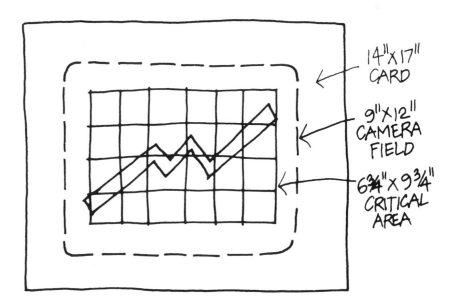

14" x 17" CARD

9" x 12" CAMERA FIELD

6¾" x 9¾" CRITICAL AREA

the card. Graphic *content* (that is, the information you feel is crucial) should be held in an area that is 6¾ × 9¾ inches. In this critical area all of the message will be seen by the viewer.

**System limitation**  If you have black and white television, the system can see and render only a limited number of shades. Remember, we spoke of tones when discussing all the varying shades of gray. In television it is wise not to be too subtle. Strong contrast is best. The same is true of color systems.

**Major types of visuals**  You decide to use title cards. And you mount your photographs on cards of the proper dimensions. Other things that can be put on cards are logos, charts, graphs, quotations, key words, drawings, etc.

*Super cards* create the effect of white letters over a live TV scene. TV panel participants, for example, are often identified by their names superimposed on the bottom part of their picture. The super card is prepared like the title card, but the lettering only appears as white; the black of the card does not reflect light and is not seen.

*Charts and maps* on television are used in weather reports. Note, however, how *large* they are. Note too that they are simplified. Many public speakers wish to appear on television with charts and maps made up for live audiences, but these visuals seldom can be adapted to television. Charts and diagrams showing too many lines are very difficult for the television audience to understand, and those used in normal written reports contain far too much information.

Television producers also use *gobos* and *crawls.* A gobo is a piece of artwork with a cutout in it; the camera views both the artwork and the scene that is visible through the cutout portion. A *crawl* is graphic material prepared on a long, narrow strip of paper and mounted on a cylinder—or on two separated cylinders—so that it can be moved continuously past the camera. Gobos and crawls are normally prepared by the studio rather than by the speaker.

If you are preparing any lettering, be sure to make it look professional. If you cannot print well, you can use *rub-on* letters. They are printed on a thin plastic sheet and when the letter is rubbed onto the art-work surface, it is transferred. Plastic letters can be arranged on a flat surface or on a slotted feltboard. As with charts and diagrams, the letters used should be simple and of a weight and size such that they can be easily read but will not be distracting.

Finally, materials to be used on television should be presented to the producer of the show at least 48 hours before air time (in many instances producers want them a full week before). Sometimes the station will prepare all the visuals for you, but on small local stations you are often responsible for your own materials. You will have a better chance of using them if you prepare them properly.

*Design all visuals to be clearly seen and readily understood.*

Remember that visual thinking means experimenting with materials and techniques. If you know the systems' capabilities, use them as a guideline to explore new shapes, new colors, new dimensions.

## Visuals for Instructional or Informational Messages

Instructors at the University of New Mexico Medical School prefer 35mm slides to any other visual format. Next to slides they like 16mm film, then video tapes, lantern slides, microscopic slides, print handouts, and finally the chalkboard. They prefer slides because: (1) except for the blackboard they are the least expensive; (2) they are colorful, which is often very important in presenting medical information; and (3) they are simplest to integrate into other instructional materials. Instructors say they rarely use models because they are so expensive.

At the Truman Middle School, in Albuquerque, New Mexico, the teachers and students have access to a media center. The media center has a printer, materials for opaques, a color lab for processing slides, and a complete video system for making videotapes. Because the school has several monitors placed in an open classroom atmosphere, the instructors use videotapes extensively in teaching. The students tape a weekly news program about the events in their school.

The determining factors in developing visuals for the instructional message are: (1) budget; (2) availability of material and equipment; (3) size of audience; and (4) size of room. Because not all schools are so fortunate as the Truman Middle School, many professors and teachers still use the chalkboard extensively.

**Chalkboard**   The advantages of a chalkboard are its immediate availability and repeated erasability. It is large and can be used for those on-the-spot comments that are generated by audience involvement in a speech. Information on a chalkboard must be legible. The problem with chalkboards is that instructors are apt to turn their backs to the audience for long periods of time while they write too much information. If the instructor wishes to put a lot of information on a chalkboard, he or she should arrive early and have it visible as the class enters.

**Photographs**   A professor invited the two candidates in the gubernatorial race to his public speaking class. The class was large, approximately three hundred students, and the auditorium seated one thousand. Students from other classes came to hear the two men debate. However, the candidates refused to appear together. The Republican candidate agreed to speak first and leave, at which time the Democratic candidate would speak.

The Republican candidate brought a huge picture of himself, six by nine feet, and the professor attached it with tape to the chalkboard. After the presentation, the candidate left, leaving the huge photograph still in place. The Democratic candidate did not remove the photograph. Instead, he referred to it in making the point that the Republican candidate was all bombast and show.

Pictures can create moods and emotions and reveal the actual conditions of an event. However, they can also be misrepresented by the speaker and interpreted according to the viewer's own biases.

*You might test other visuals this way, too.*

Before using photographs, try to put yourself in the place of the audience—physically and intellectually. First, sit in the audience seats. Actually try sitting in different areas of the room. What do you see? Does the picture change when you change positions? What do you see when you are in the front row? In the back row? If there is much room for misinterpretation, perhaps it would be better to pass the photograph around. If you do this, be prepared to have your audience distracted at varying times. Although there are many good photographs around that you can use to illustrate your speech, consider taking your own for a really fresh approach. It's not as difficult as you might think; today there are cameras that have automatic light meters and automatic focusing. It is not difficult to take your own pictures so long as you remember that there is no such thing as an objective photograph when you are dealing with people or events. You are behind that camera and it is your point of view that is recorded. But why not? After all, it's your speech and you wish to visualize it. Even if you do not consider yourself a good photographer, give it a chance. Press the button, record a moment in history. If you feel really incompetent, ask a fellow photographer to take the picture under your direction, or take a short evening course at your local high school. Remember that when taking a picture you must think of where you will use it. If you intend to use it for your television speech, take medium and close-up shots. If you wish to blow it up and make a poster, a long shot may be just as effective.

**Graphs**   The reason for using graphs is that people can absorb pictured data easier than the long verbal explanation of those data. There are many types of graphs—some of which are shown on the next page—and they present data in various ways.

A line graph is very familiar to most audiences, for it is very widely used. The line graph shows a series of facts with two variables—time and quantity. Although it is plotted on many separate data points, the curve of a line graph presents its information as a constant flow.

Bar graphs can be especially interesting if done in various colors. Comparative data are grouped into vertical or horizontal *bars* and presented as separate steps, or as separate points. It is best to draw

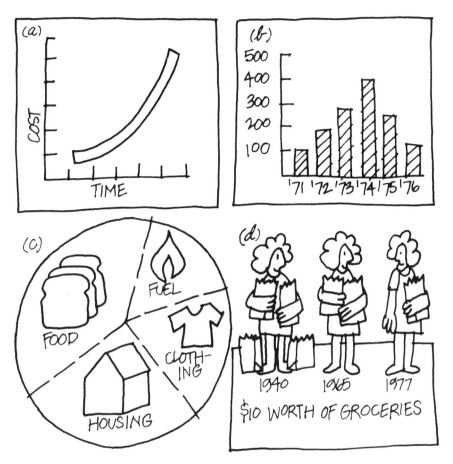

the bars on very stiff cardboard for easy handling. As in all visual messages, the key is simplicity.

The pie graph is excellent for showing relationships among the component elements of the graph. It is a little restrictive in that the pie must represent a whole, or 100 percent of whatever it depicts. The slices may—but don't need to—be given numerical values (percentages, dollars, etc.) which must add up to the whole. If the label for a given slice is too large to fit in the available space, it may be set outside the pie in the appropriate location, perhaps with a line connecting it to its slice. The pie can also be considered a form of chart.

A pictorial graph, while not as precise as the others we've shown here, is usually much more exciting visually. It can employ figures and often is the easiest type of graph to understand. In the example we have shown (Fig. 5.2d), you don't even need to know how to read the language to get the point; the numbers and the three pictures say it all.

The best graphs are simple, contain one or two ideas (at most), are easy to see, and clarify the oral information.

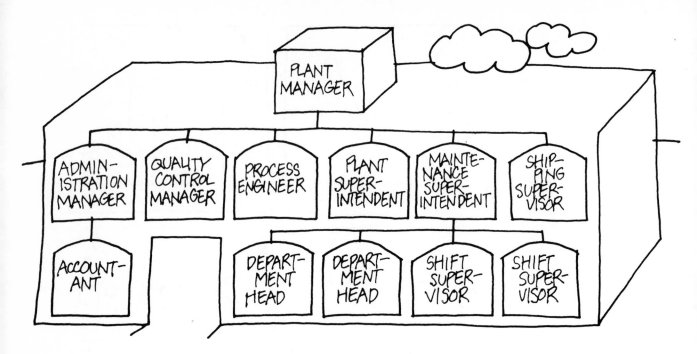

**Charts** Organizational charts are perhaps the most popular kind of charts used by speakers who wish to inform. Almost every organization, from Kiwanis to PTA, from Boy Scouts to Concerned Citizens of Ward 13, puts together organizational charts. Organizational charts can explain who is responsible to whom, the various levels of administration, the type of work for which each level or person is responsible, and the role each person plays in the organization. An organization chart is put together with a set of rules. The higher up the person or thing is on the chart, the more important he or she or it is. Equal ranking persons are on the same level, and like functions are grouped together. The organization chart does not describe a thing, but an idea. You are using a set of rules that make sense to you and your audience. A single part of that chart does not constitute a language—it is like a single symbol. As in verbal language, a symbol must be related to another symbol in order to represent a larger meaning.

Other types of *charts* include the pie (as we have mentioned) and flow charts. Flow charts generally use arrows and lines to explain how a process works and how various elements in the process relate to one another.

**Film** Most speakers do not produce their own films but rely on commercial film distributors, public libraries, museums, industry, and governmental agencies to supply them with professional films. Your telephone company, for example, can provide excellent films on communication which they lend to organizations with or without accompanying speakers. The libraries of universities have many films and also will rent films to instructors.

You should consider several things when acquiring a film. How long is it? Will film be the major portion of the presentation, while you are relegated to being its presentor? Do you have a projectionist? Do you realize that the room must be darkened, that everyone's eyes will be on the film, and that you, the speaker, will be of secondary importance?

*Films are available in various lengths and on many subjects.*

In recent years, fortunately, many short films have been produced on a wide range of subjects, so a speaker can use them to add to the verbal information he or she presents.

Once again, let us urge you to experiment with your own camera. Many people have 8mm cameras at home, used only for those family get-togethers. Although film is more expensive than 35mm slides, sometimes you need to project that feeling of *motion*. Buy yourself a primer on film making—any one of the many on the market. Keep your camera steady, don't zoom in and out except for very good reason, be sure there is enough light, and check your focus. Then go out and discover the world around you. Remember, if you are speaking about a specific problem in your community, a film about someone else's similar problem won't always work. If you are giving a speech about the dangers of open sewers, a film showing children in your neighborhood playing around those sewers is much more effective than a film about the general problem of open sewers. When you personalize both verbally and visually, you are assured of a multisensory image.

In the chart on the following page, we *suggest* that some of the materials we have discussed (A) lend themselves well to certain types of speeches (B) and certain speech purposes (C). But keep in mind that *all* supporting materials can be used at any point of this chart.

## Visual Materials for the Persuasive Speech

The best examples of visualization and persuasion come from the advertising field. From P. T. Barnum and his much publicized freaks to Madison Avenue and its hydra-headed campaigns, the American public has been treated to countless models of persuasion.

One of the most visual of persuaders was the merchant prince, John Wanamaker. His first store was called Oak Hall. He knew he had to persuade people to come into the store. He scattered six-inch posters with "W. & B." written on them all over the city of Philadelphia. This became the main topic of conversation around town. The people were mystified. A couple of days later a second set of posters was circulated, stating that Wanamaker and Brown were selling clothes at Oak Hall. Later, great 100-foot signs proclaimed the same thing. Then he sent up huge balloons, and whoever brought the balloons back got a new suit of clothes.

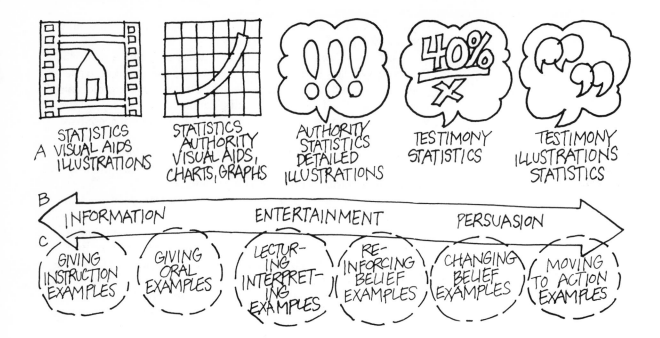

With the development of the half-tone process—an etched-line engraving technique which replaced the woodcut—America "busted out all over" with artwork. When color came into ads in the middle 1890s, persuasion by illustration was on its way.

An expressive face always captured the attention of the American public. Charles Dana Gibson always featured the drawing of a beautiful girl in his ads. The "Gibson Girls" shared attention with the Cream of Wheat chef and the Hire's Root Beer boy. Beauty and love of children went into many advertising campaigns.

After color in magazine ads the next step was electric billboard displays. H. J. Heinz rented a huge sign on New York's Flatiron Building and put up a great pickle in green bulbs, with "Heinz" written on it in white. Underneath were wild colored flashing bulbs spelling out "57 varieties," "Sweet Pickles," "Chili Sauce," "Tomato Catsup," and "Vinegar."

In this modern world, we are bombarded by visual persuasive messages every day of our lives, and every visual is designed to inform and persuade. The advertising logo contains a lot of information. The 30-second spot has been given careful attention. Decisions about color, tone, line, or direction in any persuasive message are not accidental. While the initial creative impulse in an ad may be emotional, the production of that ad is logical—and both processes involve some mental gymnastics.

When deciding to use visual materials to support your speech, don't be afraid to borrow from the verbal criteria, don't be afraid to make up your own criteria—and don't be afraid to dream.

## SUMMARY QUESTIONS

- What are the different types of illustrations mentioned in this chapter?
- When would the use of an hypothetical illustration be appropriate?
- What should you remember when using statistics for comparison purposes?
- What are the important considerations in planning the television graphic?
- What are the determining factors in preparing visuals for the instructional message?

## EXERCISES

**1** Select a topic and prepare a detailed illustration to support your main statement. Then shorten the illustration to a brief example. Finally, support the statement with a single sentence. What are the advantages of each form of illustration?

**2** Collect statements from leading politicians on the subject of energy. Then collect statements from leading scientists on the same subject. Which statements do you prefer? Why?

**3** Prepare a speech for a live audience and then adapt it for a television audience. What did you have to do to make it appropriate for each audience?

**4** Visit your local television studio and ask permission to witness a live television production (news program, documentary, panel show). What preparations did the participants seem to go through? How did those preparations differ from those of a speaker who addresses a live audience?

# ORGANIZING THE MESSAGE

Anxiously, the first trumpeter began to give his biweekly fundraising report to the other members of the college band: "Well, folks, it's getting late in the drive. We only have two more weeks to go. Region One has set a fine example for the rest of us. They have surpassed their goal by 50 percent. Let's hear it for Region One. Now, Region Two hasn't done so well. Despite all efforts, most of the people in Region Two seem to be too busy to get out and ring the doorbells. Now is that too much to ask? For the record, Region Two has only collected 47 percent of their goal. If we hope to raise the entire $50,000 and make it to the Orange Bowl, we need the full cooperation of everyone, especially Region Two. The rest of the Regions also have some problems. Let's review the specifics. . . ."

The forty young women in the classroom listened attentively as the speaker, another young woman, told them: "Ninety percent of the rapes on campus are not reported, so don't let the figures fool you. The danger is here, now, and we must be prepared to defend ourselves. First, we must learn to recognize the assailant; second, we must learn the art of self-defense—for example, the well-placed kick, the hat-pin jab, or even Karate. Third, we must know when to scream and when to run. Finally, we must report . . . report . . . . report. We must report every incident, and not be afraid to face our assailants."

The department foreman stood behind his table as he spoke to the fifteen people in his department. "The boss just sent me a memo outlining a change in vacation and overtime policies. Effective July first, all employees will be allowed three weeks vacation. You must indicate your preferences for dates six months in advance, and seniority will determine who gets what dates. Regarding overtime, effective immediately. . . ."

Whether geographically reporting the success or failure of a fundraising campaign, or chronologically reporting a step-by-step procedure for handling rapists, or topically informing employees of new company policies, these speakers were applying principles of effectively organizing their messages.

## WHY ORGANIZE?

A speech is a system whose parts all affect the whole and each other. Just as a pebble thrown into the water creates ripples throughout the entire pond, so do the various components of a speech eventually influence each other. A speech typically has three parts: an introduction, a body, and a conclusion. Organizing your speech will help you to see the parts, how they relate to each other and to the whole speech.

By the time you come to organizing your message you have a fair idea of what's going to go into that speech. You have developed a point of view, engaged in some research, further developed your message by exploring the various supportive materials, and thought about how everything will fit together. You are still in the prewriting stage, however, so you're apt to do a little more rambling and wandering as your creative impulses keep your mind in motion. Because you are unique, your method of arranging your material into some form will be unlike anyone else's. A young professor said he prepares his convention speeches like this: "I just sit down at a typewriter and let the words pour out. However lousy a sentence is, I let it go. I write on to the end. Then, the subconscious mind has done what it can. The rest is simple effort, going over the speech time and time again until, though I know it isn't right, it is the best I can do. Finally I practice before a friend whose advice helps me shape the final product."

One of the authors "talks" her writing so that she will know how it "sounds." Many radio and television writers are taught to read their copy aloud as they put it together.

Whether you follow one of these techniques or one of your own, organizing your messages will help you to synthesize your speech, to better see the parts and how they relate to the whole, to see if you have too much or too little support for a particular point, to assess the coherence and relevance of your remarks, and finally to rehearse your speech and reduce your anxiety. By being well prepared, you will worry less about forgetting major points in your speech. Some speakers give their speeches from well planned outlines, others go further and construct each sentence. In this chapter we will deal with the organization of a speech and with types of outlining.

## PRINCIPLES OF ORGANIZATION

Organization begins with the gathering of materials, the arrangement of ideas into a logical order, and the preparation of a preliminary draft of an outline; it ends with the completed draft to be used in rehearing the speech. The following five steps will help you to better organize your messages:

1 Arrange your main points in an appropriate pattern.

2 Determine the best and most appropriate order for your main and supporting points.

3 Follow the rules of coordination and subordination for your main and supporting points.

4 Prepare a mechanically correct outline.

5 Use appropriate and frequent transitions.

## 1. Arrange Your Main Points in an Appropriate Pattern

*Question yourself as you construct your speech.*

Once your central idea is selected, you must begin to arrange your main points in a pattern suitable both for your purpose and for the attitudes, interests, knowledge, and needs of your audience. Arranging your main points in such a pattern will undoubtedly help both you and your audience to remember your speech—you in the delivering of it and the audience in the retelling. Most speeches, regardless of their length, divide nicely into from two to five main points.

The most typical patterns for arranging the main points of a speech are: topical; spatial; chronological; causal; and problem/solution. How will you decide which one to use? Let's say you have decided to talk about gun control to your local Chamber of Commerce. But why this topic? Hasn't it been done to death? You answer yourself, "Yes, but in my community a gun control ordinance is coming up in the city council next week." Good point. Okay, what kind of an arrangement do you want? "Well (you say), I could give the history of gun control laws. I looked them up, and did you know that back in 1884. . . ?" Wait, do you think that *this* audience wants to start back there? "No, they are worried about the bill passing in city hall next week. Well, I have a list of all the crimes in our city with guns, from the last five years. There's been an increase of over 500 percent! We have a problem and something needs to be done. Aha! I will speak about the problem and then offer a solution."

This thinking process illustrates how you may go about selecting your pattern of organization. Actually, this speech on gun control could also have been organized topically (providing explanations of gun control laws), spatially (discussing the laws in different cities in the U.S.), chronologically (detailing the history of laws), or causally (showing the cause/effect relation between no gun control and high crimes). The selection of the problem/solution pattern was determined by the immediate needs of this particular audience. Let's look now in more detail at these five patterns.

## Topical

Now that he had lost almost 100 pounds, Marty was proud of his new figure as he stood before his 60 overweight friends and colleagues. As an FFP (formerly fat person), he could empathize with their anxieties, needs, and expectations as he outlined for them the correct amounts, types, and preparations of acceptable food products. After Marty finished speaking, Marylynn, a true heroine of the local Weight Watchers group, arose to a standing ovation when she announced the secret of her 250 pound loss: controlling the pace and place of eating.

Marty, by focusing on the major parts of a successful weight control program, and Marylynn, by citing the reasons for her victory over obesity, were both using topical outlining. When speakers approach a subject on the basis of categories, groups, parts, reasons, kinds, types, similarities, traits, advantages, etc., they are using the topical pattern. Witness Marty's main points:

I   The amount of food you consume can be accurately measured by using our special scales.

II  The types of food you eat are selected from our expertly balanced diets.

III Healthy food preparation is fully detailed in our new brochure.

Marylynn's main points also show the topical pattern:

I   Eating at a controlled pace will directly influence the amount of food you consume.

II  Eating at an appropriate place will greatly assist you in the control of your weight.

*All speeches have a topic—but not all have a topical arrangement.*

Note how topical outlining is used in the following situations. Although most of the kids were away for the summer, one five-year old boy was sitting, sweating, and shouting behind his homemade lemonade stand, "Get your lemonade! My lemonade's cold and it's really good!" Because he was citing reasons for an act, he was using the topical pattern. When a college student tells his class about the parts of his 10-speed bike, the differences between himself and the rest of his family, or the types of books he reads for pleasure, he is still using topical arrangement of his main points.

Another example of topical outlining was once used by a professional fundraiser addressing a school audience:

I   Sponsoring opening nights of popular movies or shows will typically attract large crowds and large revenues.

II  Fundraising dinners typically produce large amounts of money.

III Direct mailings to known contributors will also produce large amounts of revenue.

Although it is not required, the subordinate points of a speech may employ the same pattern as the main points. This is more often the case with topical outlining. Note how Marylynn did this with her speech on her weight loss:

I  Eating at a controlled pace will directly influence the amount of food you consume.

   a)  Eating too fast usually leads to overeating.

   b)  Eating too slowly may discourage your consumption of needed foods.

II  Eating at an appropriate place will greatly assist you in the control of your weight.

   a)  Eating in the living room, the bedroom, or the den, in front of the television, leads to heavy snacking by many people.

   b)  Eating all food in the kitchen, during regularly scheduled mealtimes, will help retrain your body and mind toward appropriate food consumption.

As we will soon see, topical outlining may be used in combination with other patterns of organization.

### Spatial

They looked tough, mean, and determined with their long hair and black leather jackets, hard faces intensely and alertly focused on their leader.

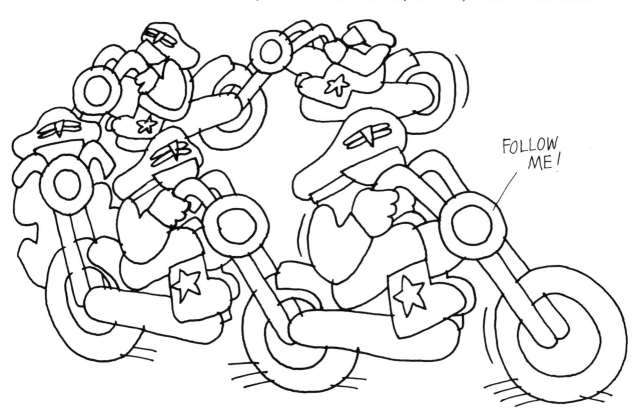

FOLLOW ME!

That one, The Enforcer, gave the others the battle plan: "Jules, you bring your group up the driveway toward the house and get the attention of the security guards. Miltie, you and your riders go around back with the fire bombs; when I give the word, you put 'em through the rear windows. The rest of you come over the side wall with me—and remember to stay behind the trees until the fire bombs go off. Then, we all bug in and grab the hostages. Let's go!"

At another time and place, a detective lieutenant gave orders to his men: "Okay men, here's what's coming down. Stafford and his partner will stay near the cars and cover Jones and Stapleton as they climb up the roof. Murdock and his partner will charge the front door, and I'll come in the back with McGuire and Blaustein. Watch for my signal, and we all go at once. We want the dope and we want the dealers, too. Let's make it work!"

Although on different sides of the law, The Enforcer and the detective both appreciated the value of spatial organization in their lines of work. Both were concerned with geography, space, and direction. Both knew the importance of entrances and exits, of near and far, of east and west, of left and right, of bottom and top. Both were concentrating on the identification, mapping, and conquering of territory.

Note how spatial outlining was used by a physical-training instructor in a recent talk to his exercise group.

I The stomach can be flattened by doing situps.

II The legs and thighs can be strengthened by stationary running or jogging.

III The arms and wrists can be toughened by regularly doing pushups.

*Some speeches are spatially oriented . . .*

Note how a million-dollar-a-year sales person for a large real estate agency uses spatial organization to address her monthly staff meeting:

I The Northeast Heights is the costliest initial investment, but the easiest to resell when desiring to appreciate your investment.

II The Southwest Valley will cost less than the Heights, but it may take longer to resell the property.

Other examples include: a Ranger's talk to the people awaiting his guided tour of a national forest:

I The three clearly marked entrances to the forest are located in its northeast quadrant.

II The five identifiable exits are scattered throughout the entire forest.

A stewardess' regular safety pitch to the 250 passengers on her plane:

I Note how the oxygen masks, needed only in an unlikely emergency situation, will easily fall from the top of the aircraft.

II You can see that our DC-10 luxury liner has several convenient exits located throughout the plane.

And a campaign manager's report on election eve results:

I Voter turnout in the northern half of the state was much lighter than anticipated.

II Turnout in the southern half reflected the active campaigning of the candidates in the larger cities.

Just as when you ask for or give street directions, so do speakers concerned with territory and its implications use the spatial organization pattern.

### Chronological

*. . . and some are arranged chronologically.*

Your vocabulary is filled with words which refer to time: sooner, later, then, now, sometime, yesterday, today, tomorrow, immediately, early, late, last (next) week (month, year, season), etc. You eat, work, and sleep by time. Major events in your lives are structures by time—births, christenings, marriages, retirements, and deaths.

Organizing messages chronologically means attending to the concept of time. Sequencing events, presenting steps in a process, historically describing systems, identifying key dates, and characterizing different seasons all involve the chronological pattern.

Patrick was beaming as he presented his recipe for shrimp and crab chantilly to his gourmet club's weekly meeting:

"First, you melt the margarine in a large frying pan and sauté the shallots, then you add the crab and shrimp and stir until it's all heated. Next, you add the wine, the salt, and the tarragon and cook down until the excess moisture is evaporated. You then spread the mixture in a lightly greased one-and-a-half-quart baking dish.

"OK, now you're ready for the top. You beat the egg whites until they form soft peaks, then add the cornstarch and beat until stiff. That is, until the egg whites are stiff, not you. Stir in the mustard, salt, and Tabasco, spread it over the seafood, and sprinkle with cheese.

"Finally, you bake it at three seventy-five for twenty minutes. It makes four servings, and contains only about one hundred thirty-five calories per serving."[1]

Just as Patrick's sequence of steps in a recipe followed the chronological pattern, so did the talk of a Girl Scout troop leader who was telling her troop how to build a campfire:

I   First, gather sufficient amounts of kindling, tinder, and fuel logs.

II  Then, build a log cabin design and place the kindling and tinder underneath the fuel logs.

III Finally, light kindling and gently fan the fire until the tinder catches.

In speaking to the members of her gym class, the gym teacher told them of their opportunities to observe and participate in a variety of sports:

I   Fall and winter sports include football, basketball, hockey, and soccer.

II  Spring and summer sports include baseball, golf, tennis, and rock climbing.

A member of a debating society briefed other members on the history of the organization:

I   Between our founding in 1944 and the Korean War, our membership grew only four percent.

II  During the next twenty years, we experienced an unusually high growth rate of two hundred and fifty percent.

III Future expectations call for a leveling off due to the founding of three competitive debate organizations.

All of the above examples followed a chronological pattern. As one writer has said, "Time talks" and we should listen to it.

I WANT TO TALK TO YOU ABOUT ORGANIZED SPORTS...

## Causal

A young woman ran into the street where she angrily shouted at the 16 teenagers who were drinking beer in the park across from her house. "You kids are going to wake up my baby! If she wakes up, I'll have to stay up with her most of the night. Then I won't get any sleep. If that happens, I'll be very angry with you bums! And if I get angry, I'll smash the windows in your cars! So quiet down and go home before I call the cops!"

*Some speeches head from cause to effect . . .*

As this woman delivered her public speech to the neighborhood "bums," she was showing how an undesirable condition (the loud, partying kids) would lead to even more severe effects (waking her baby, etc.). This causal pattern of organizing messages is typical of speakers who try to show relationships between certain factors, conditions, or forces and what follows them in the way of results or effects. In other words, what precedes may directly or indirectly cause what follows. Sometimes the reverse is true and a speaker may begin with the effect and lead to its cause(s). For example, as a bowling team captain said in accepting his league's annual trophy for the best team: "Well, you all know that we won. That's right, despite the odds against us, we won! How come? We won because of *my* sterling leadership, *my* exceedingly high average, and *my* wife's permission to let me bowl!"

*. . . (or effect to cause) . . .*

In most speeches using causal patterns, the speaker lists the causes first and then the effects, as did a woman speaking before her homeowners' association.

I   Our neighborhood is plagued with a very high percentage of young, newly married transient renters and owners.

II   The net result is a lack of concern for property upkeep.

Had she desired to further increase the causal chain, she might have added,

III   Ultimately, all our property values will decline.

Another example of the extended causal chain was demonstrated by a candidate for the state legislature in a talk to the political club at the state university:

I   The state is currently run by leaders who advocate unrestrained spending.

II   Uncontrolled spending leads directly to failure to pay off the state's debts.

III   Defaulting on these debts will certainly be followed by a poor credit rating and the inability to borrow needed revenues.

IV   The ultimate effect of all this fiscal irresponsibility is the failure of the state to provide essential services of appropriate quality.

Many times a speaker will identify a particular cause and list its immediate effects, then another cause and its effects, etc. In his semi-annual report to his stockholders one company president illustrated this pattern:

I  The recent recession has affected our financial security.

   a) Our return to investors declined fifteen percent.

   b) Our stocks failed to split for the first time in seven years.

II  The recession has affected our future growth plans.

   a) Plans for the new building have been postponed.

   b) A five percent retrenchment of all personnel is inevitable.

Most of these examples call for the elimination of selected causes due to their undesirable consequences. But, as many speakers know, this is not always the case. Sometimes the effects are so positive that the speaker may plead for adding to or strenghening the causes, as did the Army Colonel addressing his Toastmasters' Club on the subject of Army enlistments:

I  Although the draft has been eliminated, enlistments have not suffered in our volunteer Army.

II  We think this is primarily due to the increase in pay and the wide variety of available jobs.

III  To maintain enlistments, we must keep up with increases in living costs and add to the number of skills we teach.

As speakers become more familiar with the causal pattern, they soon learn to ask:

1  Do the causes produce the effects?

2  Are the effects desirable or undesirable?

3  If the effects are desirable, can the causes be added to or strengthened?

4  If the effects are undesirable, can the causes be removed without leading to other undesirable effects?

## Problem solution

*. . . and some are oriented toward solving problems.*

Mary, who was majoring in Early Childhood Education, stood on top of the chair pleading with the group of three-, four- and five-year-olds entrusted to her care at the university day care center: "Okay kids, we don't have enough toys for everyone. Let's see if we can share the toys we've got and play together. Then, everyone can have fun and play safely."

Kathy, looking very pretty in her new white dress, stood before her third grade class asking them to elect her president: "I think I should win because I can do something about the high price of our milk and the no-seconds at lunch. My daddy knows the principal, and if you elect me, I'll ask him to call him up."

Congressman Winthrop was not so self-conscious as Kathy. He pounded the podium before 2000 wildly cheering supporters and shouted, "You need to re-elect me, to send me back to Washington! You know I will vote for the new increase in gas rates. You know I support your efforts to encourage new exploration for gas. You and I know that without this new increase we will have a shortage of gas never before seen in America. You and I know that without this new increase, millions of homes and industries will suffer reduced amounts of this needed precious fuel."

Mary, Kathy and Winthrop all identified problems, showed the extent and seriousness of those problems by identifying their real and forthcoming negative effects for their immediate audiences, and proposed solutions which they thought were workable, practicable, and desirable. Such is the method of the problem-solution pattern of organizing messages: The speaker identifies a problem, presents its consequences (to involve the immediate audience), and offers a solution (or solutions) which it is hoped will remove the causes of the problem. As indicated earlier, this is a very common pattern when your purpose is persuasion.

Note how a football coach arouses his team in a half-time talk in the locker room:

I   We are trailing by 12 points. Unless we rally, and make a come-back, we're going to lose. And losing this game will have certain results:

a) If we don't win, we don't make the playoffs.

b) If we don't make the playoffs, we won't sell as many season tickets for next year as we could if we do make the playoffs.

c) And if we don't sell the tickets, you guys ain't gonna get the raises next season that you're already honking about.

II Following my strategy should produce a victory:

a) Throw more passes.

b) Use the halfback run/pass option.

c) Use the screen pass if they blitz.

Also facing an immediate problem of major consequence to herself and her organization is the membership director of a college service sorority whose membership is decreasing. In the sorority at an emergency meeting, the director presents the following points:

I Continued drops in membership will place our organization in an extremely vulnerable position.

a) We will lose our student budget support.

b) We will lose our regular meeting room.

c) We will lose our faculty advisor.

II An intensive membership campaign is our only alternative, if our organization is to survive.

a) We must schedule speakers for regular class appearances to explain our goals.

b) We must pay visits to all social fraternities and sororities, as well as to dormitories.

c) We must advertise in the student paper.

d) We must have someone at a display table in the student union every day for two weeks.

In a final example of a problem-solution pattern, the head of the local teachers' union told 2500 dissatisfied teachers:

I The budget cutbacks have destroyed our work incentive.

a) Salary freezes have cost us money.

b) Enrollment increases have harmed the instructional quality.

II It may be that our only solution is to strike.

Once an appropriate pattern of organization is selected, we are ready to organize our speech more carefully.

## 2. Determine the Best and Most Appropriate Order for Your Main and Supporting Points

Many plays follow a set pattern in which characters are introduced, a crisis develops, the "plot thickens" with a falling action or unraveling of the story line, and finally resolution is reached.

In a speech, the order in which main and supporting points should be presented is not always as clear cut as it is in most plays. As we stated earlier, we really don't know conclusively the best order for presenting our most powerful messages. Some audiences pay more attention to what you say first (when they are less tired) and others remember best what they heard last. Naturally, your purpose is to determine the most effective order in which your points should be presented. Speakers should ask the question: "What is the best order for me to use to accomplish my purpose?" The answer to this question depends primarily upon the audience and the speech's purpose.

### Audience

*Audiences can range from cordial to hostile, and you should adapt your approach accordingly.*

If your audience is hostile or your topic controversial, you probably should begin with the messages and support upon which the audience can readily agree, moving slowly toward the areas of potential disagreement. Salespersons generally follow this principle, assuming most buyers to be initially hostile. Salespersons attempt to seek common agreement on their own worth and that of their product before discussing price. (Like me, like my product, like my price.) Politicians like to tell audiences all they have done for their listeners before discussing their stand on a controversial issue.

Beginning with a point of special interest to your audience may sometimes increase your chances of being successful. For example, if you are seeking college donations from an audience of 75 men who are extremely interested in your college's athletic program, then you should stress the applications of the revenues toward rebuilding the stadium before you discuss their use for scholarships. If all arguments in your speech are of equal interest to your audience, and one argument is particularly strong in dramatic appeal, you may choose to use it last, building toward a dramatic climax. This is particularly useful when you have a series of harmful or beneficial effects derived from a particular cause. For example, a speaker addressing the Society for Prevention of Cruelty to Animals, advocating a leash law for a metropolitan area:

I   Allowing pet dogs and cats to roam our streets without a leash is detrimental to their health.

   a) They could get lost.

   b) They could get into fights with unfriendly dogs or cats.

   c) They could get killed by speeding traffic.

On the other hand, beginning with your strongest, most dramatic argument and proceeding toward an anticlimax may be best for your purposes, especially when your audience is fatigued, or you have a long speech, or it is late at night. Some speakers follow Aristotle's advice and begin or end with the most important messages, placing their other points in the middle of the speech.

### Purpose of speech

*The order of your speech may be optional . . .*

Although the main determinant of order seems to be the audience, sometimes the purpose of your speech (to inform, to persuade, to entertain) will help determine when you discuss different topics. If you want to instruct your audience or teach them something, it is usually best to begin with what they are already familiar with and proceed toward the unfamiliar. Likewise, it is also a good idea to provide your simplest information first, building toward the more complex. Just as a golfer begins by familiarizing herself with the clubs and their purposes before learning how to swing them, just as a photographer learns the parts of a camera before taking pictures, just as a chef identifies and assembles the ingredients before cooking them, so should the speaker sequence his or her points according to their complexity.

*. . . or predetermined.*

Occasionally, the pattern of organization will dictate the order of presentation. For example, speakers using the chronological pattern have little choice in determining their order. They must follow the appropriate time sequence or adhere to the logical steps in a process or identify the key dates, proceeding forward or backward. Thus a national park ranger who leads tours on mule-back down the Grand Canyon must follow a predetermined sequence in his training speech to the tourists.

---

## 3. Follow the Rules of Coordination and Subordination for Your Main and Supporting Points

As we said earlier, organizing your speech will help you see the parts and how they relate to each other and to the whole. Using the principles of coordination and subordination will help you not only to see these relationships but also to keep your message logical and internally consistent.

### Coordination

This means that the points at a particular level, main or supporting, are equal in importance to each other. All main points, for example, should share some common element with each other. Note how the addition of a third point to a speech on seasonal sports offerings destroys the consistency and chronology of the speech:

I  Fall and winter sports include football, basketball, and hockey.

II   Spring and summer sports include baseball, golf, and tennis.

III   Effective participation in any sport depends upon adequate conditioning.

*All the pieces have to fit together . . .*

The third point is not chronologically consistent with the first two, and thus is not of equal import in the speech. Perhaps it could support both I and II, or serve as the central idea for the entire speech. Dropping it from the speech is another possibility.

### Subordination

This means that one point in a classification belongs to a lower order than another. A supporting point is subordinate to a main point. Subordinate points are of lesser scope and importance than main points and should appear so in a speaker's outline. In that speech, mentioned earlier, to the 2500 members of the teacher's union, the union leader would have violated the principle of subordination by adding a third point to support the first main point:

I   The budget cutbacks have destroyed our work incentive.

    a)  Salary freezes have cost us money.

    b)  Enrollment increases have harmed the instructional quality.

    c)  The governor is making us the scapegoats for the state's financial problems.

*. . . and in the right order, too.*

Instead if placing the point (c) about the governor as a subordinate point to I, the union leader probably could have made it a separate main point (since it appears coordinate with I).

By following these two simple rules of coordination and subordination, you will undoubtedly increase the logic and consistency of your message, thus making it easier for your listeners to follow and remember.

## 4. Prepare a Mechanically Correct Outline

*And that's why outlines were born.*

Once you have arranged your main and supporting points according to an appropriate pattern and an order which adheres to the principles of coordination and subordination, your next task is to prepare a mechanically correct outline with plans for frequent transitions. Many speakers prefer to make a complete sentence outline at this stage in order to better review their entire speech. However, as preparation continues and rehearsals help familiarize the speaker with the message, an outline of extracted phrases may be quite useful. Although outlines using only key words are sometimes useful when delivering a speech, they tend to be too incomplete during the preparation stage. Whatever the scope of the outline, its utility will be enhanced by following the principles of correct symbol usage, indentation, discreteness, and clarity.

**Use of symbols**

In outlines, symbols are letters and numbers which represent points in your speech. The choice of symbols is yours and the selection is arbitrary, so you should feel free to use any symbols you desire as you prepare your outline. However, since symbols are used to show the relative importance and relationship of ideas to each other, you should be consistent in your selection and assign coordinate points the same symbol.

The accompanying example of how symbols (such as I, A, 1, or a) may be assigned to outline points may be useful to you.

---

USE OF SYMBOLS
WITH OUTLINE POINTS

INTRODUCTION

I  Introductory technique

   A. _____

   B. _____

II.  Central idea

(preview)

BODY

I  Main point _____

   A. Subordinate point _____

      1. Major supporting point _____

      2. Major supporting point _____

   B. Subordinate point _____

      1. Major supporting point _____

      2. Major supporting point _____

         a) Minor supporting point _____

         b) Minor supporting point _____

(Transition)

         c) Minor supporting point _____

      3. Major supporting point _____

(Transition)

   C. Subordinate point _____

      1. Major supporting point _____

         a) Minor supporting point _____

      1) Extended detail_____

      2) Extended detail_____

(Transition)

    b) Minor supporting point _____

  2. Major supporting point _____

    a) Minor supporting point _____

    b) Minor supporting point _____

(Internal summary)

II  Main point _____

  A. Subordinate point_____

    1. Major supporting point _____

    2. Major supporting point _____

(Transition)

  B. Subordinate point_____

    1. Major supporting point _____

    2. Major supporting point _____

CONCLUSION

I  Summary of main points _____

  A. Main point I_____

  B. Main point II _____

II  Concluding statement and techniques _____

  A. _____

  B. _____

In this example, Roman numerals were used to denote main points and capital letters for subordinate points. Arabic numerals with a period, lower-case letters with a parenthesis, and Arabic numerals with a parenthesis were used for supporting points. Note also that every point and subpoint had at *least* two ideas associated with it. If this is difficult, you may find it desirable to eliminate a subpoint or to combine it with a major point.

**Indentation**

In order to help identify at a glance the relationships among the points, use appropriate indentation. Note that the main points in the preceding sample form were at the left margin, and, as we got more specific, we indented further from the left margin. Generally, the broader the point, the closer to the left margin; the more specific the point, the deeper the indentation from the left margin. Additionally, if you use more than one line to write a point, be sure to align the second line directly under the first. See how this is violated in the following outline:

I  Eating at a controlled pace will directly influence the amount of food you consume.

II  Eating at an appropriate place will greatly assist you in the control of your weight.

Besides being visually more pleasing, the following correct outline helps us to more quickly assess the relationship between the two points:

I  Eating at a controlled pace will directly influence the amount of food you consume.

II  Eating at an appropriate place will greatly assist you in the control of your weight.

## Discreteness

*Be discreet; be discrete.*

We all know that to be discreet is to show good judgment. But to be *discrete* is to be separate, distinct, individual. So making your points discrete means placing only one idea in each unit, next to each symbol, main or subordinate. Ideas should not be run together because they confuse your listeners who are trying to see the relationship among your points. Note this violation of that principle:

I  The amount of food you consume can be accurately measured by using our special scales.

II  The types of food you eat and tips on healthful food preparation are explained in our brochure.

By separating the second point into two discrete points, we separate two ideas and avoid potential confusion:

I  The amount of food you consume can be accurately measured by using our special scales.

II  The types of food you eat are selected from our expertly balanced diets.

III  Healthful food preparation is fully explained in our new brochure.

Avoiding the uses of such conjunctions as "and," "or," "but" in the formation of your points will help you follow this principle.

## Clarity

A former President of the United States frequently said in his speeches, "Let me make one thing perfectly clear . . ." and then proceeded to speak with vague, confusing, and extended complex sentences. A good speaker does not announce his or her intentions. If you phrase your points clearly, your audience will know and appreciate it. "Clarity" means being concise and vivid in your word choice. It means short sentences with language designed to excite and appeal directly to the audience. It means using "you" instead of "it." You are clear when you say, "You all waste energy," rather than, "Statistics have shown that Americans expend more energy than is available through our natural resources." You are clear when you say, "Your interests are best served with my election," rather than, "As my record has shown, and I have voted regularly, I am the only candidate who can guarantee, and let me remind you that I voted for the last tax cut, that your best interests will be served." You are clear when you say, "I am innocent," rather than, "As the evidence will show, as the witnesses will substantiate, as my record indicates, I could not possibly have been in violation of the policy."

## 5. Use Appropriate and Frequent Transitions

Speaking is a one-time thing. Audiences need to be constantly reminded of what they've heard, where they are, and where they're going. Speakers can't underline, indent, and capitalize for emphasis. Listeners can't reread the page if they forget or miss a point. The message must be so organized and restated as to help them follow the speech. Successful speakers determine exactly how much restatement is needed for reinforcement without boring their audience. Transitions help provide that needed reinforcement.

*You can get there from here.*

Transitions are bridges which connect points to each other. As words, phrases, sentences, or paragraphs, they conclude one idea and introduce the next. They indicate the relationships among the points and remind you of your exact train of thought. This last purpose underscores their utility as a memory-triggering device of major value during delivery of the speech.

Major transitions typically occur between the introduction and the first main point, commonly called a "preview," and between all other main points. Additionally, some speakers use an "internal summary" in the middle of their speech as a further aid to themselves and their audience. All of these transitions are usually made up of one or more sentences. A grandfather saying grace during a family reunion illustrated a transition between main points: "Now that we've thanked the Lord for the quantity of his plentiful provisions, I want to say a few words about the joy I know we all feel at this assembly of our entire family."

A famous sports announcer once said, "Not only have we seen an excellent display of broken-field running, but we've also witnessed some of the most dramatic chicanery by a quarterback this year."

The "preview" is demonstrated by a teacher's explanation of a course to a new class: "Our course is divided into three sections, each of which will receive about five weeks of study: the body, including the face, gestures, touch, posture, and shape; the voice, including volume, tone, rate, pauses, and nonfluencies; and the environment, including space, territory, time, architecture, and objects."

A candidate for state office used this internal summary, connecting her first two main points with her last two: "More important than the Governor's insensitivity to the needs of the poor and his ignoring of the plight of our unemployed minority group members are the rampant corruption and outright criminal acts typical of his administration. Let's look at corruption first. . . ."

Words commonly used as transitions are:

| | | | |
|---|---|---|---|
| because | secondly | but | as |
| similarly | first | or | however |
| subsequently | nonetheless | moreover | therefore |
| since | and | thus | then |

Transitional phrases and sentences include:

| | |
|---|---|
| Not only . . . but also | Neither . . . nor . . . |
| In the first place . . . | Either . . . or . . . |
| Now that we've seen . . . | On the other hand . . . |
| let's look at . . . | Thus far we've shown . . . |
| In contrast to . . . | We also need to consider . . . |
| Similar to . . . | The question this raises is . . . |
| More important than . . . is . . . | As you can see . . . |

## SAMPLE OUTLINES

Everything we have talked about so far can be summarized nicely in the following full-sentence outline. To follow this review outline, we have included a phrase outline of a speech given by Lavinia (from Chapter 1). Note the differences in detail between the complete-sentence and phrase outlines.

Studying both outlines should reinforce your knowledge of the principles of effective organization and your interest in following them.

### Organizing Your Message

*Introduction*

*(Introductory statement)*  I  Everyone applies the principles of organizing.

*(Introductory technique)*      A.  Recent illustrations support this conclusion.
*(Illustration)*                       1.  College band member
*(Illustration)*                       2.  Speaker on campus rape
*(Illustration)*                       3.  Department foreman

                                  B.  Literary allusions support this conclusion.
*(Quotation)*                          1.  Young professor
*(Quotation)*                          2.  Author

*(Central idea)*  II  Following the principles of effective organization will make you a more successful public speaker.

*(Preview)*                       A.  Select an appropriate pattern for arranging your main and supporting points.

                                  B.  Determine the best and most appropriate order for your main and supporting points.

                                  C.  Follow the rules of coordination and subordination of your main and supporting points.

                                  D.  Prepare a mechanically correct outline.

                                  E.  Use appropriate and frequent transitions.

*Body*

| | |
|---|---|
| *(Main point)* | I   Select an appropriate pattern for arranging your main points. |
| *(Subordinate point)* |    A.   Topical outlines subdivide a subject on the basis of categories, groups, parts, reasons, kinds, types, similarities, traits, advantages. |

I   Select an appropriate pattern for arranging your main points.

A.   Topical outlines subdivide a subject on the basis of categories, groups, parts, reasons, kinds, types, similarities, traits, advantages.

*(Major supporting point)*    1.   Male Weight-Watcher member
*(Major supporting point)*    2.   Female Weight-Watcher member
*(Major supporting point)*    3.   5-yr.-old selling lemonade
*(Major supporting point)*    4.   College student
*(Major supporting point)*    5.   Fundraiser
*(Transition)*   As we will soon see, topical outlining may be used in combination with other patterns of organization.

*(Subordinate point)*    B.   Spatial outlining is concerned with geography, space and direction.

*(Major supporting point)*    1.   Gang leader
*(Major supporting point)*    2.   Police officer
*(Major supporting point)*    3.   Physical training instructor
*(Major supporting point)*    4.   Real-estate agent
*(Major supporting point)*    5.   Tour guide
*(Major supporting point)*    6.   Stewardess
*(Major supporting point)*    7.   TV newscaster

*(Subordinate point)*    C.   Chronological outlining attends to the concept of time.
*(Major supporting point)*    1.   Gourmet club member
*(Major supporting point)*    2.   Girl Scout leader
*(Major supporting point)*    3.   Gym teacher
*(Major supporting point)*    4.   Debate society member

*(Subordinate point)*    D.   Causal outlining shows relationships between preceding factors and following results.

*(Major supporting point)*    1.   Housewife
*(Major supporting point)*    2.   Bowling team captain
*(Major supporting point)*    3.   Homeowners' association member
*(Major supporting point)*    4.   Politician
*(Major supporting point)*    5.   Corporation president
*(Transition)*   Although most of the above examples call for the elimination of selected causes due to their undesirable consequences, as many speakers know, this is not always the case.

*(Major supporting point)*    6.   Army Colonel
*(Subordinate point)*    E.   Problem-solution outlining proposes workable solutions to control harmful problems.

*(Major supporting point)*    1.   Day-care center leader
*(Major supporting point)*    2.   Third-grade presidential candidate
*(Major supporting point)*    3.   Congressional candidate
*(Major supporting point)*    4.   Football coach
*(Major supporting point)*    5.   Service sorority membership director
*(Transition)*   Once an appropriate pattern of organizing is selected, we are ready to organize our speech more carefully.

| | |
|---|---|
| *(Main point)* | II  Determine the best and most appropriate order for your main and supporting points. |
| *(Subordinate point)* |     A.  The audience is a major determinant of ordering your points. |
| *(Major supporting point)* |         1.  Hostile audience |
| *(Minor supporting point)* |             a)  Salesperson example |
| *(Minor supporting point)* |             b)  Politician example |
| *(Major supporting point)* |         2.  Audience with a special interest |
| *(Major supporting point)* |         3.  Audience desiring a climax |
| *(Major supporting point)* |         4.  Audience desiring an anticlimax. |
| *(Transition)* |         Although the main determinant of order seems to be the audience, sometimes the purpose of your speech will help determine when you discuss different topics. |
| *(Subordinate point)* |     B.  Your speech purpose may help determine the best order for your points. |
| *(Major supporting point)* |         1.  Instructional purpose |
| *(Minor supporting point)* |             a)  Familiar-to-unfamiliar explanation |
| *(Minor supporting point)* |             b)  Simple-to-complex explanation |
| *(Extended detail)* |                 1)  Golfer example |
| *(Extended detail)* |                 2)  Photographer example |
| *(Extended detail)* |                 3)  Chef example |
| *(Major supporting point)* |         2.  Persuasive purpose |
| *(Transition)* |         As we have said earlier, organizing your speech will help you see the parts, how they relate to each other and the whole speech. Using the principles of coordination and subordination will help you not only to see these relationships, but also to keep your message logical and internally consistent. |
| *(Main point)* | III  Follow the rules of coordination and subordination for your main and supporting points. |
| *(Subordinate point)* |     A.  Coordination means that points at a particular level are equal in importance to each other. |
| *(Subordinate point)* |     B.  Subordination means that one point belongs to an inferior order in a classification. |
| *(Transition)* |     Once you have arranged your main and supporting points according to an appropriate pattern and order which adheres to the principles of coordination and subordination, your next task is to prepare a mechanically correct outline with plans for frequent transitions. |
| *(Main point)* | IV  Prepare a mechanically correct outline. |
| *(Subordinate point)* |     A.  A consistent set of symbols should be selected for your outline (see sample). |
| *(Subordinate point)* |     B.  Appropriate indentation helps identify relationships among the points. |
| *(Subordinate point)* |     C.  Each unit should be discrete by containing only one idea. |
| *(Subordinate point)* |     D.  Clarity means being concise and vivid in your word choice. (Quotations) |

| | V | Use appropriate and frequent transitions. |
|---|---|---|

*(Main point)*      V   Use appropriate and frequent transitions.

        *(Subordinate point)*    A. Transitions serve many purposes.

        *(Major supporting point)*        1. Reinforce ideas

        *(Major supporting point)*        2. Connect points

        *(Major supporting point)*        3. Indicate relationships

        *(Major supporting point)*        4. Remind you of train of thought

        *(Subordinate point)*    B. Major transitions include sentences or paragraphs.

        *(Major supporting point)*        1. Preview

        *(Major supporting point)*        2. Internal summary

        *(Major supporting point)*        3. Main point connectors

        *(Minor supporting point)*           a) Family reunion leader

        *(Minor supporting point)*           b) Sportscaster

        *(Minor supporting point)*           c) Teacher

        *(Minor supporting point)*           d) Politician

*Conclusion*

      *(Concluding technique—summary)*   I   Sample outlines will illustrate the major principles of organizing.

                 A. Outlining this chapter will apply the principles to a sentence outline.

                 B. Outlining a speech will apply the principles to a phrase outline.

      *(Concluding statement—appeal)*   II   Studying both outlines should reinforce your knowledge of an interest in following the principles of effective organization.

Now that we have presented and analyzed a complete sentence outline for a major speech, let's look at a shorter outline of one of Lavinia's speeches (from Chapter 1). Since this speech was much shorter, we use phrases instead of complete sentences for the main and subordinate points.

## Roosevelt: The Aggressive Campaigner

*Introduction*

      *(Introductory technique-story)*   I   Campaigning in Cleveland

      *(Central idea)*   II   Super campaigner

      *(Preview)*                   A. Hit hard

                 B. Traveled a lot

*Body*

      *(Main point)*   I   Hit hard

      *(Subordinate point)*    A. Attacked Republican image

      *(Major supporting point)*        1. Measles analogy

      *(Major supporting point)*        2. "Greatest good" analogy

| | |
|---|---|
| *(Transition)* | In his many speeches around the country, Roosevelt consistently held up the Republican policies as unsound and unworkable. |
| *(Main point)* | II  Traveled a lot |
| *(Subordinate point)* | A.  Traveled 13,000 miles |
| *(Subordinate point)* | B.  Delivered 16 major speeches |
| *(Subordinate point)* | C.  Delivered 67 minor speeches |

*Conclusion*

| | |
|---|---|
| *(Concluding technique-summary)* | I  Vigorous campaigner |
| | A.  Vigorous speaking |
| | B.  Extensive campaigning |
| *(Concluding statement)* | II  Earned confidence of Americans |

## SUMMARY QUESTIONS

- Why should a speaker organize his or her speech?
- What are the five principles which help a speaker organize his or her message.
- What are the differences among topical, spatial, chronological, causal, and problem-solution patterns of organization?
- How does a speaker determine the best order for his or her main and supportive points?
- How does coordination differ from subordination?
- What is the purpose of transitions in a speech?

## EXERCISES

**1**  Choose a topic like, "How President Carter Selected His Cabinet," and organize it into different patterns: chronological, spatial, and problem solution.

**2**  Listen to a lecture and see how long it takes you to spot the organizational pattern or patterns. What transition words help you identify patterns?

**3**  Make an outline using a number of main and supporting points. Rearrange main and supporting materials and ask someone in your class to put them together again.

## REFERENCE

1  Adapted from L.S. Pappas, *Gourmet Cooking the Slim Way* (Reading, Mass.: Addison-Wesley, 1977), p. 74.

# 7 STARTING AND STOPPING

Sweating a bit and breathing heavily, Marty and his wife dragged in the four 25-pound bags of flour and placed them in front of the 35 other members of the Weight Watchers club. A huge smile covered his face as he placed the last of the six one-pound packages of butter on top of the flour and said, "Look, I lost 106 pounds and I needed help carrying it in to show you tonight. But I had to carry this same 106 pounds around all by myself for the last ten years."

Marty could have used the preceding statements to begin or end a speech on how to lose weight, and it would probably have been a

BRAVO!

tremendous asset to his speech. As an introduction, he'd have gained his listeners' attention and provided the necessary background for their enjoyment of his speech. As a conclusion, he'd have summarized his speech and left the audience in the right frame of mind to accept his position.

Too often, unfortunately, speakers may prepare a well-organized and supported talk but neglect its beginning and end. Such practices can destroy the impact of a speech and reduce its importance.

As soon as you have prepared the body of your speech, you should design either its introduction or its conclusion. The choice is yours, but both are normally essential. Naturally, you will find it difficult to prepare either before you know what your speech will say. Although some advise that introductions typically account for ten percent of a speech and conclusions five percent, the only meaningful rule should be: Introductions and conclusions should be as short as you need to accomplish your purpose. With hostile audiences, you may need to spend most of your speech gaining their good will. With friendlier audiences more knowledgeable about your topic, you may need only a minute. With some audiences you may have no introduction or conclusion.

## INTRODUCTIONS

Wayne faced his fellow service club members, took a deep breath, exhaled part of it, and began his speech on communication problems.

"I would like to read you some sentences taken from letters written to a metropolitan office of the Veterans' Administration:

'Both sides of my parents are poor, and I can't expect nothing from them, as my mother has been in bed for one year with the same doctor, and won't change.'

'Please send me a letter and tell me if my husband has made application for a wife and baby.'

'I can't get any pay, I has 6 children. Can you tell me why this is?'

'I am forwarding to you my marriage certificate and my two children. One is a mistake as you can plainly see.'

'My husband had his project cut off two weeks ago and I haven't had any relief since.'[1]

"Undoubtedly, the senders of these letters may not have had the exact meanings in their minds as some of you may have. How often do we assume that because we know what our messages mean, so should everyone else? These letters illustrate some of the problems associated with the personal nature of communication. Let's see how grammatical nuances as well as language differences can change the entire meaning of a sentence."

Wayne's use of carefully selected quotations to illustrate and amplify his purpose contributed to this successful introduction. Starting a speech is a delicate process aimed at fulfilling a variety of purposes. Fortunately, we have several options open to us which help accomplish these purposes. After we have examined the role of the introduction, we will look at some of these options.

## Role of Introduction

The beginning of a speech generally has three purposes:

1 To gain the attention and maintain the interest of the audience in you and your speech.
2 To provide the audience with the necessary background, preparation, and orientation for you and your speech.
3 To establish a climate of goodwill so that your credibility (ethos) as a speaker is sustained or established.

### 1. Attention and interest

Without the attention and interest of your audience, you cannot proceed to accomplish purposes two and three. Your challenge is to overcome the natural inclination of most listeners to think (and sometimes say), "Why should I listen to you?" or "What's in this for me?" or "What have you got to offer me?" Let's face it, you are intruding upon one of their most valuable resources, their time (some of you may also be lucky enough to receive money for doing so), and they will want their money's worth. You must, therefore, motivate them to want to listen to you. Too often a speaker may assume the audience is just as interested and excited in the topic as he or she is. We do this all the time when we call a friend on the telephone to discuss an "extremely important problem." We assume that the listener on the other end of the receiver is feeling what we feel, is thinking what we think, and is desiring what we desire, and we treat him and her accordingly. Public speakers who do this will fail dismally as listeners tune out or walk out.

*If you can't hold them, you can't tell them.*

Your role as a speaker requires you to bring your audience closer to your thoughts and feelings. You must show them how what you say is directly relevant to their interests. You must tell them how much money *they* will lose, why *their* cars are too big, how *their* lives are in danger, why *they* need your lemonade, how *they* will win the game, how *they* can lose weight, and why *they* should vote for you. The stories, jokes, statistics, quotes, and references you use in your introduction must appeal to their interests and curiosity. We whet their appetites to want more of us and our speech. Perhaps we should identify with the unlucky speechmaker who must start his speech at a luncheon while people are still eating their dessert. "Time's getting short," says the master of ceremonies. (How does that make you feel?) Although you are competing with apple pie and unfinished stories, your task is clear.

## 2. Preparation and orientation

Once you are sure you've got the audience's attention and interest, you must provide them with sufficient background information to facilitate their understanding of your speech. The background you provide will vary as a function of what they already know. Audiences well versed in your topic may require little background, but on the other hand, if your speech contains highly specialized language or technical terms or in-house jargon, you may need considerable time to orient the audience to your frame of reference.

*Fill your audience in (briefly) on what you're going to talk about before you talk about it.*

Specifically, such an orientation may contain historical or other background information about your topic, definition of an important terminology, the boundaries of your speech (what it excludes as well as includes), and a preview (or presummary) of your central idea and main points. The formality of this orientation depends on the occasion. Researching your audience and the occasion *prior* to speaking will provide you with clues about the scope and depth of orientation likely to be needed.

Remember that audiences are investing time in your presentation; if they have to spend too much time figuring out exactly what you are talking about, they are likely to stop listening or leave. Sometimes a few simple pre-speech questions can give your audience the necessary orientation. A TV director used this technique in addressing a film class at the university near his station: "You've got fifteen minutes to shoot a festival. How do you shoot enough cutaways to build a short montage that will make it look like you were there all day?"

Some audiences may need to be formally told *exactly* what the speaker's purpose and main points will be, as with this gym teacher's listeners: "I know that you've all watched or played a football, basketball, baseball, or tennis game. That is why I would like to talk about the different sports that are played during the four seasons. I would like to specifically examine the similarities and differences among these four sports as a function of the seasonal differences in weather and environment."

## 3. Goodwill and credibility

One of President Nixon's problems during the entire Watergate episode was that millions of Americans didn't believe him. Just as politicians must be trusted to earn the support of voters, so do public speakers require the trust and confidence of their audience. If you are an expert on your topic, the chances are that the audience will listen to you and believe you more than if you lack appropriate credentials. Although credentials and qualifications as a speaker are usually given when you are introduced, sometimes you will have to supplement what has been said to underscore one of your points. Addressing a Rotary Club in a strange city, one speaker added the following remark to his speech before a very skeptical audience, "and as a Rotarian myself for over 25 years, I feel confident when I say . . ." Instantly, he noticed the audience looking up at him, when previously they seemed to be dozing and gossiping. Once, when speaking before a very hostile audience which held him in very low esteem, President Kennedy said, "It would be premature to ask your support in the next election and it would be inaccurate to thank you for it in the past."[2]

For you to be successful, your audience must believe you. Many times you will not have to worry about this at all. A friendly audience who invited you to speak to learn more about you and your subject area will probably have already established a climate of goodwill. When you are faced with a hostile audience your immediate task is to build common ground between you and them, between your values, goals, experiences, feelings, and theirs. Speaking before a hostile school board (who thought he was supportive of striking teachers), the leader of a parents' group was trying to persuade the board to begin negotiations with the teachers. He said: "We all want what's best for our kids. We all want our kids to go back to school as quickly as possible. We all want the kids to have a quality education when they go back to school."

In his attempt to stress areas of agreement between the school board and the parents' group, this speaker was likely to receive a listening ear.

Bob, an educator, faced a hostile audience of a different type—500 Mexican educators who had a very high distrust for American teaching methods. Bob had planned to deliver his talk on American educational systems in English, being promised translators by his host. But when he sensed the audience's hostility toward him and his subject, Bob immediately began to speak in Spanish. Though his Spanish was imperfect, the audience instantly applauded him and he finished to a standing ovation. Bob recognized the importance of creating goodwill between himself and his audience, and, fortunately, had the skill and the wit to do so.

*In credible speeches, you can move your audience.*

*Incredible speeches remove your audience.*

## Techniques for Introductions

The techniques we present here for inclusion in introductions can be used alone or in any combination. You should select any of the techniques that you feel comfortable with and that can satisfy your audience's immediate needs. These techniques can help you fulfill all three purposes of the introduction, but we make no guarantees or promises that they will work. As we have said all along, your topic, the audience's background, and the occasion will be your best clues as to what may work.

### References
Speakers may attempt to move closer to their listeners by making direct references to them, the occasion, previous speakers, the location,

their subject, an event, or even themselves. When President Kennedy was in Paris, he made the following reference to himself:

*I do not think it entirely inappropriate to introduce myself to this audience. I am the man who accompanied Jacqueline Kennedy to Paris, and I have enjoyed it.*[3]

Truman would often make personal references, many times in jest:

*I pinned a medal on General MacArthur the other day, and told him I wished I had a medal like that, and he said that it was my duty to give the medals not receive them. That is always the way. About all I receive is the bricks. It's a good thing I have got a pretty hard head or it would have been broken a long time ago.*[4]

Poking fun at yourself can be a good way to gain good will, especially with a hostile audience. As we said earlier, if you fail to receive an adequate introduction, one which establishes your credibility, you may need to include some personal references in your introduction as did this realtor, speaking to a group of home-buyers: "And so we need to divide the city into four quadrants to fully understand the available real estate. Although the city has grown considerably in the 25 years I have been an agent, its basic design hasn't changed much."

Avoid making any personal reference to your own inadequacy during your introduction. Apologies to audiences draw attention away from the speaker's primary purpose and central idea. Note the effect of this speaker's apology: "I notice some of the same faces in the audience that I saw in a similar panel yesterday. I think that much of my speech is going to duplicate Mr. Seiler's. I apologize to you who will have to sit through mine after you have heard his. I will try to make it interesting even though it may be redundant. Please bear with me."

This speaker's best bet would have been not to mention this at all, since there was nothing that could be done at this point. If some of the audience felt bored, they could always leave.

President Kennedy was a master at adapting to audiences, friendly, neutral and hostile. Once in Pittsburgh he stated:

*I'm glad to be here because I feel a sense of kinship with the Pittsburgh Pirates. Like my candidacy, they were not given much of a chance in the Spring.*[5]

A student of Kennedy tried to gain the goodwill of a hostile audience by referring to their good judgment with: "And I certainly want to congratulate you. Although we have had our differences in the past, your extremely good judgment in selecting speakers this evening deserves the praise of all wise people."

FOR VALOR
ABOVE AND BEYOND
BRICKS

Sometimes, a simple acknowledgment of the audience or its latest accomplishments is all you need: "Fellow Optimists," "I am pleased to be here with all you formerly fat people," "Members of the class of 1944," "As a homeowner like yourselves, I am delighted to be here tonight to voice my opinion on the new zoning laws."

*Some references are utilitarian,*

Besides referring to yourself or your audience, you may find it useful to refer directly to the subject of your speech, especially if your audience is very interested in or excited about your topic. "Since tonight is the beginning of our summer tourist season, I would like to discuss with you the steps we should take if we spot a shark in our waters," "I am happy to be here with you to reveal the truth about Watergate," "As you know, I have made five million dollars on the stock exchange. Tonight, I plan to tell you how I did it." Since these topics are likely to be inherently interesting to most audiences, referring to them in the introduction can only help your cause. If the topic is not inherently interesting, this technique may not be suitable.

*some are a matter of courtesy,*

If you are speaking on a formal occasion (e.g., wedding, funeral, banquet, dedication, graduation, confirmation, family reunion, etc.), your introduction should probably make some reference to the occasion. One speaker's Bar Mitzvah speech went like this: "Standing in this beautiful sanctuary on this momentous occasion, that of my Bar Mitzvah, carries special significance for me. It was just one year ago that I met with the Rabbi, frightened and convinced that I could never successfully stand here today. With his help and guidance and the confidence of my family, I am happy to report that today I have really become a man." Being a good Bar Mitzvah boy, he also thanked his family, the Rabbi, and the synagogue itself.

Speaking after others have left the podium will allow you the opportunity to refer to them or their topics. At an academic convention, one speaker said: "I am glad that Stu mentioned the victories of General Tubbs. I think that the late General had a lesson for all of us to learn: sinking ships are no place for confirmed cowards."

When you provide the customary social amenities: "Thank you Reverend Murphy, President Ferry, Mrs. Holder, and invited guests," you also are providing an opportunity for the audience to settle down, stop talking and walking, and attend to your speech. Wise speakers sometimes stretch these amenities for at least 30 seconds to a minute.

*and some are mandatory.*

Also, sometimes you may insult your audience if you fail to provide such courtesies. Such was the case when an oil company executive was in a foreign country giving a talk on oil exportation. He neglected to acknowledge all 34 people on the podium with him, thus offending several who actually walked off in the middle of his speech!

Occasionally, you may be speaking immediately after, during, or before a significant political, social, or environmental event. Referring to the incident may be particularly useful with some audiences, de-

pending on their reactions to it. A policeman addressing the chamber of commerce of a large city found that his talk on lowering the crime rate took on special significance for him the day after his own house was robbed. Speaking at a fund-raising dinner the night after he dropped eight points in the poll, a political candidate suddenly found himself in desperate need of new revenues.

Finally, the location or setting of the speech itself may provide a useful reference for the speaker. Invited to an overnight camp for a Sunday service, a priest was so captured by the natural beauty of the outdoor chapel that, in his sermon, he said, "How fortunate we all are to be graced with the divine gift of nature placed in our hands by the Lord. Here in our outdoor chapel, as we are even closer to Him that has blessed us, we have the opportunity to render thanks for these our blessings."

### Humor

*It's better not to use humor than to use it and fall flat.*

Avoid humor in your introductions: that is, avoid it unless you feel comfortable with it, unless it's in good taste, unless it's relevant to your talk, and unless it's funny. This last "unless" is not to be taken too lightly. There is nothing as deadly at the beginning of a speech as a bad joke. Audiences love to laugh, but the material must be worthy of their laughter. President Kennedy often used humor in his introductions:

*One of the inspiring notes that was struck in the last debate was struck by the Vice President in his very moving warning to candidates against the use of profanity by Presidents and ex-Presidents when they are on the stump. And I know, after fourteen years in the Congress with the Vice President, that he was very sincere in his views about the use of profanity. But I am told that a prominent Republican said to him yesterday in Jacksonville, Florida, "Mr. Vice President, that was a damn fine speech." And the Vice President said, "I appreciate the compliment but not the language." And the Republican went on, "Yes, sir, I liked it so much that I contributed a thousand dollars to your campaign." And Mr. Nixon replied, "The hell you say."* [6]

### Stories/illustrations/narrative

Next to references, these are probably the most commonly used introductory techniques. Real or hypothetical stories, illustrations, or narratives which relate to your speech will usually arouse the interest of your audience. In a talk to her new class, the training director of a large industry used the following story to introduce the topic of rumor flow in organizations:

*The chairman of an academic department was visiting with the retirement director of the university when the latter asked, "Have you* heard about Professor Jones's decision to retire this year?" "No, I hadn't," replied the surprised chairman. "Well, it's true; he came in yesterday to fill out the required forms." The chairman left the next day for a conference in Montreal, where he confronted Professor Smith from his department back home. "Professor Smith, I was just informed yesterday by the retirement director that Jones was retiring this year." Smith, equally dumbfounded by the news, asked, "Can we fill the slot this year?" The chairman replied, "I'll have to check with the dean on the phone tomorrow. If he says O.K., then we can announce the job opening while we're here." That night, at a party, Smith met some friends from schools in New York, Boston and San Francisco. After a couple of drinks, he told some of his friends about Jones' decision to retire, and how he hoped his dean would let them fill the job. After a lengthy conversation about budget cuts, deans, and the job market, Smith retired for the evening. At 6:45 A.M. Smith was awakened from a deep sleep by the ringing of his telephone. The person at the other end of the phone was inquiring about the "opening created at the department because of Jones's resignation." Smith angrily shouted into the phone, "There is no opening!" and he hung up. A half-hour later the phone rang again with a different voice asking the same question. Before the morning was over, thirteen phone calls were received by an exhausted Smith. One caller stated that he was awfully sorry to hear that "Smith was leaving the department" and that he hoped "Smith wasn't fired." [7]

***The keyword is "good."***

Everyone likes to hear a good story, and the speaker who has two or three which help support his central idea holds the audience's interest. Such good stories also serve to increase the speaker's rapport with the audience.

### Comparison/contrast
One of Marty's favorite ways to motivate his audiences of weight watchers was to compare weight to food: "You may not think that losing a quarter of a pound of fat is very much at all, but if you think of that quarter-pound weight loss as a stick of margarine, you will surely appreciate its substance."

The use of comparison or contrast may especially appeal to audiences of high intelligence. A training instructor for a small company was teaching a class in transactional analysis to her trainees and enjoyed success comparing an infant's recall capacity to that of a tape recorder: "Imagine an infant, as soon as it can crawl, equipped with a stereo tape recorder and microphone, crawling around his house and recording every sound (from his parents, relatives, pets, etc.) and experience that affects him. One channel of the stereo recording would be reserved for the words, messages, and tones of voice, and the other channel would record the infant's reactions and feelings to

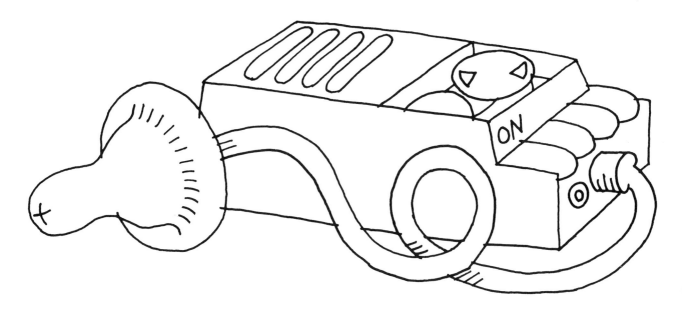

these stimuli. These tapes *can never be erased* and can be played back (both channels) at a later date in his life (perhaps years later).''

### Startling statement or behavior

Sometimes an audience is lethargic, apathetic, or distracted. In such cases you may find it useful to startle them with some form of striking statement or behavior. When Marty and his wife brought in the 106 pounds of flour and butter, their behavior was most assuredly startling for their audience. It was also effective. Discussing slow mail service, a speaker once told his audience, ''We can send a man to the moon in less time than it takes for a parcel post package to travel from Boston to San Francisco.'' The headwaiter at a well-known restaurant welcomes all guests by delivering a fluent public speech in which he recites the entire menu, describing the preparation and cost of all items within each of four food categories: fish, fowl, beef, and veal. His startling behavior holds the attention of his entire audience!

You should be cautious in your use of this technique. Gaining the attention of audiences at the expense of gimmickry can backfire. A University of Maryland speech instructor reports that one of his students once began a speech on repairing windows by throwing a brick through the third story window of his classroom. Despite his feeble efforts to regain the audience's attention as he began replacing the glass, his classmates could only stare at the broken window and think about the people walking on the street below. Speeches which begin with such shock treatment will probably fail immediately, because the gimmick distracts from the speech itself. The next time you plan to fire a gun (loaded with blanks) to illustrate the need for gun control, or ride a motorcycle into your auditorium to talk about noise pollution, or set off a smoke bomb to begin talking about smog, think again!

## Questions

When an audience is primed and ready to listen to you, a simple question may be a very effective introduction. Such questions can help get the audience interested and involved as well as provide a pre-summary for your talk. A Girl Scout troop leader's talk to her troop began this way: "We've all been told not to play with matches at home, but do we all know how to play with matches when it's okay? Do we all know how to build and start a campfire? Are you aware, for instance, that there are three kinds of wood which we can use in building our fires? Do you know their purposes?"

One question may be all you need for some audiences, "Well, folks, how much did you lose this week?"

## Quotations

You may be able to arouse the audience's curiosity by reading them a quotation at the outset of your speech. Also, you may desire to quote an authoritative source to help establish your own credibility with your listeners. If you do so, you must explain your quotation's relevance to your central idea, unless it is highly obvious. Earlier in this chapter we used several Veterans' Administration quotes which were used in a speech illustrating communication problems. Some others are:

"I am annoyed to find out that you branded my child as illiterate, it is dirty lie as I married his father a week before he was born."

"You changed my little boy to a girl, does this make a difference?"

"In accordance with your instructions, I have given birth to twins in the enclosed envelope." [8]

An attorney involved in a libel suit once quoted Truman to the jury because of the relevance of Truman's remarks to the damages his client had suffered from an unwarranted smear upon his character and reputation:

*McCarthyism . . . the meaning of the word is the corruption of truth, the abandonment of our historical devotion to fair play. It is the abandonment of "due process" of law. It is the use of the big lie and the unfounded accusation against any citizen . . . It is the rise to power of the demagogue who lives on untruth; it is the spread of fear and the destruction of faith in every level of our society.* [9]

## Statistics

Similar to the use of startling statements is the use of statistics to gain the attention of the audience. Best used when the implications of the

*I think we [may], . . . making due allowances, quote whenever we feel that the allusion is interesting or helpful or amusing.*

**Clifton Fadiman**

statistics are *clearly* relevant to the immediate needs of your audience, statistics can have dramatic impact and arouse your listeners' sense of drama and a desire for more. They can also fail dismally, if lengthy strings of numbers are read to listeners at the outset of your speech. Rather than risk boredom, avoid statistics unless they succinctly dramatize your main point. For example, in a speech to his homeowner's association, one member began by stating, "Property values will go down 20 percent this year unless we clean up our neighborhood. That means that each of your lovely new $40,000 homes will be worth only $32,000. You will each lose $8,000! How do you like that?" The speaker was successful because he appealed to one of his audience's immediate concerns—their bank accounts.

Politicians who advocate tax cuts would be better off telling their audiences that "The $11 billion cut will save each of you $250," rather than stressing the implications for the nation's economy. Doctors stressing preventive medicine should not bore their audiences with statistics about national death averages. They will probably be more successful by saying, "One out of five of you will die of cancer in the next five years." A college president once told the entering freshmen class, "Look at the person to your left. Look at the person to your right. They won't be graduating with you."

## Limited Introductions

Infrequently, an audience may already be quite familiar with you, your speech, and the background necessary to understand your speech. They may be quite excited and primed to listen to your talk. Lacking the need to be motivated, to be aroused, such audiences may not require an elaborate introduction. They may want you to get right into your speech. "Ladies and gentlemen, the President of the United States," is the standard introduction for this person because few audiences need to be aroused to listen to him. You may be able to begin with only a one-sentence opening such as this speaker's to a literary club: "As an author of five books on the Kennedy assassination, I am convinced that Oswald was part of a larger conspiracy."

Note how the speaker gained the audience's attention (by referring to his very topical subject), provided orientation (by stating his central idea), and established his credibility (by referring to his writings). Even though your audience may indeed be ready for you, if it is your first speech to that audience, you may do better with more than an introduction.

## CONCLUSIONS

Starting your speech on the right note is important. Ending it appropriately may be even more so. Since it is the last thing heard, it may

**143 Conclusions**

be all that is remembered. Thus, carefully plan a short, well-stated, interesting conclusion designed for maximum impact upon your listeners. Although its type and length will depend on your speech and audience, generally a short and simple conclusion will accomplish the logical and psychological ends of stopping your speech.

## Role of Conclusion

The ending of a speech generally has two purposes—logical and psychological—each of which interacts with the other.

### Logical

The logical purpose of the conclusion is simply to end the speech. While doing so, however, the conclusion should refer to and emphasize your central idea and purpose. Sometimes you can redirect your audience's attention back to your central idea by just restating it, as one political candidate did to his audience: "You need me in the legislature to combat the fiscal irresponsibility currently in residence." Or, when your speech is extensive or complex, you may need a more detailed summary to tie all the loose ends together, as did the speaker to the homeowner's association: "And so, my friends, we have seen the transients of our neighborhood, with their lack of concern for their property and ours, contribute to the decline in value of all our homes."

As we will see, illustrations and quotations may also help achieve the logical end of the conclusion.

### Psychological

Does your speech contribute to your listeners' sense of fulfillment or completeness? Have you left them in the right frame of mind? Did they leave the room experiencing the feelings you wanted them to feel? The answers to these questions relate to the psychological role of the conclusion. Did the listeners depart feeling happy? Sad? Sympathetic? Angry? Fulfilled? Enthusiastic? Calm? Disgusted? Were they ready to respond as you wanted?

The speaker to the homeowners' association succeeded when his listeners left the meeting quite angry. The politician failed because his audience was not too enthused over his presentation. After an Army officer's talk on the draft, his fellow toastmasters left fulfilled over the success of the volunteer army. Marty's audience at his Weight-Watchers' club felt happy, due both to his weight loss and to his startling introduction. Finally, the attorney was effective because the jury he addressed, in finding for his client, felt disgust for the unwarranted smear. The psychological thrust of a conclusion may be assisted by humor, stories, challenges, and direct appeals.

**Techniques for Conclusions**

As with introductions, these techniques may be used alone or in any combination to help achieve both the logical and psychological ends of your conclusion. Often a summary is used jointly with appeals, quotes, or humorous stories. Again, the important thing is to choose only those techniques with which you feel most comfortable in achieving your purposes.

### Summary

Particularly useful when you have lots of material, or when you are engaged in an instructional activity, summaries can be formal or casual. While probably the most common type of conclusion in use, the summary may not always be the best. If you've used lots of internal summaries or are delivering an arousing or extremely funny speech, a closing summary may be inappropriate. In such cases, summaries may negatively affect the mood you have striven to maintain; they may even bore your audience. This was not the case, however, with the scout leader's talk to the Girl Scouts or with the

corporation official's report to his stockholders. The first said: "And so I have shown you how to gather sufficient amounts of kindling, tinder, and fuel to build a log-cabin type fire, and how to set the fire by first lighting the kindling. Are there any questions?" The other concluded with: "By detailing for you the declining return to investors of 15 percent, the failure of our stocks to split, the postponement of our new building plans, and the 5 percent personnel retrenchment, I hope I have given you a better understanding of how the recent recession has affected both our present financial structure and our future growth plans."

Combining the summary with a plea for action, the headwaiter mentioned earlier concludes his masterful description of the menu with, "Now that I have reviewed for you the fish, fowl, beef, and veal dishes on tonight's menu, why don't you think about them for a short while, and I'll return for your orders."

*Tell them what you've told them.*

### Quotations

To be helpful in a conclusion, a quote should be directly related to your central idea and purpose: it should stimulate your listeners to leave the room with the appropriate feelings and ready for any desired action. For example, a politician, attempting to enlist voters and workers for his campaign, quoted Humphrey in his conclusion: "As Hubert Humphrey said in his rousing acceptance speech in 1964, I urge you to 'walk with us, work with us, help us' as we strive to build a great state for you and me."

### Illustration/story/narrative

If you know a good story or detailed illustration which can neatly summarize all your relevant main points and your central idea, the chances are good your audience will like it. For example, a speaker on communication problems decided to conclude his speech with a story which illustrated his central idea that one of the main causes of confusion is the fact that so many words in the English language have several meanings:

"I would like to leave you this evening by telling you a story I've heard recently about how *every* word in our English dictionary has, on the average, *twenty-eight* different meanings. To illustrate this, I'd like to use the word 'run': Run quickly . . . run for office . . . run last in the horse race . . . go for a beer run . . . take a quick run home . . . the salmon run . . . The vine runs over the porch . . . The story runs that the stock market will go down . . . His family tree runs back to the middle ages . . . Her stocking had a run . . . The Red Sox needed a run . . . The play runs for two weeks . . . a run of good luck . . . a run of spades . . . This illustration just runs and runs and runs . . ."

### Plea/appeal/challenge

Speakers using this technique are looking for specific actions or beliefs from their listeners. Issuing a plea or challenge is best done in speeches which are attempting to arouse or persuade listeners to lose weight, buy a car, give money or time, vote for a candidate, learn a skill or lesson, destroy a house, complete a project, etc. One dieter concluded his Weight Watchers' speech by challenging his listeners to eat "at a controlled pace and place to increase your weight loss."
The Enforcer concluded with a specific appeal to his gang for action when he said, "Then we all bug in and grab the hostages. Let's go!"
Even the young mother with the sleeping baby concluded with a challenge when she shouted at the teenagers, "So quiet down and go home before I call the cops!" The extent to which the challenge or appeal is successfully met is a direct function of the psychological purpose of the conclusion. If the audience leaves your speech feeling what you want them to feel, you have a good chance that they will respond to your plea. An enthusiastic audience, for example, is more likely than a calm audience to go to work for the office-seeker. An angry audience is more likely than an uncommitted audience to support new zoning laws for the homeowners' association. A sympathetic audience is more likely than a fulfilled audience to donate money to a service club project.

*Now, what do you want your audience to do?*

Sometimes the speaker will issue the plea or challenge in the form of a question, as did Kathy when seeking the presidency of her third grade. In effect, she said, "Given who my daddy is, can you really afford not to vote for me?"

### Humor

Humor can be a great asset to the skillful speaker who seeks to fulfill the conclusion's psychological purpose by arousing happy feelings in the audience. Naturally, if you want your audience to leave the speech feeling sad, sympathetic, angry, or disgusted, then humor would be inappropriate in your conclusion. For example, if you were concluding a serious patriotic talk devoted to the memory of a great American, a quotation or short summary may arouse the desired feelings (e.g., enthusiasm or passion) in your listeners.

Just as with any humor in your speech's introduction, the humor in your conclusion should be in good taste, relevant, and funny. A speaker once concluded a speech on communication problems in organizations with this humorous anecdote:

*The following message was communicated from a colonel to a major: "At nine o'clock tomorrow there will be an eclipse of the sun, something which does not occur every day. Get the men to fall out in the company street in their fatigues so that they will see this rare phenomenon, and I will then explain it to them. Now, in the case of rain, we will not be able to see anything, of course, so then take the men to the gym."*

*The major passed on the message to the captain: "By order of the colonel tomorrow at nine o'clock there will be an eclipse of the sun. If it rains, you will not be able to see it from the company street, so, then, in fatigues, the eclipse of the sun will take place in the gym, something which does not occur every day."*

*The captain then said to the lieutenant: "By order of the colonel in fatigues tomorrow, at nine o'clock in the morning the inauguration of the eclipse of the sun will take place in the gym. The colonel will give the order if it should rain, something which does occur every day."*

*The lieutenant then told the sergeant: "Tomorrow at nine, the colonel in fatigues will eclipse the sun in the gym, as it occurs every day if it's a nice day. If it rains, then this occurs in the company street."*

*The sergeant then assured the corporal: "Tomorrow at nine, the eclipse of the colonel in fatigues will take place because of the sun. If it rains in the gym, something which does not take place every day, you will fall out in the company street."*

*Finally, one private said to another private: "Tomorrow, if it rains, it looks as if the sun will eclipse the colonel in the gym. It's a shame that this does not occur every day."* [10]

Thus, for logical and psychological reasons, we should use either a summary, quotation, story, plea or joke to conclude our speech. As the last words spoken, they may be the only ones remembered.

## The Case for No Conclusion

Unlike an introduction, a conclusion is almost always given in effective speeches. About the only time you may leave it out is if someone else is giving it for you. Occasionally, another speaker may follow you to the podium—for example, during a fundraising campaign—and issue the challenge for you. During the October Israeli war, many American synagogues brought in representatives of the Israeli government to explain the dire military circumstances to their members. Immediately after these speeches, many of which were delivered over tele-lecture systems, local fundraising representatives issued appeals and pleas for monies to support the Israeli economy during the current crisis.

Given the dual purpose of the conclusion and the variety of techniques available to fulfill these purposes, you would be derelict in your duty as a speaker to simply conclude by saying, "Thank you," and sitting down. On the other hand, you would be just as derelict were you to recite a very lengthy conclusion, with several anticlimaxes. Once you've begun your conclusion, don't forget that your audience is anxiously waiting for you to stop. So, stop!

## SUMMARY QUESTIONS

- What are the main purposes of an introduction?
- What are some techniques for introductions? Give illustrations.
- What is the role of a speech's conclusion?
- What are some techniques for conclusions? Give illustrations.
- When may a speaker refrain from concluding his or her speech?

## EXERCISES

**1** Write an introduction for a speech on equal rights for women. Assume that the audience members are all businessmen in their 40s and 50s. Be sure to gain their attention, provide necessary background, and establish a climate of good will.

**2** Write a brief introduction for a speech to a very hostile audience. Assume that your own credibility may help reduce some of the hostility.

**3** Write an introduction for a speech to be delivered by the Dean of Students to 500 new freshmen at their orientation meeting. Be sure to use startling statements, questions, and a narrative or story in your introduction.

**4** Write two introductions using statistics. In the first, use too many statistics, which will probably bore your audience. In the second, arrive at the same point, but use far fewer statistics, relying more on summarizing detailed statistics into major statements.

**5** Write a brief conclusion which emphasizes the logic of your argument; then write one which emphasizes the psychological basis of your speech.

**6** Conclude your speech to your service club with an appeal for their cooperation in your fund-raising drive.

**7** Conclude your speech to the hiking club with a summary of the major activities planned for the coming year.

**8** Conclude your speech to the literary guild with a quote from the book you are describing.

## REFERENCES

**1** G. Goldhaber, *Organizational Communication* (Dubuque, Iowa: Wm. C. Brown, 1974), p. 93.

**2** B. Adler (ed.), *The Kennedy Wit* (New York: Bantam, 1964), p. 60.

**3** Ibid. p. 103.

**4** G. Caldwell (ed.) *Good Old Harry* (New York: Hawthorne, 1966), p. 45.

**5** Adler, *The Kennedy Wit,* p. 24.

**6** Ibid., pp. 16–18.

**7** Goldhaber, p. 93.

**8** Ibid., p. 93.

**9** Caldwell, p. 60.

**10** Goldhaber, pp. 14–15.

153

# WORDING THE SPEECH

At the Medicine Lodge council in 1867, Ten Bears, the leading spokesman for the Comanches, spoke these words before an audience of many tribal chieftains and a commission of seven representatives from the United States Government.

*My heart is filled with joy, when I see you here, as the brooks fill with water, when the snows melt in the spring, and I feel glad, as the ponies do when the fresh grass starts in the beginning of the year. I heard of your coming when I was many sleeps away, and I made but few camps before I met you. I looked for the benefits, which would last forever, and so my face shines with joy, as I look upon you. My people have never first drawn a bow or fired a gun against the whites. There has been trouble in the line between us, and my young men have danced the war dance. But it was not begun by us.* [1]

Though the commission was unsympathetic to Ten Bears, his speech remains a classic example of eloquent *oral* style. It is called "Do not ask us to give up the buffalo for the sheep."

## ORAL STYLE

*Ten Bears, former Chief of the Yamparika Band of the Comanche Tribe. From the Smithsonian Institution National Anthropological Archives.*

Chief Ten Bears instinctively used an oral style when presenting his speech to the commission because he was raised in a culture that used the spoken word and not the written word. Stories were told orally and passed from generation to generation. Only recently have Native Americans begun to record their history by writing it down. Though oral and written style have much in common, there is one significant difference.

Oral style is language that is instantly intelligible to the *ear*, while written style is instantly intelligible to the *eye*. The eye can move back over a sentence to reread it. When reading, you often take yourself on an adventure, but when speaking you take *others* along with you.

*Though we seldom notice it, oral style is quite different from written style.*

For that reason, oral style is much more conversational than written style; it contains more personal pronouns, more kinds of sentences, as well as more fragments of sentences. Oral style contains more repetition of phrases and sentences, more familiar words, more quotes, and more indigenous language. Of course, some speeches demand a formal structure. Certainly Barbara Jordan's keynote address at the Democratic National Convention in 1976 is an example of complete and grammatical sentences.

Because oral style should be accurate, clear, and appropriate to the occasion, the speaker must make certain decisions before each and every speech he or she prepares and gives. Choosing the right words for the particular occasion suggests that the speaker cares about the audience and is aware of the economy of words. While oral style should be used whenever you speak, types of oral style vary from one speaker to another. For example, some speakers have been called "eloquent." Some, like Harry Truman, have insisted on "plain-talking." Sometimes the occasion calls for a florid style, such as when speaking at a ceremonial gathering. A person's preference for certain words often determines his or her style.

Classical rhetoricians divided oral style into three areas: eloquent, middle, and plain. Good speakers have been known to mix two or more of these styles, using a few eloquent statements that contain many metaphors with some simple, short words.

Often the manner of preparing the speech helps you decide what oral language to use. An impromptu, or spur-of-the-moment speech usually is given in language that is very familiar to you. A manuscript speech which is completely written out well in advance gives you the opportunity to experiment with more eloquent language. The memorized speech should contain language you find easy to recall, while the extemporaneous speech can be a combination of your normal conversational language coupled with some easily remembered phrases and notes.

In this chapter we shall deal with words and with methods of making our words effective when we *speak*. The basic problem that occurs when you write also occurs when you speak; that is, when we try to talk about the world of things we have a limited number of words with which to try and talk about a *limitless* number of things.

## MULTIPLE MEANINGS OF WORDS

To assume that words are used in only one way impairs our effective use of language. There are advantages to simplifying the message but the disadvantages occur when we consider that for the 500 most commonly used words in our language, there are 14,070 dictionary definitions.

There are misconceptions about language that lead to barriers to communication. One is that once a word is defined, the definition remains forever.

In reality, words change their meanings curiously with the flight of centuries. Many centuries ago, "heathen" simply meant a man who lived on the heath, far from the churches. "Idiot" is from the Greek and originally meant a man in private, not public, life. "Husband" is the man who dwells in the house. "Wife" comes from the verb to weave. A "pagan" was originally a villager, and as churches were first built in cities, those who lived in villages and rural areas were not likely to attend them. So from "villager," the word "pagan" came to mean—among other things—one who has little or no religion.

We often use words to assure ourselves that *we* are important, and in doing so we give importance to the words. For example: The scholar whose views I agree with is "erudite"; the scholar whose views I disagree with is "pedantic." I am "liquidating," you are "selling," they have "gone broke." An "officer" is a civil servant whose help you need; a "policeman" is a civil servant whose presence you ignore; a "cop" is a civil servant whose interference you resent. I am "trusting," you are "credulous," he is "naive."

We also say that words are "good" or "bad." We tell our children not to use the "dirty" words. We claim certain words in our society are disreputable, or derogatory. It matters not to our audiences that words are arbitrary symbols capable of changing from one year to the next, or from one generation to the next. The fact remains that they *do* respond emotionally to certain words, and it's a good idea to know which words convey which messages. A speaker must consider that moment when he or she stands up and speaks out as one which will never occur again. At that moment his or her choice of words is very important.

Certain words are emotive; that is, they stimulate emotional responses: That's *disgusting*. Certain words are neutral: That's *unpleasant*. Certain words present concrete images, like alarm *clock, egg, apple, chair*. Certain words create abstract impressions, such as *love, food, time, space*. How much easier it is to describe an apple than to describe love!

Whatever the classification, you, the public speaker, rely upon words to convey your message.

*Be sure that the words you choose express your true meaning.*

## THE HUMAN TOUCH

Congresswoman Barbara Jordan, layman priest John Bakas, and saleswoman Rosie Hampton have something very valuable in common when it comes to selecting the right word. They employ the

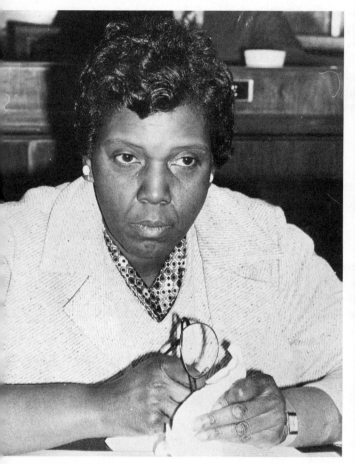

human touch in their speeches. They have learned how to "touch" someone with words.

At the Democratic Convention of 1976, in New York City, Congresswoman Jordan, after having received the first standing ovation of the evening from the delegates, thanked them and said:

*It was one hundred and forty-four years ago that members of the Democratic Party first met in convention to select a presidential candidate. Since that time Democrats have continued to convene once every four years and draft a party platform and nominate a presidential candidate. Our meeting this week is a continuation of that tradition. But there is something different about tonight. There is some-*

**154 Wording the Speech**

*thing special about tonight. What is different? What is special? I, Barbara Jordan, am a keynote speaker.*[2]

At his ordination as a deacon of the Greek Orthodox Church, John Bakas gave thanks to his parents and said:

*To my mother and father and family I dedicate this moment. It seems like it was just last Sunday that we entered this church newly arrived from Greece. My mother and father filled with joy and anxiety about this new land and this new home, said their first prayer here, thanking God for America. With tears of optimism and joy, they overcame*

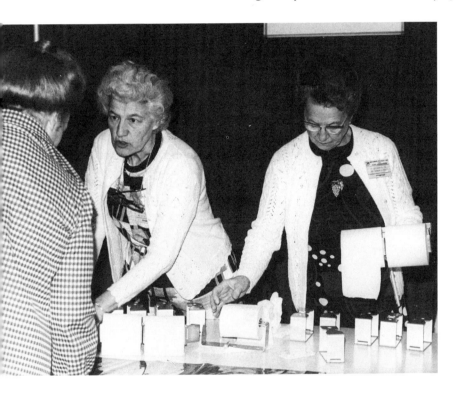

*the hardships and difficulties that all new immigrants encounter and educated my brother, sister, and myself. They never gave up and never permitted us to. They never allowed us to lose our Greek heritage, our love for the Church, and our love for the land that gave birth to our forefathers. If this moment could be transformed into worldly gold and silver, I would put it at their feet.*

Of course, the topic of Bakas's speech, his ordination, was a highly emotional one and lent itself to the human touch.

However, Rosie Hampton's subject was more difficult to humanize. Her subject was the Acme Toilet Paper Holder. Hampton attended the Park and Recreational Convention and held up the anodized aluminum toilet paper holder, not a very soft item endowed with any human traits.

She humanized it by saying:

*I take real delight in telling you about our little Acme holder. It had such a lowly beginning born out of a real need and has met that need from coast to coast and tells its own story so well when folks will try it. My husband used to go into problem areas of toilets and help them [people] work out troubles. And years later those people still remembering. [sic] Mrs. Ferrell's husband was the President of our company and he would take care of the work at home. My husband would go out on the road, selling, counseling, advising. The two of them were a real team. Now they have both died and Mrs. Ferrell and myself come here to conventions and sell our product. It is a sort of living memorial to our husbands. We helped them too, so we did not fall into this blindly after they died. Both our husbands loved people and thoroughly enjoyed the work.*

We see that the human touch is not limited to great topics such as religion and human rights, but can be used anytime a speaker addresses an audience. It is achieved by using the active voice and personal pronouns and nouns. If you reach out and touch, you are initiating the action. It's not a case of something being done *to you,* but at your *doing.* "It is reported by a reliable source," is not as powerful as "The president stated . . ." Our forefathers did not say *"It is* believed that these truths are self evident," but *"We hold* these truths to be self evident . . ."

Above all, the human touch revels in the active voice.

## LIVELINESS

Aristotle felt that listeners enjoy hearing words that set an event before their eyes. The audience likes to be a part of the event occurring at that moment, rather than hear of it in the future. The successful orator makes things move, come alive.

What makes words come alive? As we have seen, the present tense and the active voice certainly contribute. According to Aristotle, so do "metaphor, antithesis, actuality."

The following examples occurred in 1891 and in 1967. In both instances the participants employed the rhetorical devices we just mentioned. In both instances, however, *conflict* contributed to the occasion. Nothing is as lively as a *verbal battle.*

Mrs. Mary Elizabeth Lease, prophetess of Kansas Populism, was born in 1853 in Pennsylvania, moved to Kansas in 1873, became a teacher at Osage Mission, married Charles Lease, bore four children, managed a household and studied law. She studied law at home,

pinning sheets of notes above her wash tub to study while she scrubbed the washings she took in at fifty cents a day.

Late in March of 1891, speaking with little attention to notes, she said:

*Wall Street owns the country. It is no longer a government of the people, for the people, by the people, but a government of Wall Street, for Wall Street, by Wall Street. The great common people of the country are slaves, and monopoly is the master. The West and South are bound and prostrate before the manufacturing East. Money rules and our Vice President is a London banker . . . [Our legislation] is the output of a system which clothes rascals in robes and honesty in rags. We were told two years ago in Kansas to go to work, raise a big crop—that's all we needed. We went to work and plowed and planted. The rains fell, the sun shone, nature smiled, and we raised the big crop they told us to; and what came of it? Eight-cent corn and ten-cent oats and two-cent beef and no price at all for butter and eggs; that's what came of it. Then the politicians said we suffered from overproduction. . . ."*[3]

Mrs. Lease then went on to talk about starving little children and underpaid shopgirls, how the common people were robbed to support their masters and that thirty men in America had over one and a half billion dollars. She advocated the abolition of banks, and demanded that the people have the power to make loans direct from the government.

Mrs. Lease used comparisons in her talks: "common people . . . are slaves . . ." "monopoly is the master . . ." The "Vice-President is a London Banker . . ." The legislation was compared to a system that "clothes rascals in robes and honesty in rags." Her verbs were filled with action: "bound," "prostrate," "rules," "plowed," "planted," and "suffered."

The Republican editor in Wellington, Kansas said, after a Lease visit:

*At the Opera House last Monday night, a miserable caricature upon womanhood, hideously ugly in feature and foul of tongue, made an ostensible political speech, but which consisted mainly of the rankest kind of personal abuse of people in this city, among which [sic] the editor of this paper understands that he came in for the principal share. . . . All we know about her is that she is hired to travel around the country by this great reform People's party which seems to find a female blackguard a necessity in its business, spouting foulmouthed vulgarity at $10 a night. . . . the petticoated smut mill earns her money, but few women want to make their living that way.*[4]

***You can be vivid—but libel laws in 1891 weren't what they are today.***

The Republican editor also used action verbs: "spouting foul mouthed vulgarity . . ." and compared Mrs. Lease to a "miserable caricature." He used much imagery as he told how she traveled around the country. He obviously was much upset and greatly personalized his remarks. Both audiences enjoyed the verbal battle, though it was waged before separate groups of people.

The Stokes-Taft debate occurred before a single audience, but was just as lively.

In 1967 Carl Stokes and Seth Taft opposed each other for the mayor's seat in Cleveland. Carl Stokes is the great grandson of a slave; Seth Taft is the great grandson of a president. Carl Stokes was a state representative; Seth Taft was practicing law. Stokes's style during the campaign was rambling, vivid, and at times, ungrammatical (according to Standard English); Taft's style was ponderous, dry, and literate. However, on this occasion both candidates used plain talk and the liveliness was a result of the conflict introduced by Stokes, who said:

*The question before you, the voters of Cleveland, is quite simple. Which of the candidates do you believe—do you honestly believe—is best prepared to do all the things that have to be done? [Shouts, pleas by moderator for quiet] Thanks, and I appreciate the feelings, but we have to get along with our talk. Which of us is best suited by our training, job experience, and actual living experiences, personality, understanding of human beings, the ability to win cooperation from all the thousands of people whose help we will need?*

*Well, I'm going to be brutally frank with you and equally frank with Seth Taft. The personal analysis of Seth Taft—and the analysis of many competent political analysts—is that Seth Taft may win the November 7 election, but for only one reason. That reason is that his skin happens to be white.*[5]

Carl Stokes, amidst boos and catcalls, went on to explain why he believed the statement to be true. He told the audience to quiet down and let him speak. He said, "Just a minute. Just let me finish. If you don't agree with me when I get through, that's what you have ballot boxes for."

When Stokes was finished, Seth Taft arose and said:

*"Well, well, well. It seems the race issue is with us. I was charged at Carl Stokes's campaign-opening with bringing up the race issue by telling my workers that race was not a factor in the race. As far as I am concerned, it is not. It was not in the Democratic primary, as Carl Stokes pointed out. He won by the votes of fourteen thousand white voters who voted for him. Now it appears that if I say something on this subject it's racism. If Carl Stokes says something about it, it's fair play."*

It may be that you do not wish to enter public debate but are still anxious to make your speech lively. Employing the active voice, the present tense, and a metaphor or two are not the only means of adding life to your presentation. There are scores of other ways.

You can stir the senses by using: (1) action verbs, (2) adjectives, (3) alliteration, (4) personalization, (5) personification, (6) similes and metaphors, (7) parallelism, (8) antithesis, (9) the rhetorical question, (10) quotations, and (11) restatement and repetition. Using some or all of the above will also lend variety to your language and sentence structure and keep your audience awake.

**1. Action verbs**  Action verbs use the active voice as opposed to the passive voice. A great majority of American sentences use active verbs. An action verb makes the noun the subject in the sentence. The passive verb makes the noun the object. For example: The bee stung Jim (active verb). Jim was stung by the bee (passive verb).

Action verbs *do* things: they sting, sing, love, hate, caress, pierce, leap, drown, sparkle, ignite, illuminate, jingle, scream, moan and delight.

**2. Adjectives**  Approach adjectives cautiously; don't smother your noun. Modify, qualify, but don't obliterate. Forget the overgeneralized adjectives that are opinionated and nonspecific. Talk about the *spice* cake, the *European* car, the *tempting* morsel, the *golden* bell, the *piercing* scream. That's much better than talking about the lovely cake, the expensive car, the lovely morsel, the beautiful bell, the loud scream.

**3. Alliteration**  Put a little rhythm into your speech—try alliteration. Alliteration is the art of designing a *sentence so* it has *several* words that *start* with the *same sounds*. Tell the *story* about the *curious cat* that *catapulted* to *safety*, or the *Titan* that *trampled* the *tall timbers*. Or, better still, tell the Kiwanis that this is the *year* of the *Dynamic Duo*, the president and vice president will *cavort* in *chorus* at the annual *big bash* for *bursitis*.

**4. Personalization**  Use personal pronouns. Don't be afraid of becoming intimate with your audience. Create a feeling of oneness, bring your audience close to you with a sprinkling of "you," "I," "we." If you *must* use the third person (you may wish to create a certain feeling of authority) then go on and say "the president feels" the "mayor believes" *but* spice your talk with personal nouns. Don't just talk about businessmen, name them.

**5. Personification**  Personification is the practice of endowing ideas and objects with human traits, qualities, or attributes. Give your inanimate objects living characteristics. Bring the gingham dog and the calico cat alive, let time march on, and while the wheel of fortune goes spinning 'round, let the old dutch clock sit with his hands before his face, while the tongues of flame lick at the pendulum.

**6. Similes and metaphors**  Both compare objects or concepts that are basically alike. Each calls for sharp images, each should be used to both clarify and add color. In the section on clarity by definitions, we used metaphors and similes extensively.

*But watch out for tongue-twisters.*

A simile *uses* the words "as" and "like." It is a *stated* comparison between two unlike things that, perhaps unexpectedly, have something in common:

"My sister's temper is red like fire, and as searing."

A metaphor *implies* the words "as" and "like." It is an *implied* comparison between unlike things that, perhaps unexpectedly, have something in common:

> Out, out brief candle!
> *Life's but a walking shadow,* a poor player that struts and frets his hour upon the stage and then is heard no more. . .

President Roosevelt used simile and metaphor in discussing electrical power when he said, "The speaker, like a ship sailing in dangerous waters, must avoid not only unseen shoals and rocky reefs, he must be on his guard against false lights on the shore."[7]

**7. Parallelism**   Parallelism indicates a similarity of structure in sentences or phrases. Ideas of equal value in a statement are often made parallel; that is, they are expressed in the same grammatical form.

Lavinia used parallel structure in her speech to the students at Kent State when she said: "I urge you to write to your congressmen, to endorse our nonviolent policy, and to support the efforts to end this war."

Roosevelt used the same phrases in parallel form when he said, "*We cannot go back* to the old lack of hospitals; *we cannot go back* to the sweatshops of America; *we cannot go back* to the children working in factories."[8]

Putting coordinate ideas in parallel constructions helps the listener to follow your direction more easily and helps the speaker avoid shifts in person and tense.

**8. Antithesis**   Antithesis is a type of parallelism, in which the construction is balanced but the ideas are opposing. For example, in his inaugural address John F. Kennedy used antithesis when he said, "Let us never negotiate out of fear. But let us never fear to negotiate." And in his first inaugural address, Richard M. Nixon said, "We cannot expect to make everyone our friend, but we can try to make no one our enemy."

**9. The rhetorical question**   How often has someone said to you, "You don't really expect an answer to that question"? And you should honestly answer, "No, it's just a device to create interest. I'm merely introducing an idea in the form of a question. I want to stimulate your interest."

So you ask, "What's it all about, Alfie?" or your mother says, "What's going to become of you?" Or you stand up at the podium and say, "Consider the recent rise in crime in our city. Where will it

*The speaking styles of Roosevelt and Churchill are worth studying.*

lead? Where *can* it lead?" And your audience nods their collective heads and thinks, "True, true, where will it all lead?" You are really introducing an idea, and you use the question form to lead the audience to listen and perhaps probe with you. You ask the teachers "What does it mean to be tenured?" You ask the doctors "Why are we forming unions?"

*You* do not expect answers; *your listeners* expect you to go on.

**10. Quotation**   Using a quotation to add color is an easier task than using a quotation to prove something. Here, you have a limitless choice. Your quotation doesn't have to prove anything—it needs merely to be pleasing and add color.

The most fun is quoting poetry or a humorous saying or combining the two:

An attorney, trying to tell his partners that litigation was not the answer, remembered his Pope (Alexander, that is) and said:

*"Once," says an author, where I need not say,*
*"Two travellers found an oyster on their way.*
*Both fierce, both hungry, the dispute grew strong.*
*When scale in hand, Dame Justice passed along.*
*Before her each with clamor pleads the laws,*
*Explains the matter, and would win the cause.*
*Dame Justice, weighing long the doubtful right,*
*Takes, opens, swallows it before their sight.*
*The cause of strife removed so rarely well,*
*"There, take," says Justice, "Take you each a shell,*
*We thrive in courthouses on fools like you.*
*'Twas a fat oyster; live in peace—adieu."*

He could also have quoted Plautus and said: "You little know what a ticklish thing it is to go to law," or the old proverb that says "Lawsuits consume time, and money, and rest, and friends," or "It is not the saints of the world who chiefly give employment to our profession." Put a little zest in your speech: quote someone else.

**11. Restatement and repetition**   Your listeners may not always understand your meaning or appreciate a clever phrase the first time you say it, so you may wish to *reiterate* or *amplify* a statement to be sure you got your idea across.

Restatement is used to clarify and emphasize; it says the same thing over again in a different way. A speaker at a Press Club meeting restated his point in the following manner: "The fledgling reporter needs to listen to the editor who says that the three most important things to remember in any story are accuracy, accuracy, and accuracy. *I believe that accuracy is of primary importance and that every fact needs checking.*"

> *Quotation used to make our own speech gayer, our thought clearer, does not constrict or paralyze the language. On the contrary, it enlarges it, gives it more scope and freedom.*
>
> **Clifton Fadiman**

Repetition uses identical phrasing. Important names and dates should be repeated, as should important ideas. Repetition can be used after the original statement or after intervening sentences. In the two examples that follow, one person used repetition without an intervening sentence and the other supported each repetitive phrase with an explanation. Both were repeating important ideas.

In November, 1969, Reverend Jesse Jackson faced the congregation of Oleveta Baptist Church in Cleveland, raised his right hand, and shouted:

*I am somebody!*
*I am somebody!*
*I am somebody!*

The congregation picked up the chant: "I am somebody, I am somebody, I am somebody." Then Jesse Jackson began his speech before an enthusiastic audience.

In August of 1963, correspondents from Europe, Africa, Asia, Australia, and Latin America met with thousands of Americans in Washington, D.C., to listen to Dr. Martin Luther King, Jr. The highlight of his speech that day came when he told the audience:

I have a dream—*that one day on the red hills of Georgia, the sons of former slaves and the sons of former slave owners will be able to sit down together at the table of brotherhood.*

I have a dream—*that one day even the state of Mississippi, the state sweltering with the heat of injustice, sweltering with the heat of oppression, will be transformed into an oasis of freedom and justice.*

I have a dream—*that my four little children will one day live in a nation where they will not be judged by the color of their skin but by the context of their character.*

I have a dream *today.* [9]

## SIMPLICITY

While it is very important to know how to add liveliness to your speech, to embellish your words and to create vivid imagery through a variety of types of sentence construction, there are also times when the simplest and most direct words are the most appropriate. Simple statements or questions are not complex or intricate, either in their construction or their content. They are usually associated with plainness in speaking style.

When you talk about a "bird" does everyone know what you mean? Does the audience see a redheaded woodpecker, a bluejay, or a yellow bellied sapsucker? Why not just say "It's a bluejay."

When you speak about a building, how long will it take for your audience to figure out that you mean the court house, the skyscraper at 5th street, the Empire State Building? Why not say "the Empire State Building"?

Test yourself. See just how specific you are. Go over your speech and play twenty questions with your words. And if it takes more than two questions to unearth what you mean *exactly*, that's one question too many.

Of course, there are some very common words that have hundreds of meanings, so the next step after selecting the most specific word you can find is to put it into the right context.

Have you *ever* heard the starting gun go off on the word "run"? No, the starter says, "Get on your mark, get set, *go*," even though he *means* run. But if you are walking down a dark street and hear footsteps rushing up behind you, your mind says, "Run!"

The practice of selecting specific words and putting them into exact sentences is rewarding and sharpens the observational skills. You must probe your memory and increase your ability to recall—to visualize.

Don't say, "She rendered a pop-tune from another era." Say, "She sang 'Prisoner of Love.'" Don't say, "A very large number of people assembled for the meeting." Say, "Five hundred delegates attended the State Legislative Caucus."

Of course, it is possible to carry specificity too far. Consider the audience. A group of doctors understand "lacerations" and a group of laymen understand "cuts"; a group of school teachers will understand "medians" and "means," but the students will want to know their "averages."

Simplifying often means brevity. Remember, brevity is a principle, not a rule. Short words are strong, but long words can be musical. Variety is a sure cure for dullness. Monotony of sentence structure can produce monotony of tone. So keep in mind that the size of a word is not as important as its familiarity.

The following example of simplicity is from Ten Bears' speech, some of which was quoted earlier. The sentences are varied, the words are short, the meaning is clear.

**Simplicity can be beautiful.**

*I was born upon the prairie, where the wind blew free and there was nothing to break the light of the sun. I was born where there were no enclosures, and where everything drew a free breath. I want to die there, not within walls. I know every stream and every wood between the Rio Grande and the Arkansas. I have hunted and lived over that country. I lived like my fathers before me, and like them, I lived happily. When I was in Washington the Great Father told me that all the Comanche land was ours, and that no one should hinder us in living upon it. So why do you ask us to leave the rivers, and the sun, and the wind, and live in houses? Do not ask us to give up the buffalo for the sheep."* [10]

Simplicity, however, is not sufficient unto itself; you must also strive for clarity. Clarity is the most important consideration when wording your speech, and often the most difficult goal to achieve. Your speech can be alive and vibrating, but if it is not clear, if it is not understood, you have failed in your task.

Since words have more than one meaning, your challenge is to make clear the meaning you wish to convey. One way to achieve clarity is by definition.

For example, when a television camera operator was asked to give an instructional talk to the sixth grade on the use of the television equipment, she realized that she had to clarify her words because the children were learning something new. So she explained, "When the director says, 'Give me more headroom,' that means more space between the top of an object being photographed and the top of the frame. Now you probably want to know what 'frame' is; well, it's each individual picture in a length of film, or the space which the picture occupies. When we say 'freeze frame' we mean a frozen shot. Now you may want to know what we mean by frozen . . .''

**Make it simple—but clear.**

You may define a word by using a *synonym:* "A specter is a phantom of the dead." You should remember, though, that the definition should contribute to the further understanding of the word. To say that *spinosity* is a spinous part or thing means nothing to the person who has never heard of *spinous.* You may wish to define that word by example: "When you see a porcupine coming toward you, have you noticed how prickly it appears, with all those needles standing straight up. Can you imagine yourself having a lot of spines that stand out from your body? Or can you imagine just feeling prickly?"

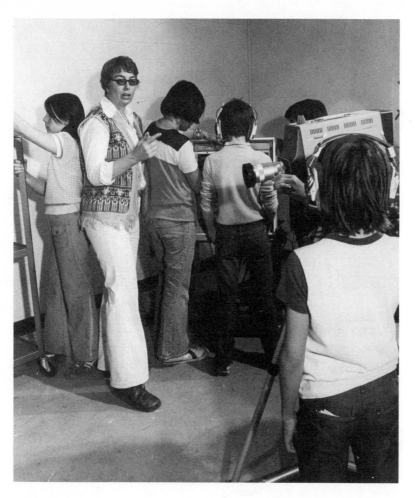

Obviously, if you wish the audience to feel prickly all over you are trying to arouse certain emotions. The example must be a meaningful one—the audience must know what a porcupine looks like and could possibly feel like, otherwise it is useless to use that example.

A very popular way of clarifying your speech is to *compare* or *contrast* a word with another item. Chief Justice Hobart made a number of comparisons in reference to Common Law:

*That statute is like a tyrant; where he comes he makes all void; but the common law is like a nursing father, makes void only that part where the fault is, and preserves the rest.*[11]

Chief Justice Hobart was not only comparing common law to a nursing father, but *contrasting* common law with a tyrant.

Here's a definition that gives an example, contrasts, and compares: "A nuisance may be merely a right thing in the wrong place, like a pig in the parlor instead of the barnyard."

You may also classify and differentiate: "This plane is like no other thing that flies [general classification: flying objects]. It has six wings, made of gossamer [but it's different]; it runs on fairy dust and it will take you to outer space faster than a space capsule."

Sometimes you may have to give an historical background to your word to set it in the right time period. For example, when Lavinia spoke of the New Deal, she had to place those words into the year 1932, giving a background of the times. She could have spoken of unemployment, bread lines, FDR, the campaign, etc. This kind of definition is most useful when you speak of concepts.

You can also define a word by telling what it is *not*: Love is not an advancing porcupine (except perhaps to another porcupine). Now try it yourself. Define "love"—or some other word—by telling what it is not.

## APPROPRIATENESS

Many a politician has made himself or herself perfectly clear, only to find that the words were not appropriate to the audience, the subject or the occasion. *Appropriateness* is characteristic of good oral style, yet it is almost impossible to set any guidelines for the speaker. Perhaps a good rule would be to take care not to sacrifice your own integrity for the sake of adapting to your audience. However, this does not imply that it isn't perfectly permissible to use different words when talking before a group of the old sports from high school days and when presenting your annual report to the board of trustees.

Appropriate use of the language is sometimes equated with good taste, but the two can be at variance at times. Good taste implies a selectivity; it combines the best of reason with the uniqueness of the human soul. Just as there is an ethic implied in the selection of your subject, or your logical and emotional appeals, so is there an ethic implied in your choice of words. Respect for the language implies respect for your audience. You do not wish to mislead, confuse or distract your audience from your purpose, nor do you wish to insult their intelligence, or strip them of the dignity they deserve as members of the audience and of the human race.

When Judge Roy Bean sat in judgment on an Irish railroad clerk who had killed a Chinese laundryman for, as the clerk claimed, insulting him, the Judge faced 200 Irishmen who intended to see their compatriot set free. A mixed audience heard the Judge declare:

*This here book, which is a Texan law book, says that hommyside is the killin' of a human, male or female. They is many kinds of hommyside—murder, manslaughter, plain hommyside, negligent hommyside, justifi'ble hommyside, and praiseworthy hommyside. They is three kinds of humans—white men, niggers, and Mexicans. It*

*stan's to reason that if a Chinym'n was human, killin' of him would*
*come under the head of praiseworthy hommyside. The pris'ner is*
*discharged on condition that he pays f'r havin' the Chinese buried.*[12]

Judge Roy Bean's knowledge of the law may have been limited,
but his sense of self-preservation was not. His words may have been
appropriate for the occasion, but no one would agree that he used
good taste in their selection.

We often applaud a speaker who uses "good taste," which
means that he was "correct" in his choice of words and displayed a
*sense of delicacy.* The word "taste" itself, as we understand it today,
evolved from a metaphor.

Rhetoricians in the 18th century equated taste with a sensibility
to beauty, and beauty, they said, was orderly, proportioned, grand,
harmonious, new, and sprightly.

It was also suggested that one could improve one's taste by: (1)
exposing oneself to new experiences in literature, art, music, and
other disciplines; (2) avoiding forced sentimentality and affected
styles; and (3) applying good reason.

But it is not for us to set a standard for taste that you, the
speaker, can follow without hesitation. We can only stress what
others have discovered—that listeners keep asking for clarity, appropriateness, liveliness, and simplicity. They also enjoy the human
touch and feel more at ease with a speaker who seems to converse
with them. As for the question of taste, perhaps a quotation from
Hugh Blair will suffice for the moment: "What interests the imagina-
tion and touches the heart pleases all ages."[13]

## SUMMARY QUESTIONS

- What is the main difference between oral and written language?
- What misconceptions about language lead to barriers in com-
  munication?
- How is the human touch achieved?
- What are a few ways to add life to your speech?
- How can you *clarify* your speech?

## EXERCISES

1   Read those parts of Martin Luther King Jr.'s "I Have a Dream" Speech
that are in this chapter and analyze his style. Find the repetition, metaphors,
and human touches that he wrote into it.

2   Select a topic that you are interested in and write a speech using plain,
middle, and eloquent styles. Explain what you added to make the speech
eloquent.

**3** Listen to a sermon, a lecture, and a lawyer's opening statement. Does the *type* of speech affect the language used? If you do not have these speakers available to you, find representative speeches from the journals called *Vital Speeches* in your school library.

# REFERENCES

**1** "Proceedings of the Council," Oct. 19–20, 1867, as reported by Henry M. Stanley in *War Path and Council Fires,* p. 124.

**2** B. Jordan, Keynote Address, Democratic National Convention, Kansas City, Mo., August 1976.

**3** D. I. Clayton, *Kansas Populism: Ideas and Men* (Lawrence, Kans.: University Press of Kansas, 1969), pp. 73–78.

**4** Ibid.

**5** E. Zannes, assisted by Mary Jean Thomas, *Checkmate in Cleveland: The Rhetoric of Confrontation During the Stokes Years* (Cleveland, Ohio: The Press of Case Western Reserve University, 1972).

**6** Ibid.

**7** S. I. Rosenman (ed.), *The Public Papers and Addresses of Franklin D. Roosevelt* (New York: Random House, 1938), p.727.

**8** Ibid.

**9** Martin Luther King, Jr., "I Have a Dream" speech at Washington Monument, August 1963.

**10** Ten Bears, *Proceedings of the Council*

**11** M. F. McNamara, *Ragbag of Legal Quotations* (New York: Bender, 1960), p. 93.

**12** C. L. Sonnichsen, *The Story of Roy Bean: Law West of the Pecos* (Greenwich, Conn.: Macmillan, 1943).

**13** H. Blair, *Lectures on Rhetoric,* condensed by G. Kleiser (New York & London: Funk and Wagnall Company, 1911), p. 24.

# DELIVERING THE MESSAGE

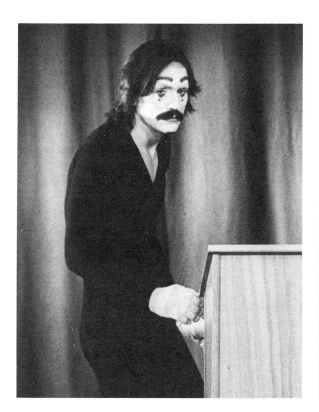

Bruce walked toward the podium, shoulders slumped. He paused there for a moment, then turned and walked away. When he was ten feet from the podium he straightened his body, walked back, and firmly grasped the edge of the podium, looking squarely into the audience's eyes. He did not say a word. Then leaning toward his audience, he smiled. Everyone applauded.

Bruce began his "speech" on the subject "Every movement has a meaning." During the course of his presentation he spoke very little, allowing his body and gestures to illustrate his points.

Bruce is a mime. He was addressing a live audience who could both see and hear him. His delivery consisted of two elements: his physical behavior and the use of his voice.

Usually when you speak you will be both seen and heard. However, in this world of mass media, there is a chance that you may sometime be asked to address a television or radio audience. While the television audience does both hear and see you, the method of delivery on television differs from that used before a live audience. Of course the radio audience obtains *all* its information from your voice.

In this chapter we will discuss the visual and the vocal parts of your delivery separately, so that you may pay special attention to one or the other as the situation demands. However, keep in mind that one directly influences the other, and in most speaking situations, the ways in which the body and the voice are used should be thought of simultaneously. Because so many speakers today address media audiences, we shall also discuss delivering the message on television and radio. Finally the different *styles* of delivery will be explained.

## WHAT THE AUDIENCE SEES

When Bruce walked to the podium and planted two feet firmly on the ground, his legs were the most physical part of the picture his audience saw. He was balancing himself with his environment because horizontal and vertical lines suggest well-being, maneuverability, and stability to the audience. Diagonal lines, which appeared when Bruce draped himself over the podium to illustrate a point, are unstable, directional, and provocative. The curved line is all-encompassing, repetitive, and warm—for example, Bruce's smile and the audience's response. Up to this point we have talked mainly about how your audience responds to the design of the message, to your sense of organization of words. We have stressed selection of words, sentence structure, and content. But just as your audience responds to verbal organization with a sense of security, so will it respond to visual organization—such as balance—with a sense of security. Balancing your body is only one of the many visuals you present to your audience. The clothes you wear, the articles around you, the pencil in your hand, the slides, graphs, films, maps, graphics you show your listeners—all are visuals and all transmit information.

### Body Movements

Let us concentrate for a moment on the messages your body transmits. Certainly you would agree that your audience reads meanings into your facial expression, into the way you stand and walk, into the way you move your hands, head, shoulders, limbs. Every movement has meaning as thought manifests itself in motion.

We like to watch graceful people. We admire the dancer, the athlete whose body is disciplined and prepared. Grace, to champions, is efficiency of movement, and every movement achieves its end by minimizing wasted effort.

For centuries, people from all cultures, particularly athletes, have studied and developed body movements. The Hindu dancer has some 57,000 catalogued hand positions, each having the specific value of an explicit word and distinct meaning. The Chinese have meanings for the various lines in one's face, and have perfected the art of face reading.

After observing people in a wide variety of situations, a Frenchman, Francois Delsarte, developed a method of teaching various body movements for speakers. Delsarte claimed that the body is divided into three parts. The head is the mental, intellectual zone; the torso is the emotional, moral, spiritual zone; and the limbs are the vital, physical zone.

*The movements and gestures one makes have even been classified as body language.*

Today, many communication researchers in America refer to body movements as nonverbal communication. In recent years, great emphasis has been placed on the important role that physical behavior plays in oral communication.

There is no question that first impressions are powerful, and are influenced by sex, uniform and clothing, body shapes and size, and facial expression.

Your walk to the podium gives the audience a chance to form instant impressions. If your listeners don't know you, and this is their first glimpse of you, they may react to your body type. Wells, a researcher in body types, using silhouette drawings, asked adults to rate three body types (somatypes). The tall, thin type (ectomorph) was rated tense, nervous, ambitious, pessimistic, stubborn, and quiet. The short, round type (endomorph) was judged older, more warmhearted, talkative, sympathetic, dependable, old-fashioned, agreeable, trusting, and less good-looking. The muscular, athletic type (mesomorph) was described as masculine, mature, self-reliant, strong, adventurous, and better looking. Fortunately, most of us do not fit into a single category but tend to be a combination of two or three body types.

Besides the information we give by merely walking to the podium, we also respond to our audience with a variety of facial expressions. The muscles in our face are capable of over 20,000 different expressions, and these expressions tell people how we feel.

## Gestures

It is not our intention to provide guidelines for how you should move or what type of facial expression you should have. The human body moves under the stimuli of emotions. The emotions you are feeling at the time you deliver your speech come from a variety of sources: the

**173 What the Audience Sees**

inner conviction you have for your message, the mood you are in at that particular moment, the attitude you have toward your audience, to name only a few. None of these emotions can be catalogued because you are unique and no one else can feel exactly as you feel at any given moment. However, the following information will give you an idea of how some observers feel about body movements and facial expressions:

1 When two parts of the body move in opposite directions simultaneously, an expression of force is achieved. Example: slamming your fist into your hand, clicking your heels together, moving your head in one direction and your arms in another.

2 When two parts of the body move simultaneously in the same direction, the expression is weak, but can be very decorative. Example: moving the hand and the head in the same direction.

3 When a movement passes through the entire body, using every muscle, bone, and joint to create a wavelike movement, the expression is all-encompassing. Example: You are truly happy to see the audience, your eyes light up, you smile, your chest rises, and your arms move to embrace them. A successive movement can work from the center outward or begin at the extremities and work toward the center.

4 We understand what is in front of us and we fear it less than other things, so a gesture directly in front of us is vital. We move our heads knowingly, and that gesture reassures the audience that we understand them. We move our upper torso and our audience feels the affection, or we walk toward them and the expression is vital and physical.

5 A gesture to the side suggests magnitude. Example: spreading our arms out, or reaching out with one hand to draw people in.

6 The fear of the unknown, however, lurks behind us, and a gesture that we do behind our backs is a negative one for the audience.

The question arises: If we assume these observations have merit, how do we apply this knowledge to our delivery? The answer is that there are no guidelines that will apply for every speech. You must apply these principles as you see fit, because body movements and expressions must come from within, from the speaker's feelings at that moment. According to Delsarte, gesture is more than speech. He said of gesture, "It is the persuasive agent of the heart." A simple movement, he felt, could express a whole being. Language is analytic and successive, and the mind speculates and reckons. But gesture grasps everything by intuition and sentiment, as well as through contemplation. Speech is the letter, and gesture the spirit. The most powerful of all gestures is that which affects the spectator without his

*Move as naturally as you can; feel comfortable with your gestures.*

**175  What the Audience Sees**

or her knowing it. One clue that a speaker is not effective may be that the audience is too much aware of movement and is distracted from the message. For example: There is nothing more disconcerting than to look at a speaker who is hanging over the podium, or looks like he or she is too tired to stand up. The speaker who clutches at any object—the chair, the podium—also distracts the audience. Body movement should supplement speech, not replace it. If an audience is made seasick by your swaying back and forth, or gets dizzy watching you pace the floor, you're probably moving too much.

Gestures that are random action, such as wiggling, twirling your hair, taking your glasses off and on, and rattling your keys, make the audience wonder whether it should have come in the first place.

While we know which gestures we don't like, it is difficult to know just which movement or expression will move an audience to shout and cheer—or to remain silent. Speakers have quieted noisy audiences by just standing still, others have raised their hands above their heads, still others have shouted louder than the audience.

**In some cases different speakers may use different movements to make the same point.**

Some speakers display strength quietly, with a gentle, even voice and simple, unobtrusive movements. Others use quick, strong movements. For example: A simple evangelical appeal which contained accusations against the North, the South, the United States Government, and the Church, was calmly delivered by a beautiful and intelligent woman, Angelina Grimke Weld, to a hostile, violent audience.

It is May 16, 1838, and the setting is a large hall in Philadelphia. The hall is magnificent. It cost upward of $40,000, and is scientifically ventilated and brilliantly lighted with gas. Gold letters over the forum read "Virtue, Liberty, and Independence." On the platform are superb chairs and sofas and a desk covered with blue damask. The occasion is the dedication of the hall. Abolitionists from all parts of the country have arrived for the dedication. Representatives of the Women's National Convention, which had been held in New York the previous year, are there. A program of women speakers is scheduled. Though the abolitionists anticipate trouble, the mayor insists that they rely on the good sense and manners of the people of Philadelphia. He therefore refuses protection to the ladies scheduled to speak.

When the abolitionists and women come, the hall is already filled. When the ladies mount the platform, there is not a familiar face in the audience. Lloyd Garrison speaks first, and is hissed. Marie Chapman comes to the podium, and boos and catcalls are heard from every part of the hall; stones are thrown from the street, shattering the windows along one side of the room. A mob surges outside the building, and diverts the speakers.

At this point, Angelina Grimke Weld, a bride of three days, steps forward. So great is the effect of her pure, beautiful presence and quiet, graceful manner, that in a few moments the confusion within the hall subsides.

Not once is a tremor or a change of color perceptible in her face. When the noise grows too loud again, she waits for it to subside. When stones fly through the open sashes, she notices them if it suits her point and ignores them if it does not. At one point the mob grows wild, and she stands calmly until the noise subsides. She has their attention but realizes she cannot hold them long. Joining hands with her sisters, she forms a human chain and marches every speaker down the center of the hall and out into the night. The next night the anti-abolitionists come back and burn Pennsylvania Hall to the ground.

## Clothing

We notice body movements, whether they are calm or frenzied, and we notice the clothes that adorn those bodies. How the body is clothed is important to the effect of the speaker's delivery.

A mayor of a large midwestern city once told a newspaper reporter: "You can sure tell the difference between you newspaper guys and television people." The mayor, who was often referred to as a "snappy" dresser, was implying that the sloppiness of the newspaper reporters' clothes was a hindrance to the job. Later he explained to a fellow politician that he thought *anyone* in the public eye should pay attention to clothes.

The early Greeks did not ignore clothing. Their heroes wore heavily draped robes that gave them added dignity and stature. Down through the ages, clothing has been identified with periods in history, with social status, and with the roles people assume. A distinguishing feature of clothing is that it constantly seems to be in a state of change. Fads in clothing designs come and go so quickly that it is difficult for most people to keep up with the times. Fortunately we are now in an age where many types of clothing are accepted in a variety of settings and situations.

A description of Clarence S. Darrow during his famous defense in the Leopold–Loeb case, shows why he was so effective a speaker, and also indicates that he wore what was comfortable for him:

*An expanse of crumpled white shirt over that relaxed chest and stomach, one thumb hooked in his galluses, the other hand extended to make a point. Striding forward in baggy gray pants and a loose, hopelessly stretched jacket pushed back on his shoulders—striding forward and then stopping, staring straight into the jurors' eyes, turning, head hung in thought as the retreating voice comes over the shoulder slowly, carefully, then all at once booming again. Sometimes witty, smiling; sometimes angry, scathing, merciless; sometimes tears streaming down his cheeks. . . .*[1]

While Darrow may have been a bit rumpled, the clothing and color combinations he selected were in accord with information we

*Actors have long known that appropriate clothing reinforces the speaker's identification with the part portrayed.*

## Live Audiences

|        | Excellent | Neutral | Poor |
|--------|-----------|---------|------|
| *Suits* | 1. Navy, solid<br>2. Dark grey, solid<br>3. Dark blue, pinstripe<br>4. Dark grey, pinstripe | 1. Medium blue, solid<br>2. Medium grey, solid<br>3. Medium blue, pinstripe<br>4. Medium grey, pinstripe | 1. Light blue, solid<br>2. Light grey, solid<br>3. Dark brown, solid |
| *Shirts* | 1. Dark brown, solid<br>2. Medium brown, solid<br>3. White, solid<br>4. Pale yellow, solid<br>5. Dark blue, pinstripe | | 1. Bright yellow<br>2. Grey, solid<br>3. Gold, solid<br>4. Green, solid |
| *Ties* | 1. Blue, solid<br>2. Maroon, solid<br>3. Beige, solid<br>4. Brown, solid<br>5. Dark blue, small white polka dots<br>6. Dark striped<br>7. Paisley | | 1. Large symbols<br>2. Gaudy colors<br>3. Big pictures |

## Media Audiences

|        | Excellent | Neutral | Poor |
|--------|-----------|---------|------|
| *Suits* | 1. Navy, solid<br>2. Dark grey, solid<br>3. Medium blue, solid<br>4. Light grey, solid | 1. Medium grey, solid<br>2. Light blue, solid | 1. Dark blue, pinstripe<br>2. Dark grey, pinstripe<br>3. Medium blue, pinstripe<br>4. Medium grey, pinstripe |
| *Shirts* | 1. Dark blue, solid<br>2. Medium blue, solid | | 1. Any with stripes |
| *Ties* | 1. Blue, solid<br>2. Maroon, solid<br>3. Beige, solid | | 1. Large symbols<br>2. Gaudy colors<br>3. Big pictures<br>4. Stripes<br>5. Polka dots |

have derived from John T. Molloy's book, *Dress for Success.*[2] Molloy spent fifteen years researching his topic, and his findings are based on information from 15,000 executives and professional men. His conclusions overwhelmingly support the statement that the clothing you wear directly affects the credibility you have with your audience.

Molloy found that men are most likely to be *liked* when wearing suits of *light grey or blue solids.* He also found that dark blue solids give men the highest credibility with the largest range of audiences. The darker the suit, the more authority it transmits, but Molloy warns that a black suit may be too powerful and suggest funeral overtones. Of course, your credibility varies not only with the clothes you wear, but also according to your personal body shape and the predispositions of the audiences.

For your further information, we have based the chart at left on Molloy's recommendations to men when dressing for a live audience and a television appearance. As the chart indicates, shirts made from light and solid colors are the most acceptable, and blue is the most popular solid.

Molloy further stated that the *tie*, more than any other aspect of men's clothing, directly affects status, credibility, and impressions of personality and ability. He urges men to buy silk or polyester that looks like silk, or a blend of silk and polyester. He also presents a guideline for selecting the tie and shirt: *The tie is darker than the shirt and the shirt is lighter than the suit.*

Of course, what you wear and the colors you finally select are personal decisions you must make every day. When speaking before a live or television audience, however, knowing how people respond to types of clothes and colors may help you avoid such mistakes as wearing a striped suit on television.

Since Molloy's chart was limited to men's clothing, we present a symbolism-of-color list that was developed from a number of sources for the general public.

## Symbolism of Color

| | General appearance | Mental association | Direct association | Objective impression | Subjective impression |
|---|---|---|---|---|---|
| Red | Brilliant, dry, intense, opaque | Hot, fire, heat, blood | Danger | Passionate, exciting, active | Intensity, rage |
| Orange | Bright, luminous, glowing | Warm, metallic, autumnal | | Jovial, lively, forceful | Hilarity, exuberance, satiety |
| Yellow | Sunny, incandescent, radiant | Sunlight | Caution | Cheerful, inspiring, vital, celestial | High spirits, health |
| Green | Clear, moist | Cool, nature, water | | Subduing, refreshing, peaceful | Disease, terror, guilt |
| Blue | Transparent, wet | Cold, sky, water, ice | | Subdued, melancholy, contemplative | Gloom, fearfulness, furtiveness |
| Purple | Deep, soft, atmospheric | Cool, mist, darkness, shadow | Mourning | Dignified, pompous, mournful | Loneliness, desperation |
| White | Spatial, light | Cool, snow | Cleanliness | Pure, clean, frank, youthful | High spirits, normality |
| Black | Spatial, dark | Night, emptiness | Mourning | Funereal, ominous, deadly, depressing | Negation, low spirits, death |

Effective delivery makes full use of all the *visible* codes, but it also includes *audible* codes. What the audience hears, after all, is speech. Speech is not a natural phenomenon. Human beings have *learned* how to speak. As far as we know, it is unique to our species.

How did it happen? How did we ever figure it all out?

Let's start with the most basic thing we have to do in order to speak—that is, breathe. Actually, the primary and unalterable purpose of breathing, or respiration, is to supply our body with oxygen (when we inhale) and rid it of excess carbon dioxide (when we exhale). The respiratory cycle—inhalation and exhalation—is automatic and is repeated every three to five seconds. It speeds up during moments of excitement and exertion and slows down during sleep or rest.

When we inhale, the diaphragm contracts and draws downward and the ribs and sternum raise and move outward. The effect of these actions is to increase the size of the chest cavity, and outside air is drawn in through the respiratory tract—nose, trachea (windpipe), and lungs—to fill that space. When we exhale, the muscles used in respiration relax, and the diaphragm, ribs, and sternum return to their original positions.

Part way up the respiratory tract—in the windpipe—are the vocal cords, or vocal folds. When they are relaxed, the air we breathe passes between them without making any sound. But when we tighten them somewhat with muscular tension, the passage of air makes them vibrate and produces sound. Now, a moment ago we said that breathing is automatic—and it is. But when we choose to, we can exercise considerable control over the *way* we breathe. If we expel only a little air, and tighten our vocal cords just so, we can make very soft sounds. And if we expel a lot of air—again with the vocal cords appropriately tightened—we can let out quite a bellow. But this is not an either/or situation; because of the marvelous sensitivity of human nerves and muscles (and given the necessary knowledge) we can produce an amazing variety of sounds. Just as important, we can arrange those sounds almost instantaneously into an equally amazing variety of combinations or sequences. And by common agreement, those combinations of sounds are recognized by ourselves and by others as speech.

That sounds simple—but aside from varying the tension on our vocal cords and the flow of air between them, what else do we do to modify the sounds we produce into speech? Well, we *articulate* and *pronounce*. Articulation, or diction, refers to the *clarity* with which we make a given sound. Pronunciation, however, refers to the *way* we choose to make that sound. That is, it's possible to *mispronounce* a sound with great clarity. For example, you may have formed a habit of saying ''expecially'' instead of ''especially.'' You can articulate the

*You don't need to be a singer to benefit from proper breath control.*

sound, but you choose to pronounce the word according to habit. Your pronunciation is affected by social conditions and residual habits from physical problems such as overbite and organic causes, or from physical deficiencies or impediments.

The following elements also affect your speech: Phonation, resonance, pitch, rate, volume, quality of voice, mood, dialects, and accents. Though we have mentioned some of these things already in this chapter, a more specific description of each follows.

## Phonation

The exhaled air passes through the bronchi into the trachea (windpipe), and then into the larynx. The larynx (or "voice box") contains the vocal folds or vocal cords. The vibration of the vocal cords produces sound. The vocal cords are more massive and about an inch longer in males than in females, and this accounts for the differences in pitch.

The aperture between the vocal folds, which is known as the glottis, is regulated by muscles.

Air is pushed up from the lungs by the muscles used in breathing. When pressure below the vocal cords is greater than that above

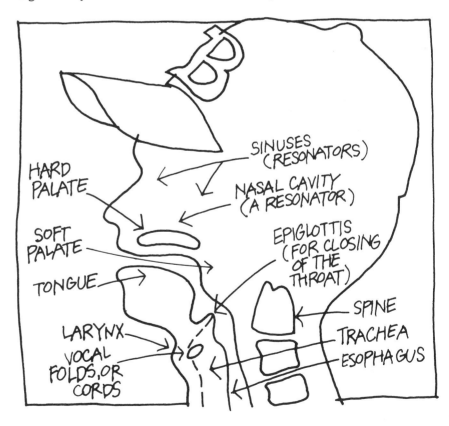

them, the cords, or folds, open upward and sideward, producing a sound wave which moves up through the pharynx. As the process is repeated, vibrations occur. These vibrations determine the frequency and pitch of the sound produced. The sound waves generated by the vocal cords change as they reach the cavities of the throat, mouth, and nose.

## Resonance

The tone from the vocal cords is not a pure one. As it passes through the throat, mouth, and nose, the overtones are amplified or dampened. The open mouth, tension, the nasal passage, all determine what overtones are amplified. Good voice is a product of proper balance between oral and nasal resonance.

## Pitch

Pitch refers to the highness and lowness of tone. Thick vocal cords produce low-pitched tones; thin, short, or tense cords produce high-pitched tones. Optimum pitch depends on the structure of the larynx and the amount of breath used. Your voice is most pleasant at about 25 to 33 percent above the lowest level of your range, as that permits vocalization without strain. If the level at which you habitually speak is below or above your optimum level, you may strain your voice (actually, your vocal folds).

Modal pitch is the pitch you use most of the time. When you wish to emphasize a word or impersonate someone else, you generally either lower or lift your voice to another tone. If you find yourself getting hoarse often, or if your quality is rasping harsh, you may be straining your voice and your pitch may be too low. On the other hand, your modal pitch may be too high if your voice is weak or has a thin quality, or if your voice is nasal or strident.

Some speakers have a very narrow vocal range. Range is the number of notes you use in speaking, from highest to lowest. A very narrow range sometimes results in a monotone.

## Rate

The rate at which you deliver a speech can be varied by several means. The most obvious means, of course, is the rapidity with which your words are spoken. However, you may also drag syllables out or cut them off short, and you may use pauses for emphasis.

Pauses should be used carefully, however. If they are too frequent and too long, the audience's attention is very likely to wander from what you are saying. Also, they may begin to wonder if you really know what you are talking about—particularly if you also use vocalized pauses, such as "ah" or "eh."

On the other hand, if you speak too fast, the audience may find it difficult to understand you—either because your speed slightly distorts your words or because your ideas are coming too quickly. The latter is particularly significant if your speech is highly technical.

If for some reason you feel that you must vary from your normal speaking speed, it's better to speak a little faster than a little slower. But speak clearly.

## Volume

The intensity of sound can be controlled by the speaker. Increased energy can amplify oral resonance, and should be adjusted to the room and noise level. If a speaker is too loud, the sound may interfere with intelligibility or even hurt the listener's ears. If the speaker is too soft, he or she may be difficult to hear. Some speakers let their voices trail off near the ends of sentences and the speech fades away. As a speaker, you should be aware of your own skill at volume control, as well as that of others. If you find it difficult to know exactly how loudly or how softly you are speaking, get a friend to help you. Stand in a room and aim your voice at various distances. For example, have your friend stand, let's say, four feet away from you, while you say to him or her, "I am trying to reach you properly at this distance." Then have your friend stand about twenty feet away from you while you repeat the sentence. Your friend can tell you whether your volume is exactly right for each distance, and then you can try to build a memory of how you sound and what effort it takes to reach the proper level.

Many times your emotional state will determine the way your voice builds or fades away. Davitz (1964) found that differences in loudness, pitch, timbre, rate, inflection, rhythm, and enunciation were related to the expressions of different emotions. For instance: affection is soft, anger is loud; affection is low in pitch, anger is high; affection is resonant, anger is blaring; affection is a slow rate, anger is fast; affection is a steady inflection, anger is irregular; affection is a regular rhythm, anger is irregular; and affection is slurred enunciation, anger is clipped. Davitz and Davitz (1960) also found that we convey our "active feelings" by using a loud voice, high pitch, blaring timbre, and fast rate. Our "passive feelings" are conveyed with a quiet voice, low pitch, resonant timbre, and a slow rate.

## Quality

Understanding the way you convey your natural feelings will aid you when you are planning your particular message and practicing the speech. Being able to recognize the different voice qualities in others will also help you develop a standard that you wish to achieve. The following voice qualities are to be avoided:

1 *Harshness:* This quality sounds strained and is generally grating on the listener's ears. People react to harshness negatively. If you are extremely tense and speak too loudly, your voice may sometimes develop a harsh quality. Breathe deeply before coming to the podium and try to conserve your voice prior to your speaking engagement.

2 *Hoarseness:* This quality often suggests that the speaker has laryngitis and that the production of voice is painful. If you do indeed have laryngitis, conserve your voice, drink something warm with honey in it—and hope that you recover quickly.

3 *Glottal fry:* This quality sounds like noisy scraping.

4 *Glottal shock:* This quality sounds like a dry cough. Both glottal fry and glottal shock can indicate a health problem or simply an unusually low voice. Glottal shock sometimes sounds breathy— that is, as though there were breath escaping with the tone. The quality is often associated with relaxed or sultry characters, such as the late Marilyn Monroe.

5 *Nasality:* This quality makes the speaker sound as though he or she has a stuffy nose. Certain regions in the United States are associated with nasal sounds. Extreme nasality can be avoided by using an open throat and making only the *m, n,* and *ng* sounds in the nasal cavities.

6 *Stridency:* This quality means that the person sounds metallic, screechy, and high pitched. Actress Margaret Hamilton deliberately used this quality when she portrayed the Wicked Witch of the West in "The Wizard of Oz." Unless you are playing that kind of role, it is best to avoid this quality. Stridency often irritates the throat.

7 *Throatiness:* This quality sounds heavy and hollow. However, it is not always unpleasant.

8 *Thinness:* This quality sounds small, and is usually associated with children's voices.

When listeners describe pleasant voices, they generally use terms like "warm," "pleasant," "rich," "deep," and "happy." Most of the terms are very ambiguous. However, they do suggest that the listener was receptive to the speaker. Many times the speaker's voice cannot be described at all by the listeners.

If you are unsure of just how your voice sounds, record it and play it back to your friends and family. Ask them for honest opinions about the quality. Ask them to describe the quality. If they mention terms like "hoarse" or "nasal," then you will have some guidelines

*And the listener, too.*

that tell you how to improve and in what areas. If your friends say "pleasant," "rich," or other complimentary terms, listen to the tape yourself and try to determine what things contribute to those positive reactions. Remember, emotions have much to do with voice quality. Try to remember your mood when you recorded your voice.

## Mood

The telephone rings. Slowly you reach over to lift the receiver from its cradle. You are hardly awake, and your voice is pitched lower than usual. You say, "Hello?" The voice at the other end hesitates, "Is that you Gerry? Did I wake you? You don't sound like yourself." Of course not; you sound better. But in a moment you become alert, your body tightens; within seconds your voice is raised a little higher than normal.

You have that same feeling of tension before an audience. One moment you are laughing with your dinner partner, relaxed and comfortable. The next moment you hear someone say, "And now we will hear from our vice-president in charge of next year's programming," and suddenly your stomach muscles tighten.

The easiest thing to say at this point would be, "Avoid tensions," but since most of these reactions are involuntary, that is no solution. So, if you can't avoid getting tense, try to *relieve* your tensions. When you find yourself tightening up, yawn, think of being submerged in warm waters with a cup of hot mint tea at your fingertips. Take a deep breath. If you're not alone, excuse yourself and retire to the restroom or a bedroom and let your head hang down, roll it around, shake your arms, take some more deep breaths.

On the day of your presentation, don't plan a lot of other things. Rise slowly, have your hot drink. Don't turn on the news; watch "Captain Kangaroo." He's much less hectic than "Sesame Street" or the "Today Show." Go out and buy yourself a new tie or a new scarf. If you are the luncheon speaker, eat lightly. Pamper yourself. You are important. You have something of value to say.

## Dialects and Accents

If you have an *accent*—that is, if you come from another country and have learned English as a second language—you may have difficulty in making your audience understand you, and will have to speak slowly. It is also possible that negative stereotyping of certain accents may cause your audience to "turn you off." If you have a *dialect*—that is, if your speech contains certain regional sounds—and your audience comes from another region of America, you may be confronted with another kind of problem. Very often audiences who have been raised to accept a given dialect as "correct," and standard American English as a sign of intelligence, have certain preconceptions about other dialects that are difficult to change. Noam Chomsky, in his book *Syntactic Structures*, reported that a sentence is considered grammatical if it is "acceptable to a native speaker."[3] When native speakers are asked whether or not a sentence is grammatical, they frequently reject it as being ungrammatical unless it makes "sense" to them in terms of both sentence structure and the speaker's pronunciation. This means that whether a sentence is grammatical or meaningful ultimately depends not on the speaker, but on the hearer.

*The accents of one region can sometimes be difficult for an audience of another region to understand.*

It is your job to discover your audience's values and opinions about dialects and accents, and then conform with, adjust to, explain, or ignore them. The decision ultimately rests with you. Sometimes if you are a member of a community, you may wish to take a chance that people will just accept you as you are and make an effort to try and understand *you*. For example, some very important people have done this. Most of our recent presidents have had dialects. Roosevelt spoke to "Ma friends," Kennedy spoke of "vigah" and "Cuber," Johnson talked to "Ma fella Amuricans," and Carter said, "Y'all come hiyah and visut."

The impact of a dialect or an accent upon an audience is difficult to measure. If a speaker's image is good, if he or she has a good rapport with the audience and has constructed a meaningful message, the chances are that the manner of pronouncing certain words will not adversely affect the audience, unless the accent or dialect makes the message difficult to comprehend.

## DELIVERING THE MESSAGE ON TELEVISION

The ability to perform in a clear, believable, and interesting manner is just as important before the television camera as it is before the live audience. The most difficult problem for you, the speaker, on television, is that you must create the illusion that the studio doesn't exist, even though you are surrounded by the reality of the studio and the production crew. Before a live audience, you can adjust to any new situation, respond to nonverbal and verbal cues from the audience, and control what the audience sees and hears. Before the television audience, you must work with the full cooperation of a technical crew, and though they may be both friendly and professional people, you are *not* in full control of your speech.

For that reason, your only insurance is to make yourself very knowledgeable about what's happening around you, and to understand exactly how you fit into the overall production. However, once the studio gets quiet and the red tally light goes on, it's just you and your audience.

We have made up a list of questions and answers that we hope will be helpful if you are going to videotape or televise your presenta-

tion. These questions deal strictly with performance of your speech, and not with the content.

*How do I get ready?*   The first step is to determine what you are going to wear. Bring a selection of clothing to the studio if you have not been advised to wear a specific outfit by the producer. Very light, dark, or rich colors are not as satisfactory as the medium tones.

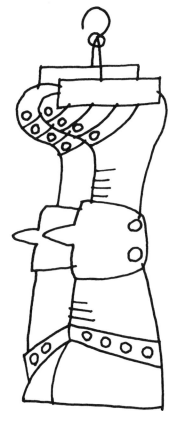

REMEMBER TO BRING A SELECTION OF CLOTHING...

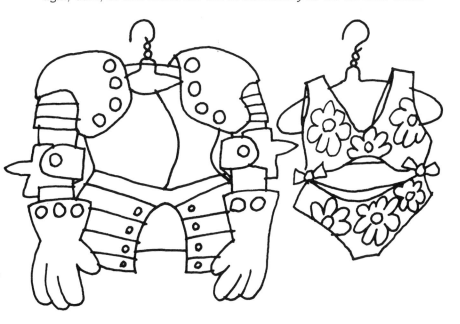

Small patterns can vibrate. Large, shining jewelry can detract from your presentation. Before going on, walk through your moves, handle all your props, speak normally from *all* positions. Get used to using cue cards or the teleprompter. Do not agree to come into the studio and tape the speech without adequate knowledge of exactly what you are going to use. Ask the floor manager to rehearse cues ahead of time, so that you are familiar with them. Some floor managers have their own nonverbal signals. If possible, complete a section and ask to have it played back. This can be done very easily with a videotaped presentation.

The production crew selects what your audience will see. Remember, your audience grew up on television and has seen some very sophisticated shows. The chances are, you will be giving your speech on a public broadcasting station or doing an editorial on a commercial station. You may also be asked to present information in an interview fashion or be a part of a panel discussion. No matter what the situation, the uniqueness of your presentation lies in the fact that it is being videotaped or televised.

*Should I use cue cards, script, or teleprompter?* If you are giving a one-minute editorial, you will wish to put your script on a teleprompter, because timing is very important. If you do this, be sure you can read the message easily. Practice. If you decide on cue cards, ask to have them placed as near to the camera lens as possible. If you are carrying a script, familiarize yourself with it, but do not hide it from the camera. Establish a contact with the audience and try to look at the script when the camera isn't on you, or when you come to a natural pause. Look at the lens, but do not stare. You will need to use your peripheral vision to see the floor manager's or director's signals. The chances are that you will be delivering an extemporaneous speech on television. The extemporaneous speech permits greater freedom of movement and improved visual personality. Since you will probably support your speech with visual materials, you can use the time the camera is on the visual to glance at your outline and refresh your memory.

*How can I look natural while looking at the camera and talking into the microphone?* That's a difficult assignment. You can look up or down before a *live* audience. You may even look around the room and wave your hands. Television, however, demands control. If you look down, the viewers may see the top of your head (especially if the director decides on an extreme close-up at that moment). If you take a little peek at the cue cards, your eyes may look shifty. If' you make a quick move, the camera may be left behind. So, on camera you must hold your gestures and movements down to a minimum, moving slowly into new positions while avoiding stiffness.

*How can I talk to a lens?* Think of the camera as a channel. Your audience is on the other end. Try to create your audience in

**Though you can't see your listeners, they are there. Speak to them.**

your mind. See a friend's face in that lens. Some performers talk to the cameraman or keep the producer's face in their minds.

*Do I always look into the camera?* No. Sometimes you shift from the camera to another person who is on the show with you. The camera can be treated as subjective—that is, as a person to whom you can speak directly—or it may be regarded as objective, in which case you can ignore it and concentrate on another person. If you are delivering information straight to the public, your camera will be subjective. If you are interviewing or interacting with someone else, your camera will be both objective and subjective, as you shift from participant to viewers. Your director will advise you.

*Can I be myself on television?* By all means. Don't be afraid to try something different if it comes naturally to you. Today's audience enjoys meeting new personalities. Perhaps your personality is exactly what they need. Remember, your audience wants entertainment and organization. They also want to understand you, so be clear, lively, and organized.

## DELIVERING THE MESSAGE ON RADIO

Before you go on the air, the producer or director will probably ask you to do a brief audition on the mike. As you speak, the control operator will check your volume and your position and distance in relation to the mike. He or she may ask you to speak louder or softer, move closer to or further from the mike. If possible, ask to rehearse your entire speech so that you may time it and check the volume throughout. Once the volume is set, try not to make sudden, unplanned changes. If you intend to shout, move your head away from the mike or slightly to one side. Avoid any actions that will vary the volume, such as swaying from side to side or shifting from one foot to the other. Avoid any unnecessary noise, like drumming your fingers on the table, rustling papers, or bumping into the mike.

When the red light goes on, you are on the air. No one can see your facial expressions, but that doesn't mean you shouldn't put your whole body into the speech. Your expressions sometimes help put vitality into your voice. Remember, your voice must carry the entire message. Radio listeners enjoy conversational speech, but they also enjoy a lively presentation. A pause on radio seems twice as long as it does before a live audience. A live audience can still see the communication that you send from your eyes, but the radio audience only hears the words, thus pauses can be deadly. You pause only to emphasize a word, stress another, or change inflection in your voice.

As in television, be aware of the passage of time. Your director will give you time signals; do not ignore them. Try to ignore the microphone and pretend you are speaking to the listener directly. Although no circular response is possible with your radio audience, try to imagine that people are responding. When one of the authors was on the air, she got to know some of her listeners who would write letters and call her after the show was over. During the show, she would sometimes mention them or keep them in mind. Although feedback is delayed in electronic broadcasting, it is better than no feedback. When possible, ask the audience to respond with letters or calls. If you are on only for a single appearance, have some of your friends listen in and critique you. Remember, you are competing for the attention of many listeners. It is therefore important that your speech contain very high interest values.

## STYLES OF DELIVERY

There are four generally accepted styles of delivery: (1) impromptu, (2) manuscript, (3) memorization, (4) extemporaneous. We will discuss each of them briefly.

### Impromptu

At a meeting to discuss the problems of juvenile delinquency, the principal of the junior high school turned to one of the parents and said: "Mr. Taylor, you're a probation and parole officer. You proba-

bly have seen and talked with many young people who have been called juvenile delinquents. Would you come up to the podium and take a few minutes to give us your impressions of what makes these kids act the way they do?"

**It helps if you can think on your feet.**

Mr. Taylor had to quickly assess the situation, note the attitudes of the listeners and how much time he had, and decide whether he should inform or persuade the audience. Fortunately, and as is typical of most spur-of-the-moment requests, he was asked to speak on a subject with which he was familiar.

An impromptu speech is not formally prepared, and works best when only one short topic is talked about. Delivery is usually more casual than with a formal speech. If you are familiar with your subject, it is easy to open with a simple statement that explains clearly your point of view. Then you may quickly use personal experiences and memories to help establish your fluency and support your purpose. You can then close by restating your point of view.

The key to an impromptu speech is to *keep it short and simple.* Generally the impromptu speech brings out your natural tendencies. If you have a limited vocabulary and are not accustomed to speaking metaphorically, you will not suddenly become eloquent. If you are speaking about a familiar subject, you will find yourself using familiar words. However, if you have been asked to speak about a subject with which you are not familiar, you may find yourself at a loss for words. In that event, simply make a statement that you have not researched that area but can comment on your personal feelings. After all, the audience obviously wants to hear you say something.

## Manuscript

The direct opposite of the impromptu speech is the manuscript speech. Speakers at conventions, ceremonial events, and before mediated audiences use this type of presentation. Politicians who worry about being misquoted often write out their speeches and distribute them to the press shortly before they present them to the public.

There are certain advantages to the manuscript speech: You can time it to the minute; you can be sure you won't forget anything; and you can pay more attention to *language.* However, since people are *listening to* your speech, and not reading it, all the guidelines for oral language should be adhered to. Use direct and personal references, use repetition, use a style that is lively, etc. Prepare yourself by reading the script *aloud* several times to avoid a dull, mechanical reading. Mark your script so you know the highlights. And above all, *avoid reading* your speech to the audience. You should know it so well that you can maintain *eye* contact with your audience about *70 to 80 percent* of the time.

## Memorization

If you choose to memorize your speech, there are benefits and hazards to that. Benefits include having absolute control over what you say and how you say it. You can experiment with language, writing out the speech in advance and learning it. You can time your speech and stay within the time limit.

Hazards include becoming tense and forgetting a passage—or even the entire speech.

Most speakers memorize *portions* of their speeches, especially the introduction and conclusion or a passage that they wish to quote. Politicians who give the same speech many times memorize key passages. Memorization and the ability to speak impromptu often produce a speech that sounds natural and impresses an audience.

## Extemporaneous

Most speakers prepare and give their speeches extemporaneously, that is, they present the speech from a partially memorized or notated outline. While the speech appears spontaneous, it has been very carefully prepared. Most of this book is aimed at the extemporaneous speaker who knows his or her categories of interest and how they fit together, and who has rehearsed sufficiently to ensure a smooth presentation.

## THE FINAL STEP

## Remembering

You now know the various styles of delivery, and you have an idea of what your audience, live or mediated, sees and hears. You are aware that visible and audible signals together make a double impact upon your listeners. The question you ask yourself next is, "How in the world can I remember all these things?" Well, you can write your speech down and read it, as suggested earlier, or just jot down a few important quotes, or even speak without notes. You know that the situation helps you make up your mind.

No matter what method you choose to follow in delivering your speech, you do have to remember a *great* many things. You must remember that you want to make your entrance from the left, or smile at the head table, or tell a joke you just heard, or a hundred other things. Years ago rhetoricians wrote about "memoria", which, to them, meant the faculty of remembering, or memorizing one's speech. The story of Simonides of Ceros is often quoted to dramatize the importance of a good memory. Simonides was a poet, and after reading a long poem at a banquet, he was called from the room. Almost immediately after he left, the roof fell in, killing and disfiguring the remaining guests. Simonides was able to match the bodies and names of the guests by picturing the seating arrangement in his mind.

The speaker today, however, needs to exercise his or her memory on a broader plain. Simply recalling something is not sufficient. The speaker needs to select subjects that he or she can understand and be able to remember under pressure.

At a sales meeting, a shoe salesman said, "I started out being scared to death. Then I realized, and I don't know exactly when it hit me, that I knew something about my subject. Maybe I learned along the way and it just became easier. I seemed to prepare less, but was really more prepared. Certain phrases, stories, examples, were stored in my memory and I could call them up whenever I wanted."

In developing your memory you should use whatever method works for you. However, we believe that sharpening one's observational skills and becoming very knowledgeable about a topic definitely helps when the material has to be recalled.

## Rehearsing

Developing your memory skills will definitely aid you in making decisions about rehearsing your speech. Rehearsing a speech need not take place before a mirror, or in the security of your bedroom. Abra-

ham Lincoln rehearsed speeches before fields of corn and pumpkins. You may talk in the shower, behind the steering wheel of your car, or in the back yard before your German Shepherd.

Rehearsing can mean fixing a phrase in your mind or just going over the outline. You must determine what is best for you. However, some speakers find it valuable to read the outline aloud first, then give the speech without notes. Some speakers review their outlines silently many times before attempting the speech. The important thing to remember is to grasp the *total sequence* of the speech. Try not to wander during the sections of the speech. After you have a good idea of how the speech flows, think about polishing your delivery. Don't be afraid to vary your delivery in the effort to find the right phraseology. This will keep you from making your speech sound "canned." The amount of time you spend on rehearsing the speech depends on the length of the speech and your memory skills. Whatever you do, don't practice so much that you get tired of the speech and your spontaneity is impaired.

## Delivering

An understanding of the effect of audible and visible activity, a good memory, time to rehearse—what else do you need to deliver a speech effectively? Let's imagine that the time has come. You walk up to the platform, smiling at the people you pass on the way—or you are already seated on the platform and rise to approach the podium. You begin by acknowledging the introduction. You are sincere, modest, confident, enthusiastic, and animated. Then suddenly you realize that something is happening *right at that moment*. All the practice is important, but more important is the realization that what is happening right at that particular moment never happened before. Your speech is brand new. The audience is laughing at places you never dreamed would amuse them. You receive a round of applause when you use certain phrases. You respond to the audience's enthusiasm by slipping in an extra story. You still finish within your allotted time because you changed your pace a little here and there. You forget to say "Thank you" at the end as you had rehearsed, but it doesn't seem that anyone minds.

Congratulations—you have delivered a speech. No matter how many times you speak about the same subject, it will never be the same speech. Your audience, the occasion, your mood, the setting, will always be slightly altered. The most important element that you bring to any speech is the feeling inside you that you are a part of a happening, an event. People may later talk about it and someone may ask for a copy of your speech, but nothing will ever be quite like what happened at the moment you stood up and spoke out.

## SUMMARY QUESTIONS

- How is force achieved through gestures?
- What is the most negative gesture discussed?
- How does color affect an audience?
- What is the process of inhalation and exhalation?
- What is the first step in developing a good voice?
- When is your voice most pleasant?
- How do you prepare for a television appearance?
- What are the four styles of delivery?

## EXERCISES

**1**  Be aware of body types. When a new person enters any group, you are to mentally jot down your reactions to his or her body type.

**2**  Read an article or a book on voice and diction and try to analyze your own speech patterns. Use a tape recorder.

**3**  Pretend you are giving a speech to a live audience and to a television audience. Adapt your voice to each audience.

**4**  Plan a short (5 min.) speech and deliver it three ways: with manuscript, by memorization, and extemporaneously.

## REFERENCES

**1**  Arthur Weinberg (ed.), *Attorney for the Damned* (New York: Simon and Schuster, 1957).

**2**  J. T. Molloy, *Dress for Success* (New York: Warner Books, 1976), pp. 37–91.

**3**  Noam Chomsky, *Syntactic Structures* (Atlantic Highlands, N.J.: Mouton, 1957).

# 10 SPEAKING IN GROUPS

In her senior year in college, Lavinia and three of her classmates sat down and spoke out on the subject of police-community relations. After the Hough Riots in 1966, and a police ambush by a group of militants, the citizens and the police were having trouble communicating. Each member of Lavinia's group selected a specific topic in the general area of police/community relations and each person spoke about the same length of time. They spoke about the police attitude toward various ethnic groups, the attitude of specific communities toward the police, the media's role in promoting distrust between the various groups, and, finally, the need for more open lines of communication between citizens and police.

People generally gather in groups to learn something, to share information, or to solve problems. There are various types of goals and methods of problem-solving that are specifically group oriented. Because groups exert influence on virtually all activities in our society, you need to understand the group communication experience in order to participate effectively in groups.

Group-oriented speaking events include the symposium, the panel discussion, the radio and television discussion group, and the small group private discussion. We shall discuss all of these *types of presentations*, and, in addition, talk about *the types of goals people strive for when meeting in groups, the roles people assume in groups, the concept of leadership, problem-solving and decision-making in groups*, and, finally, *delivery in group situations*.

## TYPES OF GROUP PRESENTATIONS

**The symposium**    Members of a symposium present individual speeches of approximately the same length with the same subject *area* in mind. Sometimes the main subject is divided into segments and each participant speaks on a particular part of the topic. Other times the people involved may wish to present their *views* on a single subject. After the participants of the symposium have given their

short speeches, they are very often asked to discuss their points of view, which they do with other members of the symposium and with the audience. Symposiums often shed light on a subject and inform rather than deal with problem-solving.

**The panel discussion**  Participants on a panel enter into a more spontaneous discussion under the direction of a *leader*. An agenda is planned and a problem that is affecting the community and the members of the immediate audience is discussed. Often spontaneous problem-solving takes place with contributions from the members of the panel and the audience participating. Panel discussions can also evolve around subjects of interest to the audience that do not present problems.

**Small group and private discussion**  The private discussion is a problem-solving situation. There is generally no audience present as there is with the panel and the symposium. However, committees that are appointed by mayors and governors, for example, hold open meetings where members of audiences can be asked to address the committees and are often acknowledged. In private discussion groups, each member of the group is asked to contribute actively in the proceedings. Such groups include workshops, study groups, reading clubs, training sessions. Private *closed* discussions are also conducted by committees, boards, councils, conferences, and staff meetings. In those latter groups the prime purpose is to solve problems and formulate policy. Private groups almost always use a chairperson or a designated leader, but the atmosphere is often informal and the language is conversational. This does not mean that a member cannot at times present a formal speech before the committee.

**Radio and television discussion groups**   Both public and private types of discussions are conducted on radio and television. Therefore, the radio and television discussion is not a *type* of group in the strict sense of the word, but another setting in which all types of discussion can take place: i.e., the panel interview, the dialogue, the panel discussion, and the symposium. The audience that is stimulated does not have the opportunity for immediate feedback; however, many discussions ask for people to call in questions and responses. More people can be involved via the electronic media but it is more difficult to do because the participants cannot tell how they are doing. Preparations for the event should be more extensive than for the live group situation.

## TYPES OF GOALS

The first stage in many group situations is to identify the *goal*. For example:

**Alternatives**   A group convenes and members say, "We have to make a decision among a number of *alternatives*. Let's select the best of the bunch, or the best of two." This kind of group may have met to endorse a candidate. In a southwestern city 33 people ran for mayor in an open primary. Various citizens' groups, plus the local newspapers, met to decide which candidate they wished to endorse. Often group members decide which person is the best in the line-up, and not necessarily which is the best person for the office.

**Information-gathering**   Many groups have *information-gathering as their goal.* The members of the Cable Advisory Board in a southern city had as their initial goal the gathering of materials and information about cable television companies in cities in America. This was their first step in making themselves knowledgeable about the subject of cable television. They felt that only if they knew what other cities had done or were doing about cable TV could they then make decisions and recommendations about cable TV in their city.

**Action**   Many groups assume the *action* goal. People like to gather to "get the job done." Members in groups gather to run a raffle, vote on a president, build a stadium, pass a law, give a party. Action groups include legislative bodies, social committees, campaign committees, and many others.

## THE ROLES PEOPLE ASSUME IN GROUPS

Those of you who will speak as members of a panel or a symposium will generally share the responsibility of presenting information to an audience. A subject may be assigned to you or you may select your topic, much the same as though you were preparing an individual speech. *Public* group speaking situations and *private* discussion groups, however, both are influenced by the *task* and *maintenance* roles assumed by the participants.

### Task Roles

Task roles govern the completion of the group's immediate goals, such as making a decision, solving a problem, or completing a project. *Task* behaviors include a number of activities such as the following:

1 *Initiating:* defining the problem, setting the rules, and contributing ideas. For example, "As I see it, the city is physically drab and lacks spirit. We need to elect a new mayor to bring some excitement into this city. Let's begin by looking over the available candidates."

2 *Information giving and seeking:* asking for or giving opinions about his or her own—or the group's—attitude toward a suggestion. For example, "I think Gregory needs a few more facts."

3 *Elaborating and clarifying:* providing additional information about a particular suggestion or idea. For example, "I think Lavinia is trying to say that we have not won total equality yet."

4 *Orienting and summarizing:* reviewing the significant points covered in an attempt to guide the direction of the discussion. For example, "I think we've covered the Civil War fully, so shall we move on to the next 100 years?"

5 *Consensus taking:* checking to see if the group is ready to make a decision. For example, "It sounds like we are in agreement on the first point, is that so?"

### Maintenance Roles

Behaviors incorporated into maintenance roles include the following:

1 *Harmonizing:* resolving differences and reducing tension, sometimes with the use of humor. For example, "Hey, if I wanted to hear an argument, I would have invited my husband to the meeting."

2 *Compromising:* offering a compromise on an issue or a change in position. For example, "Isn't there somewhere in between where we can all agree?"

3 *Supporting and encouraging:* praising, agreeing with, and accepting the contributions of others. For example, "I think your idea is really great, Lavinia."

4 *Gate-keeping:* facilitating interaction from all members. For example, "Gregory, what do you think of your mother's idea?"

5 *Standard-setting and testing:* checking out the group process, people's feelings, group norms, to evaluate the operation of the group. For example, "I feel uncomfortable going on to the next issue until we have examined all of the programs. Do you all share that feeling?"

## Self-Centered Roles

In addition to group task and group maintenance roles, members may assume self-centered roles which facilitate the solving of individual problems. These *self-serving* behaviors include:

1 *Blocking:* refusing to cooperate by rejecting all ideas. For example, "I don't like Lavinia's idea any more than I like Gregory's."

2 *Withdrawing:* remaining indifferent, daydreaming, avoiding the topic. For example, "Why don't we just do it ourselves."

3 *Dominating:* interrupting, monopolizing conversation, being authoritative. For example, "Now just one moment there. I really think what I said covered that."

4 *Being aggressive:* boasting, criticizing, fighting. For example, "Oh shut up. Who's interested in your opinion anyway?"[1]

## LEADERSHIP

The concept of leadership is closely related to the above lists of functional roles in a group. In a public group-speaking situation a moderator is usually chosen to introduce the members who will speak and to generally take control of the event. Of course, at any time during the discussion the various members can assume the roles we mentioned. However, the semiformal nature of the situation assures an orderly event. In a private discussion group, on the other hand, any member can assume the role of leader at any time. This is due to the fact that we now define a group leader as the "task" leader and the "socioemotional" leader. We used to believe that good leaders exhibited certain traits, such as responsibility, status, capacity, honesty, self-confidence, etc., but current findings indicate that leadership is more a function of the *relationship* among the group's members. Pace and Boren (1973) define leadership as doing ". . . those things that facilitate group *interaction* and that *move* the group toward completion of the task. Effective leadership necessitates accomplishing both of these objectives."[2] As we noted in the preceding section on roles, these objectives can be functionally assumed by any group member, therefore any member can assume the role of "task" leader or "socioemotional" leader at any time. It is, however, difficult for one person to assume both roles. It is also interesting to note that a "task" leader's popularity does not increase as the group progresses towards its goal, whereas a "socioemotional" leader, or a person who does things that *facilitate group interaction*, enjoys more popularity.

*There's more than one kind of group leader.*

Tannenbaum (1958) identified seven possible leadership behaviors ranging from the total authoritarian to the extreme democratic. Under this continuum it is possible for a designated leader to:

1  Make a decision and announce it.

2  Sell his or her decision.

3  Present his or her ideas and invite questions.

4  Present a tentative decision subject to change.

5  Present a problem, get suggestions, and make a decision.

6  Define the limits and ask the group to make the decision.

7  Permit the group members to function within the limits defined by the leader or leaders.[3]

In summary then, leadership is a function that can be assumed by several group members throughout the life of a group whether the group meets for a very few sessions or over a long period of time—provided the leader facilitates either the group's *accomplishment* of its objectives or the group's *resolution* of its feelings.

## PROBLEM-SOLVING AND DECISION-MAKING

Just as much as we like to persuade people in our leadership role or in our role as public speaker, we like to talk things over. Presidents of corporations often hold meetings to discuss policy before they present their views to the stockholders. City councils all over the country hold meetings at which they privately discuss their decisions and solve problems about city matters before they present their views to the public. Citizens convene on advisory boards, members of the armed forces and security councils of the United Nations sit down and determine policy. All this happens because democracy is conducive to good group discussion.

Most people who get involved in group discussion and group presentations usually want to share ideas and information for the purpose of *solving problems.* The differences between public speaking and group discussion is that group discussion aims at being more objective. People who seek to persuade cannot be completely objective. In fact, most people who engage in public speaking arrive at the podium with a specific point of view in mind, whether they wish to inform, entertain, or persuade.

People involved in group discussion and problem-solving, on the other hand, want to share ideas. They feel that open and free discussion will better solve problems and are eager to work together for the best group judgment.

It is true that some groups inherit problems, or have problems delegated to them. By the time a problem has been delegated to a group, someone has answered the question, "Can a group solve this problem better than an individual?" Much research has been done on the questions, "Should problems be solved and decisions made by individuals or groups? Which is more effective?" Davis (1972) believes that "An average group does produce more ideas and better quality ideas than an average individual working alone."[4] However, researchers Bouchard and Hare (1970) point out that "When group output is compared with output of the same number of persons working individually, individual output (adding each person's different ideas only) is higher than the group output. . ."[5] Bunker and Dalton (1972) conclude that "Certain kinds of groups can be more effective than individuals solving certain kinds of problems."[6] They believe the *nature of the task* is the key factor in answering these questions.

In a recent summary of the research on strengths and weaknesses of groups, Maier (1967) identified the following *group assets:*

1  Greater sum total of knowledge and information.
2  Greater number of approaches to a problem.
3  Increased acceptance due to participation in problem-solving.
4  Better comprehension of the decision.

He also identified group *liabilities:*

1  Social pressure (members try to be accepted by other members).
2  Valence of solutions (both critical and supportive comments).
3  Individual domination.
4  Conflicting secondary goal: winning the argument (i.e., winning becomes more important than finding the best solution).

*As a speaker, you share your ideas with others; in a discussion group, all share their ideas with one another.*

Finally, Maier listed several factors which could be *either liabilities or assets*, depending on the skill of the discussion leader:

1 Disagreement (possibly resulting in hard feelings or conflict resolution).

2 Conflicting interests versus mutual interests.

3 Risk-taking (groups more willing to assume risks than individuals—called the "risky shift phenomenon").

4 Who changes (possibility that if persons with constructive solutions change, the decision may suffer more than if those with less constructive solutions change).[7]

If, in spite of all the assets and liabilities, you find yourself in a group which has either assumed or been assigned a problem, you may benefit from knowing certain techniques which might enhance the quality of the decision or the solution of the problem.

*There are techniques for everything—even for handling problems.*

Several researchers, including Brooks (1971) adapted the late Richard Wallen's model for group problem-solving which contained the following steps:

**1. Identify and analyze the problem**  Reduce the problem to terms and examples recognizable by most of the group members. You may find that many members do not believe a problem exists. There may be confusion over the location of the problem or its importance to the organization. Too often the group may confuse the symptoms of the problem with the problem itself.

**2. Generate possible solutions**  Once the problem is identified and understood, the group may begin the task of solving it. Sometimes groups generate specific criteria or standards for acceptable solutions before they generate solutions. This may limit the thinking of the group as they attempt to suggest only solutions which meet their criteria. Of course, some groups may be able to work within some very carefully defined limits. In that case, all members should have a clear understanding of those criteria. Otherwise, the group should be turned loose to creatively generate as many solutions as possible within the time available.

One technique developed specifically for the purpose of generating a quantity of alternative ideas is called "brainstorming." (Osborn, 1953). Some rules to follow in brainstorming sessions are:

a) Set a time limit (usually 10 minutes to 1 hour).

b) Designate one person to be group recorder.

c) Generate as many ideas as possible within the time limit. Quantity is desired; even wild ideas may trigger more practical ones.

d) Avoid evaluation, criticism, and any form of judgment (good or bad) until the session is over.

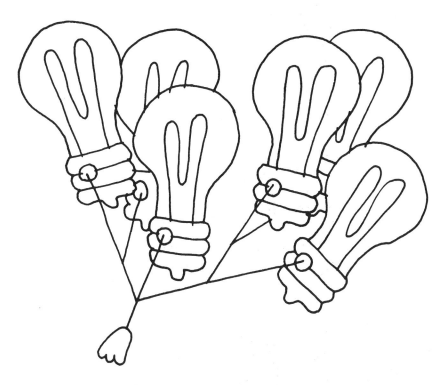

**3. Evaluate solutions** After the list of possible solutions has been generated, it is time to review each suggestion according to its merits and feasibility. At this point, criteria can be developed according to the group's needs. Each potential solution should be tested, using personal experience, expert opinions, current surveys of existing data, and planned scientific research.

**4. Make a decision** The method by which a group arrives at its final decision is a function of the amount of time available, the past history of the group, the kind of task being worked on, and the kind of climate the group wants to establish.

Pace and Boren (1973) have outlined seven commonly used decision-making strategies, all of which are some form of authority, voting, or consensus.

a) *Decision through bypassing.* An idea is suggested, but not discussed or voted upon. Then another idea is suggested, but also not discussed or voted upon. This continues until the group decides to adopt one idea in particular.

b) *Decision through power.* The person with the most power in the group either decides alone or endorses someone else's suggestion.

c) *Decision through vocal coalition.* "Railroading" of a decision by a loud minority illustrates this behavior. A president of a school board may propose an idea, turn to her top two assistants for support, then look to the group for endorsement. By this time members may feel too threatened to volunteer a deviant opinion.

d) *Decision through majority vote.* Often the simplest way to arrive at a decision is to take a vote or to poll all the members. The idea receiving more than half the votes wins. This form of decision-making, while highly democratic, may prematurely cut off discussion or set up unwarranted "win-lose" coalitions. The effect of the latter may be felt long after the vote is taken.

e) *Decision through plurality.* Sometimes a majority is impossible, and rather than spend additional time, a group may decide to accept the idea supported by the greatest number of its members.

f) *Decision through consensus.* Seeking consensus is usually the most effective form of decision-making, but it usually takes longer. Consensus has been described thus: "If there is a clear alternative which most members subscribe to, and if those who oppose it feel they have had their chance to influence, then a consensus exists." (Schein, 1969)

g) *Decision by unanimity.* This form of decision-making, while infrequently employed, represents complete agreement by all members on whatever solution is produced.[8]

After the decision has been made, the group is ready to implement its solution and, hopefully, evaluate its effectiveness.

## DELIVERY IN GROUP SITUATIONS

Your position in the group often determines your approach to your *speaking method.* If you are a *leader,* or an officer in a group, it may be your task to call the meeting to order. Although you and the members of your audience have much in common, it would be up to you to create the atmosphere you wish to have permeate the meeting. If the group has been having a bull session prior to your presentation, you may wish to stand and be formal, adjusting the physical layout to a speaker/audience situation. If you wish to retain a somewhat casual atmosphere, you may ask everyone to get comfortable around a table. You will have to ad-lib, introduce any newcomers, and conduct the question-and-answer period. The most important qualities you must display are tact, enthusiasm, open-mindedness, and humor.

If you are a *member* of the group and do not open the discussion or meeting, most of your speaking will be either impromptu or extemporaneous. However, you may read a report or some information that must be delivered accurately. As a member of a group, it is wise to follow the example of the leader. If the leader wishes that you stand and report, do so. *It is a courtesy* that implies that you respect the leader's office. As a speaker, you have probably been assigned a time limit. Stick to it. If you are a part of a panel, try to speak only when you have relevant material.

You may become involved in a group discussion in a symposium, panel, or committee meeting. The committee meeting is the most informal of the three, but may contain as many as twenty persons. Committees are usually formed to study materials, exchange ideas, and formulate policy. Therefore there should be little or no wasted time. The panel is a somewhat smaller group. However since an audience is generally present, the atmosphere is more formal and the time limits must be strictly enforced.

If you are part of a *panel discussion group* you probably will be asked to present a short presentation (five to ten minutes), and later entertain questions from the audience. Treat your subject as carefully as you would a speech you would give alone. However, try to interact with the other members of the panel. Try to sit so that you can see all members of the panel. Avoid the straight line. Pull your chairs in a semicircle.

If you are asked to speak at a *symposium*, then the chances are that you have been asked to present a short speech. However, in a symposium it is absolutely necessary that you know what the entire program is going to be and which part of it is your special project. You may be asked to introduce the subject, or analyze it, or examine a solution.

Chances are that in any one of these group situations, you may tackle a problem of fact, value, or policy. You may be asked to appraise the goodness or badness of a situation (value), address yourself to the question, "Should we support the downtown improvement program?" (policy), or debate the issue, "Is the mayor alive and living in town?" (fact).

No matter what your task is or what your role is in any of the many situations where you are one of many speakers, your style of delivery will probably be less formal and you will be seated or standing close to your audience. Your gestures and expressions and body movements, while much more relaxed, need not be expansive. You do have the opportunity of treating each member of the group as an individual and having eye contact with each and every person. You can refer to members by their names to personalize your remarks. Lastly, because this is a more informal type of setting, this should not indicate that you need less preparation. When you are not the only person involved in the speaking situation, more organization and more careful adherence to time limits should be the rule, not the exception.

*Whatever the size or type of your group, your speaking responsibility is the same— to present your information clearly and effectively and within the allotted time.*

## SUMMARY

In private and public group discussions and presentations, both leaders and participants must share the responsibilities for making the meeting successful. Members of groups usually engage in problem-solving and have goals of acquisition, alternative choices, or action. Groups function better when members all participate, when a subject is clearly and succinctly stated and understood, when the subject is fully explored, and when the discussion is organized. We suggest that you study this area further if you feel much of your speaking will be done in a group situation. There are many good books about small groups and interpersonal communication on the market today.

## SUMMARY QUESTIONS

- What are the various types of group presentations mentioned in this chapter?
- What are the three types of goals and how do they differ?
- What is the difference between "maintenance" and "task" roles? Can you name at least four in each category?
- Do self-serving roles facilitate individual or group problem-solving?
- What is the role of the "task" leader and of the "socioemotional" leader? How do these roles differ?
- What did Maier identify as the liabilities and assets of groups when compared with individuals?
- What are the four simple steps in problem-solving originally developed by Richard Wallen?
- How does delivery in a group situation differ from delivery in an individual public-speaking situation?

## EXERCISES

1   List the number of groups to which you belong. Which group do you enjoy the most? The least? What specific factors influenced your choice?

2   Visit an organization you are very curious about. Spend at least a day observing the many ways people solve problems in groups. How many group activities could you document? Were some groups more effective than others? Why?

3   Engage in a symposium session in your class. Study the presentations of the members of your symposium and then observe them when they give individual speeches. Did their delivery change? How about their ideas? Did they seem to have good ideas in the group or individually?

**4** Facilitate a brainstorming session for from four to six people. Ask for suggestions on how to solve a current school or community problem that has been identified by the school or local newspaper.

**5** Observe a faculty meeting, a student senate meeting, or a faculty senate meeting. How were the decisions made? How did the leaders in each of the groups handle conflicts? Did members assume leadership roles?

## REFERENCES

**1** K. D. Benne and P. Sheats, "Functional Roles of Group Members," *The Journal of Social Issues* **4** (1948), pp. 41–49.

**2** R. W. Pace, and R. Boren. *The Human Transaction* (Glenview, Ill.: Scott, Foresman, 1973).

**3** R. Tannenbaum, and W. Schmidt, "How to Choose a Leadership Pattern," *Harvard Business Review* **36** (1958), pp. 95–101.

**4** K. Davis, *Human Behavior at Work* (New York: McGraw-Hill, 1972).

**5** T. J. Bouchard, Jr., and J. Hare, "Size, Performance, and Potential in Brainstorming Groups," *Journal of Applied Psychology* **54** (1970), pp. 51–55.

**6** D. Bunker and G. Dalton, "The Comparative Effectiveness of Groups and Individuals in Solving Problems," in *Managing Group and Intergroup Relations,* J. Lorsch and P. Lawrence (eds.) (Homewood, Ill: Irwin-Dorsey, 1972), pp. 204–208.

**7** N. R. F. Maier, "Assets and Liabilities in Group Problem Solving: the Need for an Integrative Function," *Psychological Review* **74** (1967), pp. 239–249.

**8** W. Brooks, *Speech Communication* (Dubuque, Iowa: W. C. Brown, 1971).

# 11

# IS ANYBODY LISTENING?

## LEVELS OF LISTENING

When Dr. Warren Guthrie addressed the members of the 13th Tecnifac Seminar-workshop in visual communication at Holyoke, Massachusetts, in 1958, he asked, "When do you listen?" Not waiting for a reply, he added: "At the risk of being rude I am going to suggest that most of us never listen to anything at all. We hear about a quantity of things, but we never listen. This news program in which I participate, and which I have mentioned previously, is an interesting case in point, because the advertising agency which produces it is constantly concerned only with the number of people who hear that program. We are on an Ohio network of seven stations, and they have discovered, happily enough, that about three-quarters of a million people hear the program with some regularity. That's nice because it keeps me employed, and solves the problem of both teaching and making a living. But while they are constantly concerned with how many people hear that program, nobody ever asks, 'Does anybody listen?' They are concerned only with the fact that it is heard; whether or not it is listened to, seems to me to be a vastly different sort of thing."[1]

Since Dr. Guthrie's speech, concern about our listening habits has been voiced by many other communication scholars. Dr. Guthrie's ideas on listening, however, still make a lot of sense. He claimed that there are four levels of listening:

1 I can hear.
2 I hear and can repeat back.
3 I hear, I can repeat back, and I obey.
4 I hear and I participate in the communication process.

*Most of us miss number four now and then.*

Unless we have serious organic problems, we can all claim the first level of listening: "I can hear." We hear the crickets, the sirens, the rustling of the trees, the radio blaring in the background, perhaps someone calling us. Nothing is *happening* to us, we're not *really* listening—but we can hear. We operate much of the time on this level. A police officer has his radio going most of the time. He hears signals coming over the airways, but nothing happens to him until a certain signal that identifies his car reaches him. We sometimes adopt this same level of hearing even with those closest to us, as when a spouse goes on at length about the problems faced at work. If this happens fairly often, we may adopt the practice of making assenting noises while letting our mind wander to some other subject. And it isn't until we hear something like "So I just told them I quit, and walked out," that our attention is really engaged.

Dr. Guthrie voices a complaint about a stiuation that most of us have experienced at one time or another: We are talking to a colleague when his or her phone rings. Our colleague answers the phone, listens for a couple of minutes, then covers the mouthpiece and says to us, "Go ahead, I can hear you." What this actually means is, "I'm not listening to either one of you, but keep talking and you'll get out of here pretty soon."

"But," you may say, "I *do* hear everything the teacher says. See, I even take it down. I can repeat it back." Congratulations, you've graduated to the *second level of listening,* but according to Guthrie that isn't really listening either. He says it is sometimes disconcerting for a teacher to realize that a semester's lectures can be put into a little notebook and handed back with no change at all. That level of listening says "I'm obliged to sit here and hear all this but I don't have to participate in anything you have to say."

A lovely elderly actress picks up some extra work by giving readings to community clubs. She said that when she first started she was somewhat disconcerted when some of the older ladies seemed to be half asleep during her most moving scenes. Later they would compliment her and even repeat a line or two, but most of the time they were quoting without realizing the intent of the words. She became reconciled to the dozing when she found out that many of the very elderly ladies were brought to the readings by their daughters.

Unfortunately most of them were missing their naps, so they were hearing and being polite while struggling to stay awake.

The *third level of listening,* which Dr. Guthrie claims is still not listening at all, is that level which many of the Armed Forces settled for. It is a response you give when you understand the command, you can repeat it back, and you are prepared to carry it out.

If *we* don't really listen on those three levels, how do we reach the fourth level, where we *do* listen? Dr. Guthrie says "We listen when we participate, when we take part, when we are actively involved in the communication pattern."

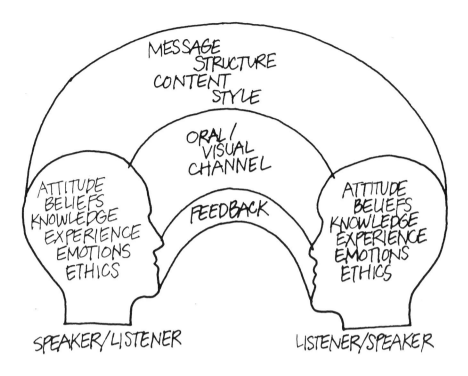

What is the *communication pattern*? We have heard of communication models, so perhaps understanding a model might help us understand what Guthrie meant by the communication pattern. Scholars agree that speech communication involves at least four essential elements, specifically: the source, the message, the channel, and the receiver. In public communication the source is the speaker. Naturally there are many other sources of communication that do not require a speaker, such as books, newspapers, and letters, to name a few. But speech communication cannot exist without speech and public speaking cannot exist without the speaker.

The speaker, as we have indicated in other chapters, is influenced by past experiences, conditioning, the speech situation, purpose, knowledge, attitude toward self, and belief in others.

The message, the second element in our model, has content, structure, and style. We have devoted most of this book to the construction of that message, which expresses the speaker's ideas through the use of symbols. We have also spent a great deal of time addressing ourselves to the creation and application of those symbols.

Speaker and message can certainly exist by themselves. A speaker can spend hours, days, or weeks just working on that part of the communication process. Prior to giving his acceptance speech at the Republican National Convention, President Gerald Ford met with

*What you say is important, but how you say it is important, too.*

speech writers, pored over acceptance speeches by other presidents, and participated in writing and rewriting his speech. He could have decided, at that point, to give up the entire speech and start again. But, being confident of winning the presidential nomination from the Republican party, he decided to go on.

The next element in the model is the channel. President Ford delivered his speech over many channels. The speech was carried to the audience physically present mechanically, by the action of sound waves; it was carried to the audience physically elsewhere electronically, by the action of electrical waves. A channel can limit or shape a message because of its peculiar characteristics.

The receiver, or listener (or hearer, too), is the final element in the communication model. However, even if someone receives or hears a message, there is no guarantee that *effective* communication has taken place. Listening to a message on some of the levels mentioned here does not guarantee effective communication.

*How often have you, with your mind on something else, completely missed the point of what a friend has just told you?*

It can be argued that on a one-to-one or interpersonal small group level, effective communication can take place if listening does not involve evaluation. Merely nodding your head and encouraging the speaker to talk while you listen with either understanding or sympathy is enough. You can help your friend by just being there and hearing some sad or happy stories and making no verbal comment. However, for the public speaker and his or her audience, *effective* communication cannot take place unless both speaker and audience *are really listening on the highest level.* That level requires that there be a judgment process; that level means that you are concentrating, you are open-minded, and you are critical and evaluative. That level means you are responding and listening at the same time. Both speaker and listener constantly exchange roles.

How can we become better listeners in the public speaking situation? In order to improve our listening skills we must destroy certain myths. One is that listening is a natural process, another is that hearing and listening are the same, and yet another is that we sometimes speak to a mass audience. Even when we are speaking to more than three or four people, even when we are speaking to hundreds, each person is listening on his or her own level, individually interpreting or ignoring our message.

Listening is the most common of all communicative acts. Good listening is important and essential to good speaking. Surveys of communication habits indicate that we may spend as much as 60 to 75 percent of our time listening. Nichols and Stevens (1957) suggested that for more effective listening we think ahead of the speaker, summarize what the speaker is saying, identify the speaker's evidence, understand the effect of our emotions on our listening ability, and watch for distractions.[2]

## EFFECTIVE LISTENING PATTERNS: GENERAL

As a member of an audience, you should, of course, pay close attention to what the speaker is saying. But as a speaker, you should also pay attention to what the audience is telling you. In each case, you want to be a good listener, and we will discuss some of the things you can do to achieve that objective. First, as a member of an audience:

1 *Create a good listening atmosphere.* Do so by being sure that you can *see* and *hear* the speaker easily. Don't be afraid to shut a window or close a door to block out extraneous noise. And don't be afraid to get rid of an unwelcome guest, if that becomes necessary. During a speech to a political club, an invited speaker was trying to inform the audience about the problems of neighborhood deterioration. One of the members of the audience who was a little inebriated kept interrupting with, "How long ya gonna talk?" Finally, the political candidate who had invited the speaker to speak that evening rose and said, "I brought Mr. Smith in ta edjacate yez, and if yez don't shut up and listen, I'll trow yez out." The tipsy gentleman shut up and the rest of the audience applauded. While you may never have to take such drastic measures, there is no reason why you should allow those distractions, whether you are the speaker or a member of the audience.

*Nobody gets off to a great start every single time; show others the patience you would like them to show you.*

2 *Don't dismiss the speaker as uninteresting before giving him or her a chance.* Sometimes an opening statement may not go very well, the speaker may be nervous and be a slow starter. You tolerate movies that take time to unfold, and you will often read half a book before your interest is really aroused. Why not offer the speaker the same courtesy? Why not listen intently and search for something you can use in your daily life? A phrase, an idea, a bit of information, can sometimes open the door to understanding. Don't get so irritated at a single word that you turn the speaker off.

Although it is easy to criticize a person for seemingly being unfeeling and uttering a word that is irritating to you, it is possible that the speaker is unaware of your feelings. Give everyone a sporting chance.

3 *Don't turn a speaker off if you can't understand some of the material.* Make an effort to listen, perhaps take notes and have the speaker explain what he or she meant later, in the question-and-answer period.

4 *Concentrate.* Sure it's easy to let your mind wander, especially since you can listen at a speed of at least 600 words per minute and the speaker can only deliver 100 to 300 words per minute. If you are versed in the art of speech making, you can be a better listener by

anticipating the next point the speaker will make. If you know something about organizational patterns, it won't be hard for you to quickly go over what the speaker is saying as the speech is being made. Evaluate while you listen. Listen for those main ideas, principles, and concepts. Listen for the proposition and identify the evidence as you hear it. Don't just sit back and relax. Concentrate, and keep on concentrating.

**5** *Be open-minded.* This is the most difficult skill to develop. Most of us like to hear ideas that reinforce our own opinions. When we hear an opposing view, we sometimes are eager to refute the speaker in our minds immediately, instead of listening to his or her arguments. (As a speaker, of course, you should also be open-minded when a member of the audience yells "prove it.")

*Being open-minded doesn't mean you have to agree with opposing views —just that you are willing to evaluate them.*

**6** *Don't be afraid to be critical and evaluative.* After all, good listening means that you are open to mental stimulation and are eager to be informed. Ask yourself whether the speaker is defining his or her terms. Ask yourself whether the evidence is sufficient, the reasoning valid. Then, if the speech is followed by a question-and-answer period, you will be flattering the speaker by asking thoughtful and provocative questions.

**7** *Try to remember what the speaker says.* If you are concentrating, being open-minded, and evaluating, your task is simpler. You *will* remember. If you need to take notes, do so. If you don't have a pen and pencil handy, jot down phrases as soon after the speech as possible. How many times have you wished you could remember what a speaker said? A speaker has information to pass along to you, information you may wish to use at a later date.

*Remember, everybody knows something that you don't.*

**8** *Be aware that you can learn a lot from intelligent people, even though they do not hold your views.* Daniel Webster felt that listening was a better learning method than reading. By not listening actively, you may miss a new slant to an idea. By being too preoccupied with your own emotions, you may miss a bit of information that may change your life.

**9** *Remember that listening is the subordinate role in the speaker/ audience situation.* We like to remain in control, to do the speaking while others listen. That's a human reaction, but it's not what you're there for. We know of someone who once tried to reverse those roles, with uncomfortable results. Our informant said he was at a convention and was being unusually loud and disrespectful of the speaker. As he put it:

"I was kind of playing to my audience: the people at my table. I really wasn't listening. I'd catch a word here and there. When the speaker would say something, I'd make an aside to the people at the table. The room was not that large and my remarks could be heard

by most of the audience. At one point when I had just shouted something to a friend at another table, the speaker paused and, looking at me, said: 'I am suddenly reminded of an incident of my childhood. When I was very young, I really wanted a shotgun. You know how boys are who are raised on the farm. My grandpa and I were buddies, and one day he brought me this old shotgun he'd had when he was a kid. He gave me a lecture on the safety features and made me promise I would be careful. Well, I was busting with happiness and couldn't wait to try it out. So I set up some cans, being careful to heed my grandpa's warnings and watch carefully for humans. Well sir, I had just raised my shotgun and taken aim, but in my excitement I didn't see a form moving toward my tin cans. It wasn't until I pulled the trigger that I saw grandpa's old mule. Yep, I shot her. I was scared to death to tell grandpa, but he came through and accepted it all philosophically. He forgave me, but he said he didn't know about that old mule. He cautioned that mules rarely forgive and he said they almost *never* forget. He said that the old mule might come back and haunt me.

"Then, looking right at me, the speaker said 'You know, I do believe he was right, because I think that ole jackass is right here today.'

"Everone had a good laugh, and I joined in. Heck, I deserved it. But it sure made me a better listener."

Those are some of the things you can do as a member of the audience to establish effective listening patterns. But what are some of the things you can do for that purpose when you are the speaker? Well, for example:

**1** *Listen to your audience's responses,* especially if you intend to speak on the same subject again in the future. Ask yourself whether they laughed long enough at your jokes, whether they seemed disinterested when you were quoting figures, whether a particular story got the response you wanted. All these audible and visible signals should be evaluated, not just seen and heard.

*Your listeners don't have to give you their attention; you have to earn it.*

**2** *Recognize that the audience will not always listen on the highest level.* Assume rather, that the audience will hear you on the first three levels *most* of the time. It is your job to "listen" for indications that they are just hearing you. Then, when you are conscious of their level of listening, it is your job to redirect them to your topic, to try to attract their attention again. A zipper salesman related this story: "I was talking to a group of salesmen who obviously had heard about these zippers before. I noticed several guys dozing. On the table in front of me was a huge pair of scissors. During the speech, I reached over and dropped it on the floor. The noise was so loud that two members of the audience fell out of their chairs."

We're not advocating that you go to extremes to gain your audience's attention, but a little excitement might start them listening again.

**3** *Be aware that audiences tend to resist change.* If you want to change your audience's views, you had better do it slowly and step by step. They will not just passively let you exhort them to change their views, especially if you demand that the change be immediate.

## EFFECTIVE LISTENING PATTERNS: SPECIFIC

**1** *Listen for ideas and make inferences.* Can you listen to the speaker and determine the conclusion before it is given? This may give you a clue to the ability of the speaker to present his or her ideas clearly and logically.

**2** *Listen for negative words.* Pick out the words that are irrelevant or that produce sensory images that distract you and toss them out of your mind. Learn not to dwell on these words.

**3** *Listen for the central idea.* Take the time between the speaker's pauses and summarize the idea in your mind. Mull it over. Say to yourself, "Well, old Joe wants to run for the Senate again. Maybe I'll listen to his points."

Many listeners accept the first idea the speaker presents and consider it a central idea. Listen closely and try to distinguish between the many ideas a speaker articulates and the central idea. How often was the central idea stated and restated, and in how many different ways?

**4** *Wait.* Listen for the full idea before either making inferences or summarizing. If you are listening to a lecture, wait before taking notes.

The way to distinguish one idea from another is often by means of the transition word. When Senator Ted Kennedy came to Albuquerque to support a congressional candidate, Robert Mondragon, he said, "I'll give you three reasons why you should support Robert Mondragon." Then he held up three fingers and said, "One. . ." Listen for the transition words and associate the main *divisions* of the speech with those words.

**5** *Listen for words that tell you what the pattern of organization is*—after you have found the central idea and recognize the main divisions. For example, if the speaker says, "This problem existed in 1698," and then goes on to quote more dates and eventually brings you to the present, you may conclude that the organizational pattern is chronological. If the speaker clearly states that he or she recognizes the problem and intends to present some answers, you know you are in for a problem-solution speech. The reason you wish to determine the pattern of organization is because it will enable you to better understand and evaluate ideas within the framework of the entire speech, you can think ahead, and you can summarize the speech as it is being given.

**6** *Listen for supportive materials.* What evidence really convinced you? You may say after a speech is over, "I like Joe and maybe would have voted for him, but all he did was tell stories. I wanted some statistics, some hard facts."

However, you may also recognize that you can be convinced because you felt good after the speech was over. Listen for the material that made you feel patriotic, happy, sad, comfortable. If the speaker has made you feel safe, discover what it was that eased your fear. Research in public speaking indicates that an audience responds immediately to appeals to their basic motives, while a listener listens for those appeals. Did the speaker appeal to the preservation of health and avoidance of pain? Did the speaker appeal to freedom, equality, social prestige, pride, comfort, safety?

**7** *Listen to the style, that is, the language as well as for ideas and key words.* Was the speaker formal enough? Informal? Were the sentences too long and you lost track of the idea? Too short and choppy?

**8** *Listen to how the speaker sounds.* When does she or he use a higher pitch? A lower pitch? Does the speaker stretch out certain words? By the middle of the speech can you find a pattern or pur-

*You have the right to require that the speaker convince you before you act on what he or she says. And your audience has the right to expect the same of you.*

pose for the speaker's use of pitch. Do you find yourself enjoying certain sounds? Do certain words have a decided impact on your senses?

Many communication experts advise against judging delivery and advise paying attention to the content. We feel both areas are important for anyone listening to a public speech. Understanding why certain voices help you retain interest or what sounds distract you will aid in understanding the speaker. You may feel that a speaker has a terrible voice, but the information is worth listening to, so you listen for ideas. On the other hand the voice, the manner, and the content may equally add to the total performance. Being aware of all the verbal and nonverbal acts that moved you makes you more appreciative of a good speaker.

## QUESTION-AND-ANSWER PERIODS

Now that you've listened to the speaker with the help of these general and specific guidelines, how do you test the results?

Perhaps the most practical way to determine whether you were listening on the highest level described by Dr. Guthrie would be to participate in a question-and-answer period. Speakers are more commonly opening their talks to question-and-answer periods, after taking a limited time to make their initial statements.

Speakers invited to the University of New Mexico often hold dialogue with the audience. For example, Gene Rodenberry did so when speaking to thousands of students at U.N.M. in 1976. The students came not only to hear his stories and see a specially made film, but also to query him on the making of "Star Trek."

When Hunter Thompson came to the University of New Mexico, he preferred just speaking briefly and opening the session up almost immediately to questions. He received some hard questions about his writings.

*Question-and-answer periods can be as stimulating and satisfying to the speaker as to the audience.*

Often when the speaker is well known, many questions are aimed at his or her past activities. When Werner Von Braun came to Cleveland to address the Cleveland State students, he was asked questions about World War II, although he had been in America since the later 1940s and working with the space program since its inception.

However, for the speaker who does not have an illustrious (or notorious) past, the question-and-answer period is mainly aimed at further explaining or amplifying the speech.

For this reason every speaker must know more than what is contained in his or her speech. A woman who works for a company that is highly oriented toward electronics resigned from the Speakers

Bureau because she was given a speech that was highly technical in nature. She memorized the speech and then handed it back and said she would not present it. "After I deliver that speech," she told the person who had given it to her, "that's the extent of my knowledge about electronics. I'm not going to get up before any audience, especially engineers, and deliver a speech like that." No amount of coaxing would get her to change her mind. She knew that she could never handle a question-and-answer period, so she preferred not to deliver the speech at all.

A highly spirited question-and-answer period may indicate that both speaker and audience are listening on the highest level. However, nothing is as frustrating to the listener as to ask a question and have the speaker respond without actually answering the question. Politicians have a way of avoiding questions, but that is often deliberate. Most speakers honestly try to answer questions, but often fail to because: (1) the person asking a question may be using slang or other expressions which have multiple meanings; (2) statements may be so general that they can be interpreted in a variety of ways; and (3) the speaker is trying to assimilate a great deal of information in a very short time, so errors in understanding naturally occur.

When these problems arise, it is wise for the speaker and the audience to engage in paraphrasing. This is a method of determining whether or not you've understood what someone has just said, and its primary purpose is to increase the accuracy of the communication. When paraphrasing, you don't merely repeat or restate what the person has said. Ask yourself what the questions meant.

> *Questioner:* Do you think the government should guarantee us a living wage?
>
> *You:* You mean, should the government create more jobs as Roosevelt did in the 1930s?
>
> *Questioner:* Yes. If there aren't enough jobs, then the government should find work for *everyone.* Don't you agree?

"Don't you agree?" is an open question and can lead to a long involved answer. Learn to recognize open and closed questions and be aware of the time it takes to answer each kind. Generally, closed questions need merely "yes" or "no" answers or are specific enough to warrant a short answer. For example, "What is your degree in?" is a closed question and demands a mere "Engineering," or "Communication," answer. However, a question such as "Where do your interests lie?" may call for a long explanation. In question-and-answer sessions, it is wise to narrow general questions into specific ones and answer briefly so that you can entertain many questions. However, if the audience is hesitant and you wish to begin the questioning yourself in order to get something started, an open question is more apt

*It's just good sense not to put yourself out on a limb.*

*Specific questions allow (and require) specific answers.*

to start someone talking. A question like, "How do you feel about abortion?" will get more response than "Are you going to vote 'yes' on the amendment?"

When the photo-club member gave his speech on photography to a high school class, he used some *direct* questions at the end of his speech. When he realized that no one knew the answers, he proceeded to answer the questions himself. He said, "Well, that's the story on the types of lenses. Hope you will get out your cameras and start shooting. Let me ask you a question. When do you think you would use this wide-angle lens? [no answer] Well, how many of you went to the basketball game last night? [show of hands] Would you use it to take a picture of the audience?"

The students started talking about the game and various types of lenses and shots were discussed. The question-and-answer period then became an excellent learning session.

If you have been listening intently *during* your speech to the audience's verbal and nonverbal responses, you will be better equipped to handle a question-and-answer period. By that time you should know whether the audience wishes to stay on for a discussion period, is anxious to leave, or needs a little prompting.

## SUMMARY QUESTIONS

- What are the levels of listening?
- What are the component parts of a communication model?
- What are general steps to becoming a good listener?
- What specific steps aid you when listening to a public speech?
- What is meant by paraphrasing a question?

## EXERCISES

**1**  Tape record a speech you are about to present. Play it back and listen for the central idea. How soon can you identify it? Play the speech again and determine how clear your organizational pattern is. What are the words that identify the pattern?

**2**  Listen to the six o'clock news for three nights and identify the organization of each story and the arrangement of local, state and national news. Compare the newscasts with those on another station.

**3**  Keep a diary for one day and record the sounds you *hear* during the day. Go back and read the diary and place meanings to the sounds. Did they have meanings or did you make some up?

**4**  Give a speech and see if you can identify those persons in the audience who are actively listening. Single them out and ask them questions.

# REFERENCES

1   W. Guthrie, address to the members of the 13th Tecnifac Seminar Workshop in visual communication at Holyoke, Mass., *Is Anybody Listening?* Spring, 1958.

2   R. Nichols and L. A. Stevens, *Are You Listening?* (New York: McGraw-Hill, 1957), pp. 5–6.

# 12 SPEAKER: YOU'VE GOT A PROBLEM!

*Lots of things can happen to foul up a speech . . .*

Have you ever arrived at the podium and discovered that you left your speech manuscript at home? Have you ever arrived at the auditorium expecting an overflow audience of 600 and found only 38 people spread throughout the entire room? Has the opposite ever happened, where you expected 50 and found 500? Has your audience ever fallen asleep while you were speaking? Have they ever yelled at you to "sit down!" Have they ever walked out while you were talking? Have you ever set up your slide projector and discovered that the bulb was burned out and there was no replacement? Or worse, have you ever found that your only copy of a valuable slide was slowly burning inside a jammed projector? Have you ever walked happily to the podium, taken out your speech manuscript and yelled in pain as the host inadvertently spilled a hot drink on both your pants and your speech? Have you ever waited impatiently while the host droned on with a fifteen-minute introduction to your five-minute speech? Have you ever started to speak and had all the lights go out, leaving everyone sitting in total darkness? Or worse yet, after the lights went out, had the police inform the host that a bomb threat was just phoned in?

If you think these are far-fetched situations; if you are convinced that they have never happened or never will happen to you; if you believe that these speaker-, audience-, or environment-related problems are the exception and not the rule, be assured that they do, nevertheless, arise. Sometimes, despite our advance preparations, we are confounded by unexpected problems which threaten to sabotage the program, disrupt our speech and destroy our confidence. Air conditioners break down, equipment fails, too many or too few people show up, the chairman is derelict, or the audience is hostile. Just as we feel we're ready to leave via the closest window, we should remember the immortal words of Sam Rayburn, "Wait a minute." We would add, "Keep cool." As we said in Chapter 2, place this speech in proper perspective: How important is it really going to be to your career and welfare? As public speakers, we must all accept the possibility that things may happen that are beyond our control.

*. . . but that's not the end of the world.*

227

So when the unexpected occurs, take a deep breath, have faith in the fact that the audience is just as surprised at the unexpected as you are (and is on your side), make whatever adjustments you can, and continue your speech, assured that you are not alone.

To illustrate the fact that even polished speakers face unexpected and sometimes bizarre events, we asked several hundred public speakers (toastmasters, members of industrial and university speakers' bureaus, and working Americans) to give us detailed examples of problems they have personally encountered during their public speeches. We also asked them what steps they took to handle those problems and what effect those steps had on their presentation. This information has helped us develop a highly practical approach to identifying potential problems, offering possible solutions, and testing the principles offered in this book.

We have selected some of the more typical responses to our survey, grouped them into one of three general categories—speaker-related, audience-related, and environment-related problems—and present them now for your own development and enjoyment.

## SPEAKER-RELATED PROBLEMS

We have already spoken about the importance of a speaker selecting a topic which is appropriate for both the audience and occasion. Sometimes the speaker's topic will be predetermined. One speaker wrote to us that one of his most "interesting" evenings as a speaker occurred when he decided to ignore the topic selected for him and address an issue he felt the audience "needed to think about." As we will see, this can be risky:

*What you say should be consistent with what you do.*

"This entire venture began on the wrong foot. I found out ten days before I was to deliver the speech that my name and the title of the speech had been published in the paper without the chairman of the program ever contacting me and asking me to speak. Needless to say, I was surprised at this, particularly since I did not wholeheartedly agree with the title of the speech. The program was a workshop for the officers of the Home-School Association of the parochial schools in the diocese. My speech had been titled, 'Why I Would *Only* Teach in a Catholic School.' I am a teacher in a Catholic high school, but at the time I was to deliver the speech, I was applying for a position in one of the public school systems to teach a course. Hence, I could not, in all honesty, deliver this speech as titled.

"I felt I had two options: I could, in good conscience, refuse to speak; or else I must alter the topic of my speech. I chose the latter, since I felt I really did have something important to say to this group. Tit for tat. I did not notify the chairman of my alteration. I had been given the name of another speaker on the program whose situation was identical to mine, although he was to speak about 'Why I Would Only Send My Children to a Catholic School.' We jointly came to the decision that we would both speak our mind and bear the brunt of any difficulties together.

"My talk with the other speaker was crucial in this decision. We were both going to say things that the people at this workshop didn't want to hear but that we felt they should hear.

"The night of the presentation arrived, along with its problems. We were both under the impression that we were the only speakers on the program, but when we arrived we discovered that the Superintendent of the school system for the diocese was speaking. This was disastrous, since we were about to address the many ills of Catholic education, thus reflecting on him and his position. We decided, at the last minute, to address the ills without the vehemence previously planned, thus minimzing embarrassment for all.

"This turned out to be the right decision because the Superintendent voiced agreement with many of those ills, realizing they were presented in good spirit.

"Nevertheless, all three presentations were received rather poorly. The people at the workshop had come prepared to hear about all the great things in the Catholic schools, and instead were given a list of what's lousy. It must be kept in mind that this was a workshop. It was not a social or honorary dinner. If it were, I would have declined to speak.

"I felt my presentation was good for the workshop, regardless of the popularity of my views. In some cases, the determining factor of one's speech topic should be how popular it will be, but not at a workshop."

Although we agree in spirit with this speaker, we think he might have minimized his surprise and some of the audience's apparent hostility by doing some simple things. Although the Superintendent's appearance was beyond his control, he could have double-checked with the program chairman without revealing his own topic. He did make the wise decision to avoid open hostility by moderating the tone of his attacks. We think he could have gone further by demonstrating the importance of his topic (in his introduction) while emphasizing the similarity in backgrounds between himself and his audience. Further, by starting with areas of agreement (which he admits were several), he would have gained their trust and receptivity to later potential differences.

*Not many things have to be presented in only negative terms. Try to include some positive elements as well.*

The airline industry probably enjoys more captive audiences for their many, varied "public speeches" than any other business, and yet, despite the importance of the subject material, probably has very few active listeners. This may be due to the delivery of the hosts and hostesses, the environment of the speeches, or the monotony of the messages.

A stewardess of a major airline wrote:

"I was giving the standard speech, the whole oxygen bit, when I suddenly really looked at the rows of people before me. Some were talking, some were reading, and others had already started to doze. It dawned on me that not a single one of them might know what to do in the event of a disaster. To me that was a real life or death problem." She decided that the content of the speeches she must read was not very interesting to the passengers. She told us, "When I read them exactly, everyone is bored and nobody listens. So I don't read them exactly anymore."

An airline captain who agreed with this stewardess would vary the language of his speech in order to heighten its interest level for his audience. Instead of just complying with FAA regulations by saying, "Although I've turned off the 'Fasten seat belt' sign, for your own comfort and safety, please keep your seat belts fastened and secure while you remain in your seats," he opted for the more folksy and interesting:

*Suit your language and your
style to the audience and the
situation.*

"Folks, welcome aboard. On the right side of the plane you can see the Sandia Mountains. Our weather looks nice, the temperature in Denver is 17 degrees, and our arrival will be on schedule at 8:08 p.m. The seat-belt sign is off, so you can stretch, but if you stay in your seat, we'd appreciate it if you would please keep your belt on. Have a nice trip, and we sure thank you for flying with us."

One airline gives specific instructions to its personnel about the manner in which they are to make announcements. Among their rules are the following:

1 Naturalness of expression is the key to successful announcements.

2 Announcements must sound sincere and friendly.

3 Hold the microphone at a distance most suitable for the volume of your voice and speak at a normal telephone volume.

4 Keep the rate of your speech constant and slower than normal.

5 Do not use humor—passengers travel for business, vacation, illness, or death.

6 Do not use airline slang or terminology which passengers may not understand.

Another airline believes that slang or airline terminology may be necessary at times to prevent passengers from getting too nervous. Their instructions to their personnel include, "In making reference at any time to the mechanical difficulties that occur occasionally, the best way to keep from destroying confidence is by using the term 'mechanical adjustment.' " ("We are extremely sorry, but it is necessary for us to delay your flight because of a mechanical adjustment. Our maintenance people are making an inspection to determine the cause and will let us know just as soon as they can estimate the time necessary for the adjustment.")

We know that a speech whose content is inappropriate in purpose, subject, content, or language may create unnecessary problems for the speaker, but sometimes a speaker's delivery can have the same effect. Newsletter editor Lawrence Ragen writes that:

"Public speakers who try to give power to their words by pausing for several seconds every few sentences succeed only in boring their audience. The silence in the room builds tension in the listeners, who recognize the speaker's attempt to add drama to his platitudes, but cannot articulate their embarrassment."

Businessman Edward Hess reveals that his own attitude as a speaker may impede his performance:

"I had a 'flash' inspiration one time when I was thinking up a topic for a speech. It seemed really brilliant. I was very excited as I

**231 Speaker-Related Problems**

wrote it down, and the whole speech seemed to flow from my pen. I gave it a lot more thought, and worked up what I thought was a really fine speech. Then a month went by before I was scheduled to give the speech. In the meantime, of course, I was busy thinking of a thousand and one other things, and gave only passing thought to the topic of my speech.

"Came the night of my speech presentation, and I grabbed my notes and went off to my meeting. When it was my turn to speak, I got up and presented it. Perfectly, normally, you would say. Right! But in the interval between the idea and the presentation, the idea had gone flat. It was and is an excellent idea, *but the time delay destroyed my crusading fervor, and I did nothing to rekindle it before getting up to speak.*

"I tried a deliberate experiment for my next speech, when I realized what had happened. I gave a speech on the use of words in the Declaration of Independence. I deliberately worked up my enthusiasm before the speech, especially the few hours prior to its presentation. The speech went well and was very well received. I had several favorable comments on the sincerity and enthusiasm of the talk.

"It is now a habit of mine to really get myself 'up' for any talk. I have to be my own coach giving a half-time pep talk before the big game. It works!"

Boy Scout Director of Support Services, Carl Barnes, agrees with Mr. Hess on the importance of speaker attitude:

"I still haven't conquered the problem associated with giving the same talk twice in one day. It is a personal attitude. I'm never as good the second time, or at least that is the way I feel about it." Mr. Barnes also tells us of the attitudinal problem associated with the case of "your good friend pantomining to you that your fly is open." He offers the best solution to that problem as "beating the hell out of him afterwards."

*Most people who appear before audiences get themselves into the right mood first. Professionals may do it in seconds—but they do it.*

## AUDIENCE-RELATED PROBLEMS

In addition to unexpected problems evolving from speaker errors, unforeseen circumstances due to audience logistics, demographics, or attitudes may also plague your speech. As some speakers told us in their letters, you may be unprepared for the size of your audience, its age, or its receptivity to you and your speech.

Judith Laughlin, Executive Director of the Erie County, N. Y., Department of Anti-Rape and Sexual Assault, tells of an evening that started off with audience-related problems and acquired others as it went on:

"It was in June that I was to address the County Judges and Police Executives Conference. The group meets monthly at different local restaurants and there are usually between 75 and 100 members in attendance. This month, however, since most of the members are male, and the topic was on sexual assault, it was decided that spouses be invited. Of course, arrangements for dinner and the meeting were made well in advance, and in this case reservations for approximately 200 persons were made.

"For large audiences such as this, I use a film to start off my address, follow it by a 15-minute talk, and then give the audience several minutes to write down questions. I quickly review them, choose the most common, and then answer them for approximately 20 minutes. My presentation, including the film, generally takes just about one hour.

"Since this presentation was to be held in a restaurant, with 200 persons expected, and I was to be at the head table, I lined up an experienced audiovisual-aid person to take care of the film, set up the projector and screen, and run the film. The equipment and film were tested ahead of time.

"Well, on the night of the meeting, I arrived about one-half hour before dinner, met the audiovisual person, and decided on where to set up the projector and screen. Everything was right on schedule at this point.

"The next thing I knew, the room was crowded—so crowded you could hardly move. This June night was especially warm and it was apparent that the air conditioning was not working.

"I was then escorted to the head table and seated. It was at this point that I realized that there were about 300 people—100 more than expected. There were not enough seats, and it was very hot. To make matters worse, extra tables were brought in and people were sitting on top of each other. Next, dinner was served—head table first, of course. Now, it was evident that the restaurant had not prepared enough food for everyone who showed up. Eventually, about two hours later, when everyone had finally eaten, the program portion of the meeting was about to begin. I was to be introduced by a judge with whom I had collaborated previously on several projects. The judge rose, thanked everyone for coming, and then proceeded to give me an unbelievable introduction. The next thing I knew, the entire audience had risen to their feet and was applauding. I almost died—how do you follow a standing ovation before you have even begun?

"I stood up, humbly thanked the judge and the audience, and quickly moved into the presentation. I was introducing the film when I realized the microphone wasn't working. I thought, 'OK, just project your voice and you won't have to do it for more than 40 minutes, since the film will take 20 minutes.'

**. . . all the unfortunate things that could happen.**

"The lights were dimmed and the film was rolling, when all of a sudden the projector completely malfunctioned. The audiovisual person tried for several minutes to get it going again, but to no avail. It was then that I felt like leaving through the closest window. Three hundred hot people, starting an hour late, an unbelievable introduction, no microphone, and now no film—and I had only prepared a 15-minute talk!

"Well, I couldn't get the window open, so I had to stick it out. I apologized to the audience for the problem with the film and said something like, 'With so many important people jammed into this hot room, maybe all the excitement that the rape film might generate would be too much and someone much higher up had planned it this way.' That got a good chuckle.

"Since I no longer had the film to fill in certain information, I was going to have to ad lib. While they were getting comfortable, I quickly reviewed my notes and made a brief introduction on a napkin. I knew my subject matter inside and out, so I at least had that comfort, and that comfort led to confidence.

*But if you are resourceful and well prepared . . .*

*. . . you can still make your audience glad they heard you.*

"I spoke for 30 minutes about the topic of Rape and Sexual Assault. First, I gave the audience a definition, followed by a descripton of the victim, reasons why it was a male and female problem, what's now being done for the victims, and how such programs will benefit society. I was aware of the audience and their response was positive. This response increased my enthusiasm. Since the time was now very late, I decided just to open up the next 15 minutes to questions and answers. The audience was terrific. They asked me a lot of questions and I answered all of them. They made remarks and interacted frequently amongst themselves. After 45 minutes, I decided that I should bring closure to the discussion. I did this by passing out pamphlets that I had brought and telling them how to reach me if they had any other questions. I then thanked them for being so patient, especially under the conditions of the evening, and sat down. Would you believe—another standing ovation.'"

Judith Laughlin is an experienced and highly professional public speaker, but after reading of her experiences, one can't help sympathizing with her for what she went through that unforgettable June evening.

Many speakers have had audience-related problems of just the opposite type—not enough audience to speak of, and hardly enough to speak to. Chemistry professor Gordon Harris writes:

"I am convinced that the worst fate which can befall a public speaker is to face a very small audience when he expects much better. Politicians have to face this situation frequently, but the normal arrangement involves an invited speaker for some special gathering with a predetermined audience expectation. On one occasion, I was part of a panel of four experts on the subject of atomic power—this was back in the 1950s when it was still a very mysterious thing. We got together on a winter evening in a large university lecture hall and found that our audience, excluding the organizers, was one less in size than the panel. We went ahead anyway, but certainly without much enthusiasm, and completely convinced of the apathy of the academic community at that time."

Professor Peter Lupsha faced that same problem. His experience let him with a different philosophical view:

"Once when I was playing hotshot prof. at Yale and trying to support a marriage by consulting on the side, I reorganized a government for the city of Sheldon, Connecticut. Being egotistical and young and conscientious, I did a pretty good job (I think). And as those years were years of government mandated citizen participation, I had to give my alternatives before the community in the local high school auditorium.

"The night came and I had spent the day preparing as if it were a doctor's oral (at the time I believed one could change things). I arrived a fashionable five minutes late to find *three* people. Out of a community of 30,000, and for a well-advertised, publicized meeting, *three* people showed.

"Being up for confrontation to the masses, this large empty hall was quite traumatic [to me], so tightening my J. Press tie, I huffily declared that if the people didn't give a shit about Sheldon, neither did I. And turned to leave. At which point a small voice clearly said, 'Young man, I am a citizen and a taxpayer of Sheldon. I gave up an evening with my family to hear what you have to say, and I would like to hear it! I don't care if I'm the only person who cares to hear it, I do, so let us proceed.'

"Rather chastened, I [gave my speech]—such perils before an audience of three—and I learned that it's the job of the researcher and scholar to listen and learn and translate his knowledge honestly, forthrightly—even if it's to an empty hall—for it is the ideas and the synthesis and the one listener, if any, who count—not the ego, the status, or the roar of the crowd. You deal with the unexpected by being totally and completely honest."

*What you have to say* is *important . . .*

Judge August Pyratel handled the same problem in yet another manner: He *comforted the audience* when he faced only a dozen people at what was supposed to be a major annual convention. His audience was composed of educators, and the person who introduced him apologized profusely for the small number of people. Judge Pyratel opened his remarks with:

*. . . no matter the size of the audience.*

"Don't feel badly about your numbers; remember that the greatest teacher of them all had only twelve disciples. There are twelve of us here. Let us learn from each other. Perhaps we cannot change the world, but we might try to move city hall a little."

There is little that Professor Harris, Professor Lupsha, Judge Pryatel, or you can do to influence the size of the audience (unless you are in the business of marketing yourself or your speech). This is usually beyond your control. However, when faced with an audience much smaller than you'd anticipated, you can make adjustments in your speech and delivery to adapt to the unfortunate circumstance. You can probably reduce your formality by taking off your coat, sitting instead of standing, moving closer to the audience, avoiding a microphone, speaking extemporaneously instead of from a manuscript, reducing the time of your speech to encourage more dialogue and interaction with your audience. Judith Laughlin has already provided us with some advice on handling the opposite situation—that of confronting a much larger audience than planned. Politicians generally prefer the latter and help arrange it by booking rooms with smaller capacities than the expected number of listeners.

Speakers may also be startled by audiences whose demographic breakdown differs from what they've been told. Mr. Barnes of the Boy Scouts once encountered an audience that didn't fit his prepared speech:

"Recently I was invited to speak to a service club. I have a rather standard talk I use which includes the usual humorous stories with serious subject matter sandwiched in between.

*Again—resourcefulness!*

"When I arrived at the meeting hall, I found that the youngest person there was at least 55 years old. My prepared speech was totally unsuitable. I tucked it in my pocket and spoke on 'experience' being the best teacher and that old solid institutions constitute the backbone of our society. I learned a lesson about researching my audience beforehand."

But you can't always depend on advance research to give you all the answers. Events may happen even as you get ready to speak which will affect your purpose and content. Veterans' Affairs Coordinator Clarence Dye provides just such an example, which he aptly calls the "bombed audience":

"About a year ago, I gave a talk to a newspaper guild. The speech was to be given after dinner, which was preceded by a cocktail hour. The cocktail hour went one hour longer than it was supposed to because dinner was late. The problem was that most of the audience was under the influence of alcohol by the time it came for my speech. I made a mistake and gave my serious lecture. The interruptions were horrendous. From this I learned that one gauge of an audience is the quantity of alcohol consumed, which must be judged from the length of the cocktail hour. I have hit this same problem once since then, and I met the problem by giving a humorous, if extemporaneous, speech on the same subject. This same incident pointed out to me that, for the most part, audiences want to be entertained rather than informed."

*Tipsy audiences may require a light approach.*

We would add that entertainment from the speaker is especially likely to be the preference of drinking audiences.

Besides an audience's demographic and logistical composition, speakers may also be surprised by the audience's attitudes toward them, their speech, or the occasion. Psychiatrist L. K. Fischer reports on how he handled just such an audience:

"I remember having to talk for an hour to psychiatric residents on psychological testing of children, when I knew that they were not in the least interested in kids. One student came into the class late, sat down and promptly fell asleep. I waited until she nodded slightly, went over to her seat and said, cheerfully, 'It's time to wake up,' which seemed to please the other students."

Dr. Fischer was probably correct in trying to gain the attention of an audience that wasn't too interested in his remarks. Mr. Dye recalls a situation where he would have been delighted if his audience had fallen asleep.

"Some years ago, I was talking to an audience of about 80 people who did not respond in any way to whatever I said. I tried humor, jokes, serious thought, talking softly and loudly, moving about, etc.—all to no avail. I had never met this situation before, nor have I had it since that occasion. I finally tried to insult the audience, and even that had no effect. The horrible thing was that I had to talk to the same group the following week. The second talk had the same result as the first.

*Forced audiences may tax your ingenuity.*

"In this case, I had nothing in my repertoire that I could use—I tried everything. But I did learn the lesson that one cannot force an audience to listen. As a result, I have since that time refused to address groups that are forced, for one reason or another, to attend the speech."

A nightmare for most speakers occurs when an audience's hostility erupts into outright heckling. Situations like these will test the nerves and skills of even the most seasoned speakers. One college president we know did not handle such an incident very well. He was invited to speak to a gathering of students to answer their questions about financial matters. Since there had been several student demonstrations against proposed tuition hikes prior to his speech, he had reason to suspect (and thus prepare for) a hostile audience. Suspicion turned to reality when, just as he was being introduced, a student yelled out, "Why don't you stand up so we can see what you look like!" Shortly after his first answer, another student shouted, "Stop evading the question and answer it!" Finally, after repeated heckling, the college president started to take the offensive. When one student said, "I disagree with your answer," he replied, "I expected you would." To another student he said, "I'm amazed at how little you know." To a third, he replied, "Again, we seem to be re-inventing the wheel."

We make no defense for a hostile audience, but our advice to the president would have been to stay home until he learned how to handle one. His first mistake was in not immediately telling a few jokes to loosen up the audience, preferably jokes at his own expense. Second, he should never have engaged in a shouting match with the students. This only increased their wrath and the resulting heckling. A better approach would have been to calmly wait till they finished heckling and then continue with his prepared remarks. More jokes or an open plea for common courtesy (as politicians often use) may also have proven effective.

Biologist John Storr (from whom our university president could have learned much) shares with us his experiences in dealing with hostile audiences. Note his unique technique for gaining rapport with his skeptical listeners,

"One of the most difficult parts of a presentation is the first two minutes. If one can overcome the initial 'who is he?' and gain the confidence and sympathy of the audience, then the rest of the lecture will go smoothly. On several occasions when I have been talking to high-schoolers as a university professor, the initial reaction of the students is one of complete skepticism. On several occasions the microphone supplied was a standing mike, and as I began to talk the microphone started to slip. Rather than breaking the thought by grasping the mike and trying to make an adjustment, I simply bent my knees and kept my face in the same relative position to the mike itself and kept on talking without a break. This kind of action can often break the ice, so to speak, and that initial laugh and acceptance by the students makes the difference between an unsuccessful lecture and one which is very well received and remembered. Breaking the ice, then, is a major problem if the speaker is far removed, as in the case of a university professor in a high school audience, from the audience in terms of social position or standing."

*There are ways to reduce— or at least, avoid increasing—audience hostility.*

*It may be possible to turn a liability into an asset.*

## ENVIRONMENT-RELATED PROBLEMS

Although often unexpected, the sudden problems due to speaker or audience factors are frequently curable without much loss of time and face. Unfortunately, those resulting from the environment, natural or man-made, create the most headaches and shatter the confidence of even the calmest speakers. This is probably because we have so little direct control over the weather, national crises, equipment failures, fires, poor dinners, and broken ventilation systems.

Rock star Elton John would, if rain interrupted his outdoor concerts, pour cups of water over his head to empathize with his audience. Then he would continue his performance. However, sometimes the environment may force a speaker to cancel. Such was the case with the several victory speakers awaiting the arrival of Congressman Jerry Litton of Missouri, who had just beaten two opponents in a 1976 senatorial primary. When news of Litton's death in a plane crash reached the speakers, the tragedy precluded all but spontaneous prayer.

Clarence Dye tells us about some problems he once encountered in his environment due to what he calls the "nightclub setting":

"I was once one of a number of speakers at a youth convention. Because of a large turnout, my room was too small and we were

switched to the hotel dining room, which also served the hotel's nightclub. Many of the audience were not even in sight from the small stage. The loudspeaker system had been hurriedly brought in and did not work properly. So I could not be heard nor seen by many in the audience, which numbered over 500.

"My solution to this problem was to have the audience move the tables and chairs to one end of the dining room and to have them sit on the floor at the other end. I then moved the loudspeakers to that end of the room. By having the audience sit on the floor, I could be seen by them—and the loudspeaker system, while far from perfect, was at least adequate to that end of the room. One practical conclusion from this is that I now would rather talk in the room scheduled than do an abrupt change."

The problems that were most often cited by those responding to our survey dealt in one way or another with broken or malfunctioning equipment, primarily audiovisual aids. Chemist Gordon Harris describes such an incident:

"I think the one thing which causes the most difficulty and embarrassment to speakers on scientific or technical subjects is the inadequacy of audiovisual equipment. I hardly ever give a public lecture without using slides, which I generally take a great deal of trouble to prepare. Ninety percent of the time everything works out well—the projector and screen are suitable, the projectionist knows his business, and everything is set up on time. But there can be foul-ups!

"I recall one occasion when I was lecturing in Europe and had brought with me some new-fangled . . . slides. As I commenced the talk, and turned on the first slide, I noted that it was slowly darkening, then starting to curl up, and finally, to melt away completely. The projector had a very powerful arc lamp and heated the slides so much that they literally melted away. I've avoided plastic-mounted slides ever since that date, though most projectors in use in this country do not result in accidents of this type. Needless to say, my lecture proceeded with considerable difficulty since I was totally dependent on the slides!"

Speaking on television can create new hassles, especially for those unfamiliar with the medium. Carl Barnes warns us of a problem he has often encountered.

*In the absence of a visible audience, ignore environmental distractions.*

"When appearing on television I have, at times, had a problem with the camera taking a close-up—moving in until you see yourself reflected in the lens. It can be distracting. The solution is simple. Ignore the camera and remain natural."

Scientist Thurman Grafton found it very difficult to "remain natural" when his projection equipment failed.

"The most catastrophic problem to ever strike me in my years as a public speaker occurred when I was on the program of a professional meeting held in New York City in 1964. The title of my presentation, 'Vivarium and Research Laboratories for 100 Chimpanzees,' was explained in the abstract given to every participant of the meeting as a description of a multimillion-dollar facility for this purpose. In fact, the presentation consisted entirely of a description of 72 35mm slides showing the physical plant, equipment, techniques, etc. The slides were in the automatic slide changer magazine for a . . . projector which preceded the carousel most commonly used today.

"I had only described about six slides when the magazine slide changer jammed. The machine would neither advance to the next slide nor return to the previous slide. Neither could the magazine be removed. With an audience of about 250 people in the room, I felt confronted with the following immediate considerations:

1 Pray the stage would open up and swallow me. It didn't.

2 Stall briefly in hopes the projectionist would soon correct the problem. He didn't.

3 Proceed with the description of the facility without the slides. I didn't.

**4** Try to hold the audience by a combination of serious discussions of philosophic background and direction of both basic and applied research in aerospace medicine utilizing chimpanzees, interlaced with amusing anthropomorphic anecdotes of chimpanzee behavior which had previously entertained the family at the dinner table.

"The last alternative is the one I pursued, with what I considered to be relatively considerable success. In the 20 minutes it took to get a technician to disassemble the projector, correct the problem, reassemble it, and be ready to proceed, I would estimate that I lost probably 30 persons from the room. Since this presentation was scheduled immediately preceding lunch, I was very pleased with the outcome."

The most detailed response on the subject of equipment failure was provided by biologist John Storr. His suggestions are particularly useful when one is confronted with microphone, lighting, and projector problems.

"1. *Turning out lights to darken a room* — I have found that making sure that someone is in charge of turning off the lights, or that I know when the lights are to be turned out and have tested the actual switch, is most helpful. This ability to have the lights turned out on cue is important in not causing a break in the thought and the mood of the lecture. It is amazing how many times the person in charge of the program will say, 'I know when the lights go out,' and when the time comes either the switch does not work or the lights are only half turned out, or some other misfortune takes place.

*Try to be sure that those assisting you know what they are to do.*

"The other major problem with lights is in having accepted a commitment to give a talk in a certain place, then, on arrival, finding that there are no curtains in the windows, etc., or lights which are supposed to turn off which can't be turned off. One of the solutions to the problem of having too much light in the room from windows is to be sure to place the projection screen over one of the windows and have the audience face toward the window. This means that the screen itself is darkened fairly well with the light being cut off from the window itself. Consequently, the projector can be used even though the brightness of the projection is lost to a large degree.

"2. *Microphones* — While standard mikes on lecterns or standing microphones are satisfactory, use of a lavaliere type of microphone which hangs around the neck is a much more satisfactory solution, giving the speaker a great deal of ease in being able to move from place to place without any loss of words, which so often happens if one moves even slightly from the major position [at a fixed microphone]. A much better presentation can be given when one has the ability to move around.

"3. *Projectors* — Despite the fact that many individuals say that they know their projector or have cleaned the projector, the number of times that the lens of the projector is dirty, or in the case of movie projectors, the gate being very dirty as well as is the condensing lens, is amazing. I always carry a clean handkerchief with me, and very often a flat stick, such as the kind found on a sucker or ice cream bar, and use this to clean the gate thoroughly. As a result of cleaning both the lens, which should be cleaned first, and the gate, I find that the color of the projection and the intensity of the light can sometimes be greatly increased, changing a mediocre projection into one which is sometimes excellent. Neverthelesss, cleaning the gate will also prevent the film from being scratched. I have, on occasion, taken along a film into a shcool and allowed the projectionist to go ahead without supervision. As a result, a $200 film print was scratched and completely destroyed by wax which had built up from other films and had collected on the gate to badly scratch my film."

The only addition we would make to speaker Storr's excellent suggestions is *not* to use a handkerchief on the lens of any projector. Try lens cleaning paper, which will not scratch the lens as handkerchiefs often do.

A third major environmentally caused problem which can increase your frustration level is to have a host or program chairperson either fail to give you a sufficient (or accurate) introduction, or bore your audience with an unnecessarily long and detailed one. The inadequate introduction deprives you of your just worth, and the long, drawn-out introduction, which may sometimes be mistaken for the speech itself, may reduce your available time so much that you deprive your audience of their just worth. John Zeis provides us with an example of the insufficient introduction:

"I sent the toastmaster a copy of my detailed resume. She then selected only those facts that she wanted the audience to hear about me. She left out some very important information about my wife, which related to the speech at hand. Since then, I have learned to keep my resume as brief as possible."

*You can provide the person introducing you with only necessary information . . .*

Carl Barnes experienced the opposite problem:

"Several times a poor introducer has given me a problem. Particularly one who makes your speech for you as a part of his introduction. I try to clue the introducer in beforehand by saying, 'Keep the introduction short; these people don't want to hear about me.' I find that if your talk gets off to a good start, you've pretty well got it made."

John Storr once again provides some very detailed suggestions on how to minimize problems associated with your introducer.

"As a standard rule, I carry along, or send in to the individual who is going to do the introduction, a broad list of various aspects to my background. This might include such things as where I was born, what education I have, what special field of education I was in, some reference to special things which might be of interest to the audience such as, in my case, the fact that I have spent 4,000 hours underwater, or that I have produced a series of films for educational television, or that I have participated in some expedition, or am a member of some particularly unusual group, or have taught some place, or visited some place.

"My suggestion to the introducer is to pick out those individual facts which are felt to be of interest to that particular group. Usually, however, I do find that the person who is to introduce you has not taken the trouble to read the list, or is so confused that one has to make a quick judgment of the particular audience that one is speaking to and suggest three or four interesting facts to the introducer. Very often being able to sit beside the person who is introducing you and chatting with them and bringing in interesting facts about yourself or about what you have done, during the course of the dinner or before the presentation, is a very good way because they often find that some particular piece of your background fits into the aims or interests of the particular group. [The introducer] often can find from your background that there might be some little thing that you have done which is of interest to the group or fits in with their philosophy. Those kinds of things can easily be mentioned in your conversation and will greatly help the person introducing you."

*. . . or you can provide more than is really needed, so that the introducer can select what is appropriate for the audience.*

When Congressman Jack Kemp was speaker at one college's commencement exercises in 1976, the person introducing him made an introductory speech that went on for more than four minutes. It consisted primarily of an exhaustive listing—with numerous figures—of Congressman Kemp's activities, memberships, positions, and honors in college, the military, professional football, and politics. Well before the introductory speaker finished, the audience was obviously restless. But Congressman Kemp relieved the tedium and got a favorable response from the audience when his first words were, "I can hardly wait to hear what I'm going to say."

Probably one of the most unusual environment problems we heard of was sent in by a man in Cincinnati. He wrote:

"I was going to be inaugurated into the JC's and the dinner started late, the speeches were long. Along about 10 p.m. they still hadn't gotten to me. We suddenly heard a banging on the walls. Seems the annual bowling league dance was setting up. By the time I was introduced the wall between the hall was down and the band was starting up. I got 'Thank you' out and that was it."

After reading the above collection of speaker-, audience-, and environment-related problems which often surprise you as you march to the podium, you should see some commonalities in the advice provided by our fellow speakers:

1 Reduce the chances of being caught without a speech (because someone else gave yours, the wine spilled on it, or the audience was too hostile) by bringing a back-up speech with you. You're the expert, you have the knowledge and experience and can go beyond the prepared speech, as Judith Laughlin did, and, if necessary, deliver impromptu remarks of relevance to your listeners.

2 Be ready with back-up equipment (or knowledge about equipment), as was John Storr, so you won't be destroyed along with your faulty equipment.

3 Be ready with some appropriate jokes and amusing anecdotes, as Thurman Grafton was, to handle any unfortunate surprise delays or changes in the program.

4 Above everything else, be calm, cool, and collected; place your speech in its proper perspective; then take a deep breath—and have fun.

If all else fails, keep an accurate record of exactly what happened and send it to us for inclusion in our next edition of this book. We can't all be as fortunate in our speaking careers as steel executive J. F. Heinz:

*Good luck always helps . . .*

"I've been Bethlehem Steel's executive speechwriter for the last six years or so. I've accompanied our top people on most major speaking occasions and have received full reports on all speeches I didn't attend. In addition, I've had a hand in scores of speeches delivered by 'lesser' executives, and have spoken dozens of times myself. (In our Community Awareness program alone, local personnel gave 268 talks to community groups in 1975.)

"Believe it or not, I can't recall a single instance of the kind of mischance or embarrassment you have in mind. The possibility is always in my mind, and we take a lot of precautions to minimize the risk, but we've been spared, thank goodness!

*. . . but so does careful preparation.*

"As a matter of interest, we always try to 'scout' the area in advance, check the PA system, pay attention to the height and adjustability of the mike, look over the lectern, and make sure the lighting is satisfactory. One important, fussy precaution: we always have a duplicate script on hand when our top people are speaking.

"Assiduous attention to detail helps. So does just plain luck!"

## SUMMARY QUESTIONS

- What are some of the more common unexpected problems that are primarily related to the speaker? How can you prevent them from happening?

- What are some of the more common unexpected problems that are primarily related to the audience? How can you prevent them from happening?

- What are some of the more common unexpected problems that are primarily related to the environment? How can you prevent them from happening?

## EXERCISES

**1** Tape record five speeches on campus or in the community. Were there any problems associated with the speaker, audience, or environment? If so, how did the speaker handle them? Was she or he successful? Write a brief report for a class discussion or a speech to inform in which you describe these problems and solutions.

**2** Interview three public speakers (toastmasters, politicans, members of university or industrial speaker's bureaus, athletes, entertainers, etc.). Ask them to describe the two experiences they remember that caused them the most problems due to an unexpected occurrence at the time they were to speak. How did they handle the problem? Were they successful? Summarize your results and present them to the class in a panel discussion or in a speech to inform or persuade.

**3** Heckle a friend of yours while he or she is giving a speech before your class. How did your friend handle the heckling? Did he or she get angry? Flustered? Polite? Rude?

# 13 STAND UP, SPEAK OUT: ANALYZING SPEECHES

## THE LISTENER AS CRITIC

One of life's great pleasures is discovering a new bit of information and passing it along to a friend. Listening to speeches, reading speeches, rediscovering the speeches of the past puts you in the enviable position of acquiring knowledge. As a student of speech and as a public speaker, you have the right to question the content and the presentation of public speaking and your relation to it. You have the right to examine and test the truth of a speaker's arguments, the appropriateness of his or her language, the poignancy of the style. By doing so you can acquire an awareness of the intricate manner in which speeches are put together. You may even develop a standard that will help you not only appraise speeches, but become a better speaker.

Because the field of rhetorical criticism is a large one, we do not intend to cover even a small part of it. Quintilian, the Roman schoolmaster, said that rhetoric could be a very easy and "small matter" if it could be included in one short body of rules, but he believed that rules had to be altered to suit the nature of each individual case and each time, occasion, and necessity.

Although we agree with Quintilian that rules are often altered to suit each individual case, nonetheless, a general body of rules does exist. These rules, or methods, have been handed down to us by Aristotle, and we have adapted them to contemporary situations throughout this book. For example, we have stated over and over that a speaker should select a topic that is appropriate for the audience and the occasion and that is timely or significant. We also urged that the speaker should assume an ethical responsibility toward both his or her topic and audience and attempt to build a rapport with the audience. We have suggested various ways of starting a speech, adapting a message to the audience, supporting a message, organizing a message, wording a message, and concluding a message with logic and/or vigor.

*As a good speaker, you will be better able to evaluate other speakers.*

Those same suggestions for effective public speaking that we have already presented in this book can be used by the critic to judge whether a speech is successful. Knowledge of the many ways to construct a speech makes you a better critic because you know what to listen for. You can listen to a speech and recognize the specific arguments that convinced the audience, or you can instantly evaluate the appropriateness of the language or the manner in which the speaker put the audience at ease. You can recognize the specific techniques because you, the public speaker, have also used them.

Therefore, the first step to becoming a good critic is to understand the basic concepts of public speaking and the second step is to become a good listener. As we mentioned earlier in this book, there are several levels of listening. The highest level demands that you participate in the communicative act. By doing so you are constantly alerted to the organizational pattern, the arrangement of arguments, the way the speaker uses language, and the manner in which the speaker addresses himself or herself to logical and psychological needs of the audience.

By listening and participating you will discover that many speeches often have an immediate and specific purpose and are given to specific audiences. Other speeches are merely aimed at creating good will and can, like a sermon, be given many times to different audiences with little change.

By listening and participating you may discover your own method of judging speeches that will ultimately help *you* in your own speaking endeavors. After listening to a number of speeches you may decide that you wish to pay attention to the content, or to the logical appeals, or to the style of the speaker. You may eventually wish to compare two or more speeches, to study many speeches within an historical movement, or to analyze the speeches of one person through a lifetime. Or you may wish to merely listen to speeches so that you can become a better speaker yourself.

## ANALYZING SPEECHES AND SPEAKERS

To introduce you to the fascinating field of rhetorical criticism we present excerpts from speeches given by people from different parts of America, taped especially for presentation in this book. We have grouped these excerpts into six categories representing some of the most important principles of public speaking discussed in the book:

1  Adapting the message
2  Supporting the message
3  Organizing the message
4  Starting the speech

**5** Wording the speech with appropriate language

**6** Stopping the speech

(We realize there are many other things that must be considered when analyzing speeches—such as the occasion, the historical background, and the speaker. However, there are many very good texts that can take you further should you wish to pursue the subject of rhetorical criticism.)

At the beginning of each excerpt is a very brief identification followed by a reference number. The references (at the end of the chapter, as usual) give fuller identification and some background. To the left of the excerpt we have included our brief analysis of the significant public speaking principle(s) illustrated in the sample. In most cases, these are followed by appropriate text references to aid you in reviewing the principle in more depth. Reading these excerpts and analyses should help you grasp the magnitude and variety of occasions and topics used by our friends and neighbors as they stand up and speak out.

## Adapting the Message

*The speaker confronts a potentially hostile audience with some facts to counter possible rumors the listeners may have heard. (Ch. 2)*

*The speaker uses restatement as a stylistic device for the purpose of clarification. (Ch. 8)*

**1**   *Tallahassee briefing*[1]

Before we officially begin, I'd like to say a couple of things about some rumors that I've heard, and I'd like to straighten out the record. As we announced yesterday, and I'd like to repeat it again today, the financing of this audit project is being done without any county funds. The entire funding of the audit project, which is limited to direct audit costs for travel, printing, food and lodging, and computer costs, is being handled through separate grant moneys. The second statement I wanted to make is that it is my understanding, and it was verified in a conversation I had today with the superintendent of schools, that all information will be summarized by myself and my colleagues, and we will handle distribution of all information from the audit project. It will all be distributed back to all people in the school system. There is an audit committee which was established last January, and that committee will get the complete report so that they can work with us in developing recommendations. I hope this clears up any misunderstandings you may have had about financing and reporting back results of the audit.

*The speaker does not use any techniques to reduce overt hostilities in audience. Instead, he encourages more heckling by*

**2**   *President of university confronting hecklers*[2]

First of all, the statement which you made was not literally correct. I said I was in support of Women's Studies College as an entity, but was totally opposed to its policy of saying that its courses would only be for women. And you know that as well as I do! . . . I did answer *shouting back at hecklers and insulting them. (Ch. 2)*

*Speaker attempts to clarify the problem.*

your question, but I don't mind going beyond that . . . I am convinced, and you may disagree with me, that such means of handling the problem is much more effective than the means of going out and tearing up things and taking over buildings, etc. (Student—"I do disagree.") I expected it! . . . My position is the following: that you have absolutely every right to do that which you feel is important. However, under no conditions do you have the right to deprive others of that which is legitimately theirs! (Student—"You slammed the administration doors in our faces last Friday!") That you'd better believe!

**3**   *Macra Fortkort giving prayer at commencement exercises*[3]

*Speaker's prayer is adapted specifically to the occasion at hand, with ample references to the listeners and their needs. (Ch. 2)*

*Speaker uses many action verbs and emotional langauge to set a spiritual mood. (Ch. 8)*

Father, we have gathered to honor the accomplishments of these graduates in a ritual that reminds us again that every infant is a new beginning. May these men and women carry with them the spirit of St. Francis, and may they live out their lives doing the truth. We have come to know, Father, that truth is exceedingly subtle at times. Be with them, then, and with us all as we begin the struggle to flush truth and to realize Your model as a continuing, surprising event in our lives.

**4**   *Dolores Aguirre giving airline departure speech*[4]

*Speaker's calm, nurturing, slow delivery is particularly suitable for an audience of many scared passengers flying for their first time. Her personal references to the listeners, along with her smiles and gentle tones, help create much good will for her and the airline. (Ch. 2)*

This is Continental Airlines, Flight 204 for Los Angeles with two intermediate stops, one in Houston and one in El Paso. At this time we'd like to introduce your flight attendants to you. In the rear cabin serving you will be Candy and Linda. In the forward cabin, Howard and Tom. My name is Dolores.

**5**   *Patrick Sweeney giving political speech at Cleveland*[5]

*Speaker follows three candidates who talked about crime as Cleveland's number one problem. He chooses not to ignore their comments, but to refer to those comments, thus adapting his message to what has already been said. He then goes on to broaden the meaning of the word crime. (Ch. 2)*

*Speaker uses repetition as a stylistic device and to hammer home his main idea. (Ch. 8)*

*Speaker uses specific examples.*

Ladies and gentlemen, I concur with those who share the podium with me today. Crime is a serious issue. Crime is more than statistics. Crime is stabbings in the schools. Crime is terror in the park, drugs on every street corner and fear on every face.

From anyone's point of view, crime is an issue. But let's not limit our vision. It's also a crime that the garbage isn't picked up.

It's also a crime that the elderly of Cleveland can't be made to feel needed.

It's also a crime that a Republican Convention means more to City Hall than the needs of the citizens of Cleveland.

It's also a crime that the city of Cleveland has sold inferior coal at premium prices and the public records are spirited away under cover of darkness.

**6** *Chief Garmire speech at the Crime Conference*[6]

It is, indeed, a unique experience for a layman to address a conference such as yours. A more accurate statement would be one that substitutes the term "challenging" for unique. The challenge to a layman is, of course, one of communication.

In reviewing the titles of the papers to be presented and the roster of those attending, one is immediately struck by the esoteric nature of the subject matter and the divergent interests of the participants. Various academic disciplines are involved, ranging from engineering to physics to computer science to criminalistics. Numerous and various institutional interests are represented: industrial, law enforcement, military, universities, research institutes, and consultants, to name a few.

*Speaker adapts his message to a very diversified audience, names all the different factions attending, and then goes on to say that everyone at the conference has one common interest—technology. (Ch. 2)*

**7** *Coach Walter Gantz giving a pep talk to his runners*[7]

Last year when you were younger and they were tougher and we were running on a course that we did not know, we lost a very close race. This year you are all stronger; they are not. They are a young team. This is our course, and I expect us to demolish this course, to demolish that team and come out victorious. Now I know it and you know it, that running is tough, running is probably one of the hardest sports anyone can engage in. It's going to hurt today. Accept it. You guys are strong and developing. I want you to get that pain—to look forward to it. It's going to come and get you. Take it, accept it, work with it, defeat it, conquer it, *kill* it. And when it hurts a lot, smile to yourself and say, "It's got to hurt more because I've got to go a little faster." And when you finish, and when you pass those guys in front of you, you'll feel good. That is the satisfaction in running, in racing, finishing, knowing that you conquered yourself and you conquered this course and you conquered the other guys. I expect each one of you to be able to do that. I want you to come out of here today with a victory for each individual. Now let's put our hands together and get into yourselves, and let's go!

*Speaker appeals to the emotions of his listeners and adapts to the immediate audience. Since his goal is to arouse his audience to high spiritual levels of feeling, he chooses the best approach possible—to discuss the pending pain of the runner, and how to "conquer it." (Ch. 4)*

*Many active verbs keep the speech vibrant. (Ch. 5)*

*Use of hypothetical illustration makes the athlete's task for the day very vivid. (Ch. 5)*

## Supporting the Message

**1** *Tom Cantone speaking on rent control*[8]

What else does it mean to New York City? Here I will point this out. This strikes out tax-producing buildings which are then abandoned. As an example, General Telephone and Electronics, which employs 2000 people, wanted to put up a new building in New York City. They happened to find a location that was under rent control. They cannot get these people to move out from the rent control. In some cases these families were offered $15-17,000 to move out. They said no. You take it before the courts. It is a long drawn out battle. This costs General Electric money. So what do they do? Stanford, Connecticut. That's where their 2000 employees are today. And here is a

*(Speakers one through five use detailed illustrations, examples, and stories to support their main ideas.)*

*This speaker's detailed story supports only one point. (Ch. 4)*

*Speaker gives one example after another to arrive at a conclusion (inductive reasoning).*

*Illustrations are short and relevant. (Ch. 5) Statistics are brief and simple.*

good loss of the tax base. Other examples are the Shelton Hotel. The Shelton Hotel costs $30-35,000 a month to maintain. There are 26 occupants in that hotel. They are paying $100 a month. There is a development company that wants to buy the Shelton Hotel. They can't get the 26 occupants to leave. They cannot be forced out and the courts will not move them out. Consequently, what is going to happen, the owners of the Shelton Hotel are going to abandon it and there goes another tax base. Okay. We'll see what this means to New York City. New York City has over one billion dollars in real estate taxes that are in arrears or have been defaulted on. That is New York City. . . .

*Speaker makes a statement of fact and supports it with example (deductive reasoning).*

*Speaker uses statistics to support part of his message, explaining their meaning and relevance to the audience. (Ch. 4)*

*Statistics are interwoven with a hypothetical illustration, thus using two types of supporting materials. (Ch. 5)*

*Descriptive passages make the story more vivid. (Ch. 8)*

Someone was paying $61.00 for an apartment, they could be relatively assured that five months from now they were not going to be paying $161.00 for that same unit. Look at the ramifications of this today. Well, some of the ramifications of this. Many of these units have not changed. The same base that was established in 1943 still exists today in 1976. If you were paying $61.00 in 1943, you're paying $61.00 in 1976. However, your landlord is paying 1976 taxes, the landlord is paying 1976 maintenance costs. All down the line he has had to absorb these economies. But the consequences have been the neglect of the building. The building needs a new paint job, he is not going to worry about it; it is not going to increase his income. From there, what happens? It goes on and on. The plumbing gets defective. It goes on and on. What do we end up with? Slums. Abandonment. Totally abandoned building. Let the city take it over. It is their problem. I paid $10,000 for it. It got my $10,000 out of it. Forget it. It is gone.

## 2 Walter Rettig speaking on "What Price Bureaucracy?"[8]

*Speaker immediately sets the scene for a chronological pattern of organization. (Ch. 6)*

*Speaker uses extended analogy.*

I'll take you back to the year 967 BC, a time that King Solomon first started to rule. He was the original bureaucrat. At 950 BC, Jerusalem was known throughout the world for its splendor. Buildings made with marble, wood from the Cedars of Lebanon. It was terrific. Came Solomon's first heavy government. He had a prime minister. He also had a labor department. A chief of forced labor. He also had a chief governor. He divided his government up into twelve groups. Now originally there were twelve tribes of Israel, but he picked up something that the politicians of today do. He wooed the districts over so that each tribe of Israel was in two different sections. He couldn't let them get together to gang up on him. This woke up the tribes. Now each one of the tribes was furnished supplies to his government for one month of the year. In each of the twelve districts. What did they have to supply? Everything! I have to read this: 188 bushels of flour per day, 370 bushels of meal per day, 10 fat oxen per day, 20 cattle pasture beds. That was the specs. One hundred sheep, deer, and other animals and fowl. They also had to supply straw and barley for the king's stables. He had a big building program one month out of

*Speaker reasons by comparison. (Ch. 4)*

every three. This was forced labor. Does that again sound familiar? Are you working for your government? Samuel warned about the consequences, the taxation and the conscription. Nobody listened. Taxation and conscription increased. People did something that we do today. They started looking up tax dodges. If you had land, if you had flocks of animals, they were very visible. They could be taxed. People started hoarding things like gold and silver. It was not visible wealth. Therefore it could not be taxed. Government costs and government taxation grew. There were more buildings. The buildings cost more. There were more government jobs, but government salaries increased. Finally there was a pretty big expensive government. The people were getting restless and finally there was a deficit. What did he do about that deficit? I hope our government doesn't do it. He gave 10 cities to King Herod from Tyre. Tyre was one of three cities that formed Phoenicia. Finally, in 922 BC, King Solomon, like all the rest of us mortals, he died. His son didn't have the personality and the drive that King Solomon had. And soon the people came to him and said, "This is enough. Too much taxation." He told them to get out of his hair. Finally, along came a labor leader, He led a revolt to the people. The country was split in two: Israel and Judea.

*This long narrative compares today with ancient times, shows many cause-effect relationships, and slowly builds to a rational conclusion. (Ch. 5)*

### 3  Ellis McDaniel, speaking on "Me and Body Language"[8]

I was looking for a way to watch someone as he talks and tell what was really going on in his mind. Now I know that was a false hope. Because what I was really looking for was a dictionary of body language. A dictionary is possible to a certain extent because there are certain standards and symbols. "V" used to be for Victory, but now has become the symbol for peace. Stan Corris gave us an example tonight, of the open-minded message that you can give as a nonverbal body language message to the person you're talking to. But generally a dictionary is not to be expected, because body language is somehow or other under the control of that part of your mind that's running your body, while your conscious mind runs your mouth. Thus, the body language to some extent is under the control of the subconscious. I don't mean to say anything more than that. Something is running your body while your conscious mind is working on the ideas, the thoughts and the words. . . .

*Speaker tries to personalize her words with sprinklings of "I," "he," and names of people in audience. (Ch. 8)*

*Speaker uses argument by definition.*

In most audiences, body language is the feedback. How important can that be? Well, perhaps if you make an imaginary trip with me. Imagine that you are Red Skelton with all of his skills and miming with all of his skills at facial expressions, and with all of the nonverbal skills that he has. And you are putting on a performance as one of his characters in front of the TV screen, but with no studio audience. No audience. Just the camera. You are trying to put on this skit, without any feedback whatsoever. I started trying to imagine myself doing that and I got butterflies. The feedback from the audience is very important.

*Speaker asks a rhetorical question and answers it with a hypothetical illustration. (Ch. 4)*

**255 Analyzing Speeches and Speakers**

**4**  *Cathy Miller's talk on meditation*[9]

We experience unhappiness when we are in a situation doing something and we don't want to be there. That makes us unhappy. In order to rectify that situation, you can do two things. Either you can split the situation if you have that option, or you can get yourself concentrating in the moment and you'll forget that you don't want to be there. That happened to me today. I was doing some work with a friend, and we were both working on this stairway on which we're both sanding. We're doing all this work so we can paint it and make it look nice. We're doing the preparation, which is a grungy job. You're sanding and caulking and tearing down things, and painting. It's all dusty and dirty and grimy. I was looking out the window, and there were birds feeding in this feeder in the back yard, and the sun was shining. I thought, "Gee, it would be nice to be outside." Then I started doing my thing again. I wasn't too much into painting when I stopped myself and said, "OK, I want to be here working three more hours, and I know this because I've decided that's what I want to do. I don't want to be in this frame of mind. I don't want to be some place else now. I want to be here now working." So I said, "OK, I'm going to do my utmost to meditate, to take my tendency to drift off from where I am, and bring it back." This way I wasn't plagued by thinking about places I wasn't going to be. I had such a fantastic day because I did it. . . .

I think for myself personally—I'm not saying this is for everybody, but for myself—knowledge has made me aware of the fact that I am unlimited in my attempts for anything. I could probably just do anything. I know that there is so much in me that I don't even know about mentally that I'll be surprised if I just keep pursuing life, about what's going to come out of myself. I have no idea, really, what is within me except that it's unlimited, and that's all I need to know. I just have to go ahead and do whatever it is and have confidence. It doesn't matter to me that much if I succeed or fail at things, because I like the doing of them. That's to me the adventure. The outcome— if it's up, all right, if it's down, well, on to something else.

**5**  *Congressman Jack Kemp's commencement address*[10]

This is a day of gratitude, not only for the students, but I am sure the families and perhaps even the faculty. My all time favorite movie, all time favorite play, screen play, is *A Man For All Seasons,* the story of St. Thomas More. In the movie, Sir Thomas More at that time was speaking to a young man who was very cynical, very super-sophisticated. This young man went to Sir Thomas More and was asking for some advice about what he should do in his life. Not too untypical perhaps. But the answer of Sir Thomas More is classic. In *A Man For All Seasons,* Sir Thomas More turns to young Richard and he says, "Why Richard, I think you would make an outstanding teacher." And Richard looks at Sir Thomas More and says, "Yes, but

*Speaker tells a long personal story to establish her credibility and to personalize her speech. (Ch. 5, 8)*

*Speaker relies heavily on herself, her background expertise and feelings to convince her listeners. (Ch. 4)*

*Use of personal pronouns makes the speech intimate and adds credibility to the speaker.*

*The speaker tells a story that is relevant to the topic. Opening with a story (or example) sets a comfortable mood and emotional tone appropriate to this ceremonial occasion. This story is used to support only one point. (Ch. 5)*

who would ever know?" And Sir Thomas More said in a transcendant answer, "But you would know. Your students would know, and God would know." Quite an audience. Yes, teaching is the ability to implicate those values both spiritual, moral, socio-economic and political, philosophical upon which our nation was founded and waxed strong. . . .

I saw the other day some statistics that say today in the United States there are over 145,000 individuals employed by the federal government and working in the regulatory agencies. Doing things like passing laws to prevent lower prices, or prices from being lowered in certain areas of our industry, like in trucking and airlines. Do you know that last year 14 airlines were fined 25,000 dollars apiece for giving discounts to passengers because they hadn't cleared it yet with the Civil Aeronautics Board in Washington, D.C.? If you want to go into business today in Buffalo, hauling freight from Buffalo and Philadelphia, Pennsylvania, you must go to the regulatory agency over trucking and railroads called the Interstate Commerce Commission, the ICC. Last year the ICC made 650,000 individual decisions over rate, routes, profit. Let me ask you a question. Of what value is the right to vote if your property, your savings, your investments, your pension, your livelihood, your wages, are controlled not by you, according to your priorities, but were controlled by someone in Washington, D.C.? Ask the British people today what it is like to have 60 percent of their total income controlled by the central government. In the United States of America, we've come to a point where 44 percent of the total personal national income of America, not the gross national product which is a very inflated figure, is now being taxed at the federal, state, and local levels. The Brookings Institute says by 1985, ten years hence, 55 percent of your personal income will be taxed at the federal, state, and local levels. By the year 2000, two-thirds of all of the national income of America will be taxed and we will reach that point very briefly. . . .

Two hundred years ago, Thomas Jefferson said that God gave us life, He gave us freedom. Today it seems to me two hundred years later we should be saying that God, who gave us freedom, gave us life. That reverence to life, that reverence to freedom, that love of God, that is so important to the future, to the past and to the present. Those architects of America's dream put it very clearly when they said that eternal vigilance is the price of liberty. Edmund Burke, the great parliamentarian, 200 years ago in the British House of Lords, said that mankind must qualify for liberty. In other words the price of freedom is responsibility. That freedom without responsibility is license, and that lives without reverence for it, is indeed a threat to life itself. You know that freedom is not free. It has a price. The price is very high. As high as it is, it is never so costly as the loss of it. . . .

We must decide whether we are going to run our own schools, whether we are going to run our own lives. It seems to me that these

*Use of a rhetorical question is aimed at getting the audience to ponder on the issue. (Ch. 8)*

*Comparing the British people and the audience in the United States is used as evidence to support the speaker's point. (Ch. 4)*

*The speaker explains to the audience the significance of the statistics he uses. (Ch. 4)*

*Speaker uses quotes and testimonial to add authority to his argument. (Ch. 4)*

*Speaker refers to authority in defining what freedom entails.*

young people that have graduated from college today ought not to sacrifice their individual choice, their individual freedom, to any politician, any political party, anyone making promises that can't be kept, and I hope this doesn't sound political because I don't mean it in that fashion. I think there are people in both parties who are talking more sense today than perhaps in the last 15–20 years. If we don't protect the integrity and vitality of the private sector of our country, there are not going to be the jobs, there is not going to be the housing, there is not going to be the transportation, we're not going to be able to find the capital that is necessary to make this nation's energy sufficient by 1985. Why tell a supplier and a producer and an explorer of natural gas that you can't sell natural gas for more than 50.4¢ a thousand cubic feet because of a rate set by the Federal Power Commission in Washington, D.C.? Why tell them that and then turn around and tell the consumers on the eastern seaboard of the United States of America that they are going to have to buy their natural gas from Algeria at $3 a cubic foot? It doesn't make any sense to me and I think what we need is a healthy dose of freedom of enterprise. Again it is not retreat, it is moving forward.

**6** *R.W. Murphy's management briefing to a group of consultants* [11]

The company has just placed a new oil-fired generating unit into commercial operation. This unit will have an ultimate capacity of 850 MW, but presently is operated at 650 MW. Now, under construction is a sister unit scheduled for service in 1979. This unit will be operated by us, but ownership will be shared with our share being 76 percent (646 MW). A second nuclear unit is under construction. This 1100 MW unit, scheduled for service in 1982, will be operated by us, but ownership is being shared, our share being 41 percent (451 MW). We are also a 22 percent owner (253 MW) of an 1150 MW nuclear unit to be built in the future. We have just filed plans for construction of a two-unit 1700 MW coal-fired station. . . .

In recognition of the need to keep our employees and, through them, the public, better informed concerning events that have a great impact on our business, we have initiated publication of new in-house organs; a biweekly newspaper and a brochure issued periodically to supervisors. We also have started using in-house videotape presentations for this purpose. These measures supplement existing related activities including the president's monthly meeting with his vice-presidents and publication of the monthly company magazine. With respect to improving communications outside the company, we have increased our participation in radio and TV talk shows and in Speakers' Bureau activities. A new brochure, prepared especially for the financial community, is periodically distributed. We have just initiated a modest advertising program utilizing daily and weekly newspapers and are considering expanding it to include radio and TV.

*Speaker uses comparison/control.*

*Use of questions to arouse interest is effective device. (Ch. 7)*

*Speaker appeals to national loyalty.*

*Speaker uses very specific figures when explaining the equipment to consultants. (Ch. 5)*

*Speaker uses simple examples without much detail to support a point. (Ch. 4)*

## 7  George Mai's pottery-making demonstration[12]

*Extended use of analogy gives audience a rational line of reasoning to follow. (Ch. 4)*

*Use of personification makes speech vivid.*

Throwing, that is the process of throwing, or working on a potter's wheel, is about 90 percent technique. In other words, it's like playing scales for a musician. There's a certain order, a certain regularity to all shapes, which is a cylinder . . . Pots are kind of like people in that even when talking about them, you speak in terms of foot, belly, shoulder, etc. . . . Throwing the cylinder is like running the scale; once you learn that, you can start thinking in terms of form. It's like when you learn the scale, you can start thinking in terms of melody.

## 8  Tallahassee briefing[1]

*Speaker explains to clear up points in the speech that might be confusing. (Ch. 4)*

What we're asking is for you to write out in as much detail as you can, what we call communication critical incidents or communication experiences. These are detailed narrative experiences which highlight communication breakdowns and strengths that you personally are aware of through your direct involvement or your direct observation. We are not interested in hearsay, rumor, or gossip; we are only interested in communication experiences which you have witnessed, observed, or participated in either by sending or receiving messages yourself.

## 9  Juan Vidarte giving a guided tour
## of an art museum's famous pieces of sculpture[13]

*Speaker clarifies possibly confusing points with explanation.*

Here we will see a sculpture represented by another people, another part of the world, another philosophy, and in this case, we will have to go to pre-Hispanic times in New Mexico and Central America. What we have here is the concept of volume which is always geared to a philosophical idea. In the case of the sculpture here, you have two opposite worlds that come into conflict.

## 10  Eddie Bisone's listing of the menu at St. George's Table[14]

*Use of action verbs like "stuffed" "topped" "sauteed" "browned" aid imagery and liveliness to the speech. (Ch. 8)*

*Speaker explains clearly what dishes consist of.*

For appetizers we have Mushroom Caps Lorenzo, which are the mushroom caps stuffed with shredded crabmeat topped with Mornay sauce and baked. We've got the artichoke hearts Au Marchaises. They're the bottoms of the artichokes filled with finely chopped mushrooms and onions with a touch of tomato and grated parmesan cheese. We have Shrimp Provencale, which are shrimps sauteed in butter, lemon, garlic, white wine, tomato, and scallions served with a border of rice. We have Coquille St. Jacques, which is the combination of the scallops and the sliced mushrooms topped with both Mornay and Hollandaise put back into the oven until the sauces are lightly browned. . . .

*Immediacy.*

Today the chef has introduced an appetizer that consists of sliced eggplant, tomato, artichoke hearts, oil and vinegar, rosemary, basil, thyme and oregano—served cold. It's very good. Those are the appetizers in addition to those listed on the menu.

**11** *Bonnie Salund's talk on being a migrant worker*[15]

*Speaker appeals primarily to the emotions of her listeners, using her voice effectively to communicate the sufferings of the migrant worker. (Ch. 4)*

I'd like to talk a little bit about the experiences my mother has gone through as a farm worker. As long as I can remember, my parents were always struggling, worrying about where they were going to be working and where's the money going to be coming in from. When my father wasn't working in the fields, he was trying to gamble. If he could bring $5.00 home, that would be really helpful, especially with six kids. So there was no question in my mind that my mother had to go into the fields and work, even if she was pregnant, even if she had five or six kids to take care of. When the kids were going to school, she had to get up at four o'clock in the morning to make breakfast or lunch for them, and get the kids ready to go to school. Then she would go to work and work as long and as hard as my father would. Then, after working real hard in the hot sun, she'd come home very tired and prepare our meal, which was very little because we were so poor. Then, she'd get the kids ready to go to sleep. Her job would just continue throughout the night. She would have to wash clothes by hand. And my father, all he would do is try to find work so we could survive.

**12** *Street hawker selling goods at a street fair*[16]

*Speaker appeals to desire of audience to save money. (Ch. 4)*

Hey folks, come on over! We've got all your musical instruments stuff reduced right now. We're letting it go real low. Come on down right now before we close up! We'll sell anything we can right now before we move!

**13** *Patrick Sweeney on politics*[5]

*Speaker says he wants to change something, then explains how he wants to change it. (Ch. 4)*

We're going to change Cleveland. We're going to trigger the human resources of this city so Cleveland can save itself. One, we propose a discretionary budget of $100,000 for every ward. People will select the priorities and the councilmen will no longer have to scratch the mayor's back to get something for the ward.

---

## Organizing the Message*

**1** *Eddie Bisone's listing of the menu at St. George's Table*[14]

*Speaker lists the categories of entrees. (Ch. 6)*

For entrees we have several seafood, beef, duck, and veal dishes. I'll begin with our seafood delicacies.

**2** *Dolores Aguirre giving airline departure speech*[4]

*Speaker lists safety requirements aboard her aircraft. (Ch. 6)*

*(First four speakers use topical outlining to organize their main points.)*

If we could have your attention at this time, we'd like to acquaint you with the emergency procedures aboard your 727 aircraft. If, at any time during the flight, oxygen should be needed, an oxygen mask will fall from the unit above your seat. If this should occur, reach up, pull down sharply on the mask to start the flow of oxygen, place it over your nose and mouth as your flight attendants are now demonstrating and continue the use thereof until otherwise advised by a uniformed crew member. Your 727 has eight emergency exits—two doors forward, the main cabin door through which you entered, the galley door right opposite, four wing exits (two over each wing) and two at the rear of the cabin. For further information, there is a card that can be found in the seat packet in front of you. We do suggest that you please read this before takeoff.

**3**  *Robyn Berman talking about rape, its myths and prevention*[17]

Today I'm going to talk about the eight major myths surrounding rape. After this, I'm going to show you a brief film and talk about some of the preventative techniques we recommend. The eight myths are: The rapist is sexually unfulfilled. All rapists are pathologically sick and perverted. Most rapes occur in dark alleys or to women who are hitchhiking. The typical rapist is a stranger to the victim. Black men rape white women. Women ask for it. Rape is impossible without consent. Women enjoy rape.

*Speaker lists myths about rape. (Ch. 6)*

**4**  *Irving Spitzberg's speech to dedicate a building complex*[18]

Ellicot Complex houses the colleges at this university. The colleges are a system of eleven academic units which provide multidisciplinary learning experiences to undergraduates through credit-bearing courses and various other educational opportunities. Seven of the colleges are residential and provide many of their academic programs in that striking architectural setting. The residential colleges include . . . The colleges and their workshops serve approximately 1400 students in their residential and academic program. There are, in addition, four nonresidential colleges on the Main Street campus. They are . . .

*Speaker lists the principal features and purposes of the building complex. (Ch. 6)*

**5**  *George Mai's pottery-making demonstration*[12]

First, you cone the clay. You center the clay and make all the particles move in the same direction. Then you throw the clay and begin to think of the different forms.

*Speaker organizes steps in pottery making sequentially. (Ch. 6)*

**6**  *Walter Rettig speaking on "What Price Bureaucracy?"*[8]

Government is too big. I will show you historically the problems with big government, beginning first with Solomon's empire in 967 BC and concluding with our own troubled times.

*Speaker uses chronological outline to organize main points. (Ch. 6)*

**7**  *R. W. Murphy's management briefing to a group of consultants*[11]

Our electric system covers an area of approximately 24,000 square miles in upstate New York. The system itself is divided into three divisions. The Western Division covers the Niagara Frontier, metropolitan Buffalo, and sections of the state bordering on Lake Erie. It extends eastward to the Rochester Gas and Electric franchise territory. The Central Division extends from Syracuse northward to the Canadian Border and eastward to East Canada Creek near Little Falls.

*Speaker describes the main functions of the electric company by spatially (geographically) organizing his main points. (Ch. 6)*

The Eastern Division of the system begins where the Central ends and ranges north and east to a point midway along the western shore of Lake Champlain; from there it sweeps southward along the Vermont and Massachusetts borders, ending at the Duchess County line.

**8** *Tom Cantone speaking on rent control*[8]

But the taxes are still going up. This to me indicates that something is wrong. Some place along the line the system is going wrong. What is it? I personally, for a long time, had never been able to answer that. But in this week's mail, I think we all received a little mail like a newspaper called the New York State Tax Guide. It is a free issue. I think it presents part of the answer. That being rent control. So what exactly is rent control? This is what I would like to discuss this evening. Rent control was established in 1943. The primary objective of rent control was to protect the low-middle income families from paying exorbitant rents to landlords. . . .

**9** *Andy Fusco speaking on the Battle of the Bulge*[8]

My battle with the bulge is not the historic battle of World War II. It is a continuing fight against a bulging waistline. Tonight somebody told me I was wasting away to nothing. Well, I haven't lost that much weight. My wife spent the first ten years of our marriage demonstrating her culinary ability. She prepared all sorts of goodies, homemade apple pie, with whipped cream, lots of potatoes, lots of steak and gravy. Not forgetting her meatballs. And a lot of homemade bread with a lot of butter on it. This was all very delicious and nutritious and very fattening. Then we both realized that I had outgrown all my clothes sideways. So for the past 25 years she has been after me to lose weight. She thinks I am too heavy for my height; I don't agree. I think I am too short for my weight. Anyway, I became serious about it some three months ago and I decided I must lose some weight or buy new clothes. I believe I reached the same decision at least twice a year for the past 25 years. So that's 50 times. When I would go after a diet in a couple of weeks, then I would go right back to my old eating habits, gaining back what I had lost, or more. But this time I have managed to stick to it. Who knows, I may develop more will power as I have grown older. I found that the first thing I had to do was admit that I was fat. Not stout and not big and not chunky—just plain fat.

**10** *Chief Garmire speaking on technology and the police officer*[6]

A brief review of police technology reveals that the telegraph call box system was not used until 1880. Next came the telephone and electric lights. Fingerprints as a method of identification became common practice only in the early 1900s. . . .

*Speaker organizes his speech causally by telling us the causes for higher taxation, one of which is rent control. (Ch. 6)*

*Speaker tells us the problems associated with being overweight and then offers his own unique solution as he organizes his speech with the problem-solution pattern. (Ch. 5)*

*Speaker uses a detailed illustration that is vivid and appropriate to the subject. By using his own experiences he adds credibility to himself. (Ch. 5)*

*Speaker adopts the chronological pattern, giving historical background of technology in police work, then describes 50s and 60s and finally brings audience up to the state of the art in the 70s. (Ch. 6)*

## Starting the Speech

*Speaker establishes good will with his listeners by personally referring to some by name. He uses a partition statement early to provide a pre-outline of what he will be saying. (Ch. 7)*

*Speaker uses personal reference to relax her listeners and establish good will. (Ch. 7)*

*Speaker gains the audience's attention and establishes rapport with them by using a humorous personal reference to one of his listeners. (Ch. 7)*

*Speaker uses a startling statement to arouse his listeners and keep their attention. (Ch. 7)*

*Speaker provides the rules and details the format for the briefing in his lengthy partition statement designed to orient the listeners to the rest of the speech. (Ch. 7)*

**1** *Eddie Bisone's listing of the menu at St. George's Table*[14]

Hi. How are you, Gerry, and how is Mrs. G? It's nice to see you all tonight. How was your trip? We're all glad that you're back with us and we hope you have a good meal. Shall I run through our menu now? I'll begin with our appetizers, then describe the soups, entrees, vegetables, and salads. I'll come back later to tell you about our latest desserts. For appetizers we have . . .

**2** *Dolores Aguirre giving airline departure speech*[4]

Good morning ladies and gentlemen. We'd like to give a special welcome to our Miami boarding passengers.

**3** *Management briefing to members of a management club of a manufacturing organization*[19]

I'm really glad to be in Warren again. This is my fourth visit to your lovely town and I've been fortunate not to have been here in the winter. But since I had dinner tonight at the same table as Terry Higgins, I now know what you do in Warren to keep warm during the winter. For a man with six kids Terry seems to be in delightful spirits.

**4** *Walter Rettig speaking on "What Price Bureaucracy?"*[8]

Have you ever gone to Washington, D.C. and visited the Jefferson Memorial? And stood in there and looked at the arch over the top and what does it say? These may not be the exact words, but it is close. "He governs best who governs least." And as you look out through the arch, look at all those government buildings, you see quite a paradox. These government buildings are there to govern us, and tell us just about everything we're going to do. Remember that movie, "Big Brother 1984"? The year is coming closer and so is big brother.

**5** *Robert Mulligan's briefing to a group of management consultants*[20]

Gentlemen, I'd like to start the meeting on time. Let me introduce myself. I'm Bob Mulligan, Deputy Director of our Power Division, and I have the administrative function of supervising our management and operations studies. The way we're going to run the meeting is I'll make a few brief introductory remarks and introduce some of our commission staff people who are here. I'll pass on to Mr. Jim Miller who is Vice President of the Central Division of Niagara Mohawk, who will be the company's chief liaison with the consultant selected by the commission. And then I believe Jim will introduce Bill Murphy who will make the presentation for Niagara Mohawk Company. Bill has about a 15-minute presentation, basically a slide presentation, and he'll also have a packet for you with introductory material about Niagara Mohawk Corporation. At the end of the presentation by Niagara Mohawk, I'm sure you people will have some questions, possibly both for the company and for the commission staff. I'll try to answer as many questions as I can. We have other staff people to answer questions too. Why don't I just introduce some of them to you now.

**6**   *Congressman Jack Kemp's commencement address*[10]

I can hardly wait to hear what I am going to say. I am very grateful for those gracious words and the very generous introduction. I think all you would have had to say is that I am a Trustee of the Rosary Hill College and I was a friend of Rosary Hill College, and that would have been enough to say. I am very honored to be with you on this, the 25th Graduation Ceremony, for Rosary Hill. As I look out on this audience I first would like to congratulate all the graduates of the Class of '76 and how proud I am to participate in your graduation ceremony. Dr. Marshall and to all the trustees, the faculty, the students, family and friends: Thank you so much for allowing me to be with you today. As a member of the family, as it were, I checked this story out with Dr. Marshall before I would ever think of telling it. But as a friend of the family, so to speak, I would like to tell you just a quick family story because I have those four children under 16, or is it 16 under four? We had our little guy in Hamburg the other day, our little four-year-old. As we were walking along, shaking hands and meeting some people, several people were coming up to him and saying, "Oh, you must be Congressman Kemp's son." Now, he is only four years old. This went on time after time and that night he went to my wife Joanne and had an identity crisis and she told him, "Tell them you're not Congressman Kemp's son, you tell them you're James Paul Kemp and you're proud of it." Next day we were out walking around again, shaking hands and meeting some of the elder statesmen of the city of Buffalo. They walked up and said "Oh, you must be Congressman Kemp's son." He says, "That's not what my mother says."

**7**   *John Bakas' speech at his ordination*[21]

Your Eminence, I have come before you to receive the sacrament of ordination to the Holy deaconate of the Orthodox Church.

**8**   *Anita Gonzales, Field Manager, Skin Care Clinic presentation*[22]

My name is Anita Gonzales. I represent Lady Venus Cosmetics made by the Cosmetic International Corporation. Thank you for allowing me to come into your home to introduce and demonstrate our cosmetics. My purpose for being here is to help you and show you how to preserve the beauty of your skin and keep it lovely from head to toe.

*Speaker makes ample references to the occasion and the audience to establish goodwill on this special day. He gains their attention and reinforces the goodwill by using a humorous story. (Ch. 7)*

*Speaker uses a beginning, simple statement of purpose. (Ch. 7)*

*Speaker begins with a simple introduction, acknowledging her audience and coming quickly to the purpose of her speech.*

## Wording of the Speech With Appropriate Langauge

*Speaker's language is lofty and general since the occasion is graduation. Here he uses an analogy to make a point. (Ch. 7)*

**1**   *Congressman Jack Kemp's commencement address*[10]

People are being denied the opportunity that I think was there when our nation was founded. It was there when teeming masses of immigrants came to America, seeking not security, but opportunity, were willing to work, to buy, to save, invest, and if we deny them the same opportunity we're turning our backs on the greatest dream that mankind has ever known in its history. "We hold these truths to be self-evident, that all men are created equal, they are endowed by their creator with certain inalienable rights, among which are life, liberty, and the pursuit of happiness." And the only purpose of government is to secure those rights that come to us not from Washington, D.C., but from God Himself. Freedom is the road to prosperity. Freedom and prosperity without spirit, without soul, is a shallow, hollow, and self-defeating volume.

*Instructions are given to a group of teachers with very clear and specific language, used along with visual aids. (Ch. 8)*

**2**   *Tallahassee briefing*[1]

It may help, as the instructions state, to sit and think for a few minutes about certain incidents, or certain people who you think are very good or very bad communicators. Then, jot down why you think they are very good or very bad. Use one form for each separate incident. We are giving you five or six forms. If you need more, raise your hand and we'll come to you with extra forms. We'd like you to work individually, please. We know the room is cramped, but try not to work with anyone else as you prepare and write down your cirtical incidents. These are your incidents and you should work alone. We are not interested in the names of people, just the details of the experiences.

**3**   *Juan Vidarte giving a guided tour of an art museum's famous pieces of sculpture*[12]

*Speaker uses very specific language as he points to the various parts of the sculpture. (Ch. 8)*

In one hand you have the jaguar, which represents the night, and in the other hand you have the serpent that represents the day. Each one is moving in an entirely different direction. This sculpture is decorated with color; you have a piece of jade placed in the eyes of the serpent, decorated with red color.

**4**   *Cathy Miller's talk on meditation*[9]

*Speaker uses language which is specifically adapted to the jargon of the college students in her audience. (Ch. 8)*

I had such a "right on" feeling, you know, that I had achieved such a great natural high through meditation. I think when you're studying, you know, you will really appreciate the benefits of meditation when you start to wander and daydream and forget, you know.

**5**   *Rosemary Mecca's announcements over the PA system in a student union building*[23]

*Speaker's language is quite*

Tomorrow at four p.m. the student radio station presents an hour *specific and brief as she seeks clarity in her short announcements. (Ch. 8)*

with our university president. If you have any questions about budget cuts, tune in and call in tomorrow at four p.m.

Hillel will hold a Purim service at 6:30 this evening and at 7:30 tomorrow morning at the Hillel House.

Stephanie Washburn, go to Room 344 please.

**6** *Police station tour conducted by a desk sergeant*[24]

After we arrest someone, their fingerprints are taken, we remove all their property from them, they are placed in a very small room, about six by twelve, with steel bars. They wait there until they go to trial or until they are released on bail. . . .

*Note how the policeman's language, while very clear and specific, is far too difficult for his audience of elementary school children to understand. (Ch. 8)*

This is the second floor where all the communications are, where they answer all calls, and where the computers are stored. . . .

This is our copying machine where we receive messages from the bureau and other stations. When we get or send messages, we make up extra copies as they go over the system. If the machine breaks down, we have another one at our disposal. We can also make up messages ahead of time for this machine here by putting it on tape, as you can see. We shove the tape through and the message is on its way. . . .

This machine here is connected to the state police computer. It is also connected to the computer at the F.B.I. in Washington, D.C. If you want to find out if a person is wanted for any crime, or whether an automobile or an article has been reported stolen, by coding it into this machine, we can get a reply back within 35 seconds. The differences between this machine and the old-style machine is not only the visual part, but also the speed of transmission. The speed of transmission on the old-style machine is 70 words per minute, while on this new machine, it's 1200 words per minute. So you can see, there's a big difference. The faster we can get the message through, the more messages we can get into the computer.

**7** *Rosie Hampton's speech on the Acme Toilet Paper Holder*[25]

*Speaker's language is simple and direct. The audience works in parks and understands the problem of messy restrooms. She doesn't avoid the problems and they understand her straight talk.*

We also recommend mounting these holders at about waist height. They are best put slightly forward of the commode. When put at this height, they will automatically be at about shoulder height when sitting on the commode. This makes it ever so much easier to get this paper off, thus eliminating another frustration, and if you have some folks who are mad at the world and bent on kicking everything in sight, they will do this little damage to the holder at waist high. *Try it.* Also, you will get few of them urinated on. The few that you find, the custodian does not even have to bend to take a knife and cut that roll off. Otherwise, just use it down to the place you can tear the little remaining paper and cone off, then open and refill.

## Stopping the Speech

*Speakers 1 and 2 conclude their speeches with specific appeals to their listeners for action they can take if they are persuaded by the speakers' arguments. (Ch. 7)*

**1**  *Tom Cantone speaking on Rent Control*[8]

I am asking you to make a commitment. Not a commitment to me, but a commitment to yourself. Find out which way they are going to vote. Determine which way your taxes are going to be spent. To do this, what I have done is made copies of the official form to find out exactly how your legislators are going to vote. What I would like to do is hand these out at this time. I would just like to close by quoting the saying that goes, "If you're not part of the solution, you're part of the problem." Let's participate and become part of the solution.

**2**  *Walter Rettig speaking on "What Price Bureaucracy"*[8]

What I am wondering about is when are we going to revolt? When are we going to protest the taxation we have? I don't know about you, but they took a pretty big piece of my wages last year. Social security, state, federal tax. What can you do about it?

*Speaker ends his stirring rendition of the menu with both a summary of his main points and a plea for specific action. (Ch. 7)*

**3**  *Eddie Bisone's listing of the menu at St. George's Table*[14]

Well, that's what we've got tonight in the way of appetizers, soups, entrees, vegetables, and salads. Do you want some time to think it over, or would you like me to take your order now?

*Speaker uses a summary, some relevant quotations, and a challenge to his listeners as he concludes his brief address. (Ch. 7)*

**4**  *Irving Spitzberg's speech to dedicate a building complex.*[18]

In addition to dedicating the Ellicott buildings, we ask you to join us in a commitment which is the essence of the colleges—dedication to open and frank debate about issues affecting the university and the rest of society. The colleges have historically been governed by a participatory consultative system which requires every policy decision to be vigorously and extensively argued. Our debates have often been with, not just in, the university. Therefore, we invite all of you to join us in debating the future of post-industrial institutions in such imaginative and striking settings as the Ellicott Complex. We believe that the future of the university and the rest of society requires more small neighborhoods built upon choice such as ours. In the words of E.F. Schumaker's new little book, "Small is Beautiful." The issue is not the overall size of SUNY-Buffalo, the SUNY system, or the state of New York, but how these institutions are organized. We believe that the model should be that of small, heterogeneous, changing neighborhoods cooperating together to solve larger problems. What do you think? Thank you.

**5**  *Andy Fusco speaking on the Battle of the Bulge*[8]

I have been losing one or two pounds every week since that time except during my vacation. I think Al Jones can tell you how good

*Speaker concludes with a humorous story designed to*

*leave his audience in the proper frame of mind. (Ch. 7)*

some of the restaurants are down in Mertel Beach. So I gained back about six or seven pounds during that time, despite the warning I was given by Irv Brewster, that on vacation you always pick up weight. But when I got back it took me about ten days to lose it back again and now I think I have taken off about twenty pounds and I can wear that leisure suit my wife bought me for Christmas. I still think she intends to buy me things two sizes too small to kind of tell me to lose some weight. I am built too heavy for my height, and I should lose about fifteen more pounds. But I still wonder if it wouldn't be easier to get taller. I could buy a pair of those platform shoes and grow a couple of inches that way.

**6**   *R.W. Murphy's management briefing to a group of consultants*[11]

In this last forty-five minutes I have given you a thumbnail sketch of our business. As I promised you at the start, there would be time for questions and now is the time.

**7**   *John Bakas' speech at his ordination*[21]

*Note that the speaker ends his rather long speech without a needed summary. (Ch. 7)*

And now your Eminence, I commit myself to your hands as unworthy as I am, for the sacrament of Holy Ordination, pledging to remain faithful to the canons of the Orthodox Church. I will adhere to the directives of my ecclesiastical superiors and promise to do my best to help Father Dogias and the community of St. George.

*The speaker does not summarize his speech, but ends it with a pledge to do his best for the community, thus selecting a psychological ending. (Ch. 7)*

**8**   *Chief Garmire's speech at the Carnahan Crime Counter-Measures Conference*[6]

We cannot avoid the future by denying to the police the technology they must have to perform their mission, for ours is a world of technology. If we are to avoid that future, then those who are expanding the limits of technology must tell us how imminent that future is so we might be forewarned. Those who are using technology as a means to solve technical problems must recognize that even greater societal problems can thereby be created. Those who are selling technology must temper the profit motive with a concern for its use. The police who use technology in the name of the law must do so within the letter and the spirit of the law. Finally, and most importantly, the public must insure that the law fosters democracy, not technocracy.

*In his conclusions, the speaker neatly summarizes all the points he expanded upon in his speech. He ends with a final sentence that not only presents his point of view, but is a plea for preservation of our form of government in the face of a technological era that might threaten its existence. (Ch. 7)*

## OTHER WAYS OF ANALYZING SPEECHES

In the preceding analyses of the speeches given by various speakers in this country, we focused on those principles that we stressed in this book. The analyses were based on the *content* of the speeches because we had not heard the speeches or were not aware of the composition of the audiences or of many of the events leading to the speeches.

To give you some examples of other ways a critic may analyze a speaker or a speech, we present our analyses of the 1976 Vice-Presidential and Presidential debates. We analyzed these debates for our local newspapers. We *saw them* on television, so delivery greatly influenced us. In the Mondale/Dole debate, we focused on style and language as the most important features for analysis. In the Carter/Ford debates, we primarily studied the nonverbal behaviors exhibited by both candidates.

## Mondale/Dole Debate: Style

Buffon, the 18th century naturalist, posited that *style* is the man himself. What a person is comes through in his or her choices of language and the product speaks of the person. In the country's first vice-presidential debate, Robert Dole and Walter Mondale attempted to translate style into persuasive power. Dole tried to master the informal speech, not taking notes, not preparing either his beginning or ending. But he lacked the poise of the master of the informal speech, Everett Dirksen, the charm of Franklin Roosevelt, and the wit of Harry Truman. He swung his words around heavily and with abandon. He gave the "bunny" vote to Carter, implied Mondale had his make-up done by Meany, cruelly cut down the League of Women Voters, and finally, wielding the heaviest blow of all, laid 1.6 million dead Americans at the Democrats' door.

Mondale busied himself with note-taking while his opponent spoke. Then, looking straight into the camera, he spoke in language containing some of the classical stylistic devices such as repetition, metaphor, and analogy. In one organized passage Mondale spoke about America's foreign policy. He stated that America's greatest strength is found in its values and beliefs and that we have not pursued a foreign policy that is compatible to these values. He supported his proposition by speaking of our policy in Africa, Greece, and Saudi Arabia, of how we supported colonial control for seven and a half years in Africa, of our commitment to the Greek Junta, and of how we "turned our backs" on Greece when she became a democracy.

Dole dismissed the entire argument with "I notice you never once criticized Secretary Kissinger," as though Kissinger was not even remotely attached to any of the foreign policy decisions.

Despite discernible ambiguities Dole barged on, using long involved sentences and numerous phrases and asides that led, inevitably, to the personal attack.

Mondale continued to turn a phrase with such statements as "never can we permit politics above all to dominate the nation."

When he chose to attack he most often used the impersonal "they." That is, he did so until Dole made his comment about the dead Americans. Then Mondale made his strongest remark about his opponent's style: "I think Senator Dole has richly earned his reputaion as a Republican hatchet man."

Finesse plays no part in a hatchet man's image. Mondale was accusing Dole of lacking style in the classical sense. Style to the scholar is artistry in language, a sophistication of manner and wit, and a new conception of political leadership.

In this debate, in which each candidate repeated the campaign rhetoric that was used on the campaign trail and no new policies or plans were articulated, the language became the highlight of the evening. And there was little doubt that the language was revealing of the man. Mondale appeared thoughtful and organized and avoided too many personal attacks upon his opponents. His language revealed that he was a logical man, slow to anger but rising to the occasion when the situation demanded it.

Dole on the other hand, was casual, spicing his words with adjectives, controversy, and personal attacks. He was more colorful and more apt to stir the emotions of his listeners.[26]

## Carter/Ford Debates: Verbal and Nonverbal Differences

After 750 combined hours of analysis, we have discovered major verbal and nonverbal communication differences between the candidates in the three Ford-Carter debates. The research was based upon an analysis of 7,378 specific nonverbal behaviors and 955 verbal references found in the 30,852-word transcripts. We found differences in eye gaze, mouth expression, shoulder and head movements, speech rate, nonfluencies, use of specific supporting materials, character references, as well as differences in overall effectiveness and speaker credibility.

Since most viewers in national surveys conducted after the three debates were unable to identify *specific* reasons why Ford or Carter "won," this research may provide useful clues about each candidate's image projected to the viewers.

### Eye gaze
Eye contact and eye contact shifts are associated with a communicator's directness (trustworthiness, honesty, competence) and a communicator's ability to put his thoughts into words. Increased eye contact can indicate individual ability to communicate meaning directly. Eye contact also gives an indication of the nature of the relationship desired by the communicator. Typically, a speaker who desires a close relationship with his listener will gaze more directly and more often at his listener.

Throughout the three debates, Carter shifted his eye gaze direction three to four times as much as Ford. Carter spent much of his time maintaining direct eye contact with the TV camera (and consequently, the home viewer) and the panel, while often shifting somewhat nervously to the podium. *It is with eye gaze that Carter shifted his behavior most inconsistently.* For example, in Debate I, Carter concentrated on the panel and the camera with nervous looks at the podium. In Debate II, he practically ignored all other directions except the TV camera. In Debate III, he reduced his TV camera eye contact and increased his looks at the podium. In no debate did he glance much at Ford.

Ford, on the other hand, maintained a consistent pattern of eye contact throughout the three debates. With the exception of Debate II, when Ford increased contact with the TV camera, he maintained almost exclusive contact with the panel, and in Debate III glanced at Carter on 20 different occasions. Since an estimated 80 to 100 million people watched portions of the debates, TV camera eye contact had important implications. The person at home may have felt that the candidate was speaking to them directly rather than to others whom they were (casually) observing from their living rooms. Carter, therefore, was "looking directly at the home viewers (and potential voters)" far more often than Ford.

In sum, *Carter shifted his eye gaze direction three to four times more often than Ford while maintaining more direct eye contact with the TV audience than Ford. Ford maintained more consistent eye contact throughout the three debates, concentrating mostly on the panelists and shifting direction only infrequently.*

### Head movement

Head activity is typically an indication of a speaker's expressiveness or an indication of tension in a communicative situation. In all three debates, *Carter shifted and moved his head more often than Ford.* In Debate III, Carter moved his head *three times* as much as Ford, mostly with short (three seconds each) rapid shifts usually typical of tension. Throughout the three debates, Ford *gradually decreased* the amount of time his head moved from 29 percent to 27 percent to 16 percent of his speaking time, while Carter *increased* the time spent in head movement from 23 percent to 34 percent to 41 percent. *Coupled with other nonverbal characteristics (fluency, speaking rate, eye gaze), we interpret these data to mean that Ford's head movement suggested expressiveness while Carter's movement indicated tension.*

### Mouth expression

The expression on the mouth of a communicator (smiling, frowning) indicates several dimensions of emotion. *In all three debates, Carter's mouth was two to three times more expressive than Ford's.* This

*Eye contact with your audience establishes a feeling of personal communication.*

means Carter shifted mouth expression (from expressionless to smiles to pressing lips, etc.), revealing his emotions more than Ford. *Although both candidates were mostly expressionless throughout all debates*, Ford was the more somber of the two, remaining expressionless for about 95 percent of his speaking time to Carter's 80 to 83 percent.

Carter tends to lick and press his lips (a possible sign of tension) as well as smile (a possible sign of satisfaction) more than Ford. Although Carter's famous "broad smile" was largely missing from all debates (occurring less than two percent of his speaking time), Carter gradually increased the number of his slight smiles from seven percent to 10 percent to 12 percent of his speaking time. Since he also increased the number of times he pressed his lips, Carter seemed to be alternating exhibiting behaviors indicative of two conflicting emotional states (relaxation and tension). *In brief, Carter's mouth was more expressive than Ford's, at times indicating both relaxation (by smiling) and tension (by licking and pressing his lips).*

### Upper body movement

The manner and amount that a person moves his body communicates much about his self-confidence, energy or fatigue, status, defensiveness and nervousness. As tension increases, body movements tend to be viewed as symptoms of several inner states. The shape of a person's body has a definite impact upon body movement and the perceptions of people about a communicator's credibility. In addition, body shape is often related to the temperament of the individual. No one person fits perfectly a given theoretical body type, but considerable information can be gleaned from just such an analysis.

For example, Ford, whose body type is close to the "athletic" type, will *probably* be viewed as stronger, more masculine, better-looking, more mature, and self reliant. Carter has a relatively "slender" body type which would be viewed *probably* as ambitious, younger, tense, cautious, thoughtful, sensitive and gentle. These perceptions often play an important role in the development of a candidate's "image" and, thus, have a part to play in how votes are cast.

Ford moved his upper body two to three times more often than Carter in all three debates. Both candidates increased their rate of upper body movement from Debate I to Debate III, although Ford reduced the amount of time spent in such movements from an average of eight to two seconds per movement. Thus, Ford's upper body movements, while more frequent in Debates II and III, were less ponderous. Carter's upper body remained relatively erect throughout the three debates. *In brief, Ford moved his upper body to release tension created by the debates while Carter held his upper body erect while moving his eyes, mouth and head.*

*Body movement can be a clue to how the speaker feels.*

## Speech rate

The average speaking rate of most Americans ranges from 125 to 150 wpm (words per minute). Speaking rate is related to the amount of information transmitted and perceptions of the competence and spontaneity of the communicator. *In all three debates, Carter spoke between 22 percent to 27 percent faster than Ford. Carter averaged 164 wpm in Debates I and II and increased that rate to 176 wpm in Debate III, while Ford spoke between 128 and 133 wpm in all three debates. Because of Carter's faster speaking rate, he was able to use 12 percent more words in 11 percent less time than Ford. Carter's fast rate of speaking apparently dispels the myth that all Southerners speak more slowly than other Americans, and may have contributed to his high ratings as a dynamic speaker.* In Debate III, Cater tended to increase his speech rate as the debate progressed, at one time *approaching 220 wpm.* Ford, on the other hand, maintained a steady rate of about 130 wpm with increases occurring when he was responding to Carter (perhaps a sign of tension).

The rate of speaking and listener comprehension tends to be related. When specifics such as statistics and detailed examples were used in Debate I, Carter's faster rate of speaking may have been a disadvantage. In the second and third debates, however, in which Carter used fewer specifics, his faster rate may have increased comprehension. Ford's slower speech rate tended to be related to his use of fewer facial and head movements. Similarly, Carter's faster speech rate tended to be related to his more frequent facial and head movements.

*Speech should be fast enough to hold the listeners' attention, and slow enough to be understood.*

## Nonfluencies

Nonfluencies tend to indicate a speaker's state of tension as well as influencing the way he is perceived by the audience. For example, more nonfluent speakers tend to be perceived as less competent and dynamic, but not necessarily less trustworthy. Nonfluencies are those breaks or substitutions which interrupt the normal communication flow (e.g., "repetition, tongue slips, er, ah, ehm").

In Debate I, Carter had three times more nonfluencies than Ford (averaging about nine nonfluencies per minute compared with Ford's three and a half per minute). In Debate II, however, both candidates had the same number of nonfluencies, averaging about two per minute. In Debate III, both candidates increased to about six per minute, probably revealing their anxiety over the serious consequences of the last debate. Carter's increased speaking rate (176 wpm) may have accounted for some of his increased nonfluency, while Ford's increased nonfluency (since his speaking rate remained the same— about 128 wpm) was probably attributed to tension. *Thus, in only the first debate was Carter more nonfluent than Ford.*

While Ford's rate of nonfluencies tended to be evenly distributed throughout the debates, Carter was more nonfluent when responding to Ford than when answering panelist questions.

In brief, *Ford's low rate of nonfluency may have contributed to his high public ratings for competence and knowledge while Carter's higher rate (in Debate I) may have contributed to his higher ratings on sincerity; that is, his communication appeared spontaneous.*[27]

## Dennis J. Kucinich[28]

I stand here in assurance that this moment has been long awaited by many of my colleagues here tonight. But the words of John Donne, who worked the precincts of seventeenth-century England, perhaps writing of you and me, can bring us comfort:

> "Our two souls, therefore, which are one,
> Though I must go, endure not yet
> A breach , but an expansion . . ."

A Valediction: Forbidding Mourning

So like John Donne's valediction, mine tonight will also forbid mourning.

*The speaker adapts to his audience by acknowledging that he has both friends and foes listening to him. He attempts to establish himself immediately as a person who recognized and accepted his mission—to speak out against those issues he felt to be hindering good government.*

Six years ago, when I came into this legislative body as one of thirty-three members, I knew that if the political and social needs of the people I represent were to be advanced in this forum it would be necessary for me to stand up and speak out. I understood immediately that my outspokenness would infuriate those in government who choose to remain silent.

It is not very comfortable to be the target of the wrath and scorn of some politicians—just because one chooses to speak out and others choose silence. But I prefer to make my enemies feel uncomfortable rather than to dash the hopes and dreams of my constituents.

So I spoke out.

I fought income tax increases and I fought unfair utility rate increases. I fought for consumer legislation and I fought for improved transportation systems for the transit-dependent people of our city whose world reaches to the limits of the local bus lines.

*As evidence that he met the challenge and spoke out forcefully, the speaker cites specific instances, such as the "jet-port in the lake," etc.*

Words were the tools I used to help implement public policy. I used words to defend my constituents against immoral, importuning tax schemes. Remember the jetport-in-the-lake, the Halprin Plan, and the Rhodes billion dollar boondoggle bond package?

I knew that whenever I took strong positions on issues contrary to the vested economic interests of the establishment I would invite vilification. But I was prepared to pay the price and would do so again because I believe in what I talk about.

*Speaker chastises those in his audience who remained silent or were in opposition to him, further admonishing them that they must stand up and speak out.*

Think about it. How many of you wanted to stand up and speak out but were frozen by fear of being attacked by special business interests, political jackals, or straw bosses who sold out their people? How many of you cowered to vapid editorial writers? How many times did fear of losing political office cause you to let important things remain unsaid?

I believe that unless we are willing to risk these simple offices we hold, that if we are not prepared to stand up and fight for what we believe, the only legitimate purpose of public service—the fulfillment of our constituents' needs—will always elude us.

What you say does matter. It must matter. It is the ability of one person to stand up and speak out which can change the course of history in a city, in a state, or in this nation.

*To support the moral side of his actions, the speaker cites several authorities: Andrew Jackson, Martin Luther King, Jr., etc.*

Andrew Jackson wrote that: "One man with courage makes a majority." It takes courage to speak out. But courage well-practiced comes not just as force of habit, but is transformed into a habit of force. And it is this force that can redirect political historical events.

What happens when just one person stands up and speaks out? What happens when one person rises to resist the prevailing consensus, to challenge public opinion or common practice, and sets out to blaze new social horizons?

Contemporary history gives us the names of persons like Rosa Lee Parks, Martin Luther King, Robert Kennedy, Daniel Ellsberg, Ralph Nader; individuals who were willing to sacrifice whatever they possessed to make their beliefs known.

Their struggle did not begin on the great stage of national events. In most cases, it began in the humblest of places. But because they were willing to press forward daily to advance deeply held beliefs, they eventually found that millions were prepared to listen. They found that their voice was the voice of these millions.

We in this Council begin with a forum which most citizens can never hope to achieve. We have the opportunity to promote those ideas and beliefs which we hold dear—to make the feelings of our constituents understood through spirited public discussion. We forfeit our uniqueness, our intellectual integrity, through silence. And worse, we often forfeit the rights of those we represent.

This City Council has progressed in the past six years.

When I began, my hard-hitting, independent approach was considered political suicide. Today present and incoming councilmen find that these same qualities are prerequisites for service in council. These qualities are demanded by the people.

*Speaker does not dwell on those in the council who chose to remain silent during his term of office but moves quickly to the present members. He attempts to*

The council leadership has changed its direction, too. Six years ago the leadership employed polarization as a substitute for action and used confrontation as the justification for nonperformance.

Today the role of city council has grown from reacting to policy to formulating policy—in finance, in housing, in transportation. More *establish a rapport with the present members by praising their recent efforts as policy makers.*

*In his conclusion, the speaker uses a quote from a man who greatly influenced his life and inspired him to enter politics at the age of 21—Robert Kennedy.*

councilmen have chosen to become full participants in the process of city government. The increased importance of the council has come about because the present administration has defaulted on its leadership, shunning its obligation to the people of Cleveland. It is standing still, perfectly still, puzzled, dazed, moribund—waiting for Council to lead. And Council has accepted the challenge.

It is fortunate for the people of Cleveland that the next council, by virtue of higher education, deeper community involvement, and plain old vigor, is better prepared to lead than any council before it. The lack of seniority and experience should not be an impediment or an intimidation to any member. We each know the needs of our constituencies. Each of you are qualified to speak to issues which affect those needs.

There are always enough causes to advance. There will always be enough work to do. There will always be problems to solve. But the resolution of public problems must come in a free and spirited public debate. This forum should be the tabernacle of the First Amendment. I urge you to remember that if the needs of a single constituent suffer from your silence, then all the power and prestige you have gained as a result of public service mean nothing.

In closing, I call to your attention a quote from the late Senator Robert Kennedy which not only answers why we must speak out, but also justifies the continuance of daily battles on behalf of the people:

> "Each time a man stands up for an ideal, or acts to improve the lot of others, or strikes out against injustice, he sends forth a tiny ripple of hope, and crossing each other from a milion different centers of energy and daring, those ripples build a current that can sweep down the mightiest walls of oppression and resistance."
>
> Robert F. Kennedy, April 1968

## EXERCISE

Using this form as a guide, rate the next speaker you hear: 3 = Excellent; 2 = Fair; 1 = Poor.

Name of speaker: _____

Title of speech:_____

___ Subject choice (appropriate for audience, occasion; timely; narrow):

_____

___ Audience analyzed (logistics, demographics, attitudes; before, during, after):

_____

___ Message researched/developed (ethically, emotionally, logically):

_____

___ Message organized (topical, spatial, chronological, causal,
problem-solution pattern; order appropriate; coordinate/
subordinate; transition):

_____

___ Introduction (gained attention, oriented, established good will;
used references, humor, stories, comparisons, startling statements,
questions, quotations, statistics):

_____

___ Conclusion (logical, psychological purposes; used summary, quotation, illustration, plea/appeal/challenge, humor):

_____

___ Language/style (clear, specific, appropriate):

_____

___ Nonverbal physical behavior (body movement, gestures, facial expression, eye contact):

_____

___ Nonverbal vocal behavior (pitch volume, rate, fluency, quality):

_____

___ Overall rating of speech: _____

Additional comments on strengths/weaknesses/improvements:

_____

_____

# REFERENCES

1  An unidentified speaker was giving instructions to a large number of
   teachers (over 200) assembled in Tallahassee, Florida to complete an
   instrument designed to evaluate the quality of communication in their
   schools' systems. The instructions were given in May 1975 in the
   cateteria of one of the high schools in town.

2  An unidentified President of a major university was giving a short talk
   and answering questions for a large group (over 500) of college students assembled in an open mall area. The president was primarily addressing the reasons for pending tuition increases and was constantly
   harassed by large numbers of hecklers. The talk occurred in Spring
   1976.

**3** Macra Fortkort, a student, gave a prayer at the commencement exercises of the State University of New York at Buffalo, 1975.

**4** Dolores Aguirre, hostess for Continental Airlines, was delivering her regular departure speech to an audience of airline passengers on a flight to El Paso, Texas. The date was October 28, 1975.

**5** Patrick Sweeney, State Representative from Ohio, was giving a political speech to the Cleveland City Club, September 26, 1975.

**6** Chief Bernard L. Garmire, retired Chief of Police, Miami Police Department, was speaking to the 1973 Carnahan Conference on Electronic Crime Countermeasures at the University of Kentucky, Lexington, in April of that year.

**7** Coach Walter Gantz of the Cross-Country Team at the State University of New York at Buffalo, was giving a pre-meet pep talk to the team, September 15, 1976.

**8** Tom Cantone, Andy Fusco, Ellis McDaniel and Walter Rettig are all members of a local Toastmaster's Club, and were delivering their regular speeches to the club. They were judged on the quality of their speeches and their purposes could vary. This meeting took place in 1976.

**9** Cathy Miller was talking about meditation to a group of meditators and novices to meditation who assemble nightly to discuss their experiences. The audience are followers of Guru Maharaj Ji, the spiritual teacher from India. This talk occurred in April, 1976.

**10** Congressman Jack Kemp delivered the commencement address for Rosary Hill College in June, 1976, before an audience of 1000 students, faculty, and parents assembled in Kleinhans Music Hall in Buffalo, N.Y.. Mr. Kemp, an accomplished public speaker, discussed the American Bicentennial and the graduates' role in the free enterprise system.

**11** R. W. Murphy, an executive with Niagara Mohawk Utility Company of New York, was giving a management briefing to a group of consultants assembled in the Syracuse offices of the utility on April 20, 1976. Murphy described the company and its operations to the consultants who were about to submit bids for a special project.

**12** George Mai was giving a demonstration on making pottery to passers-by. His audience was constantly changing, so his attention was fixed to his pot, not his audience. The visual aspect of the speech greatly supported his words.

**13** Juan Vidarte, museum guide, was giving an oral guided tour in a museum of modern art. His audience is small (from five to seven people), but his voice boomed loud to attract others. He was constantly moving around to describe different pieces of art.

**14** St. George's Table Maitre d', Eddie Bisone, delivers his highly oral rendition of the continental menu at this famed restaurant in Buffalo, New York. This particular version was delivered in February of 1976 to a group of six diners.

15    Bonnie Salund, a migrant worker from California, was telling a group of interested listeners about her experiences as a migrant worker in Spring 1976, and the audience was mostly young people.

16    An unidentified street hawker used a microphone to attract customers to his booth at a street fair. His speech was rather ineffective, as no customers were forthcoming on this Spring afternoon in 1976.

17    Robyn Berman was conducting a workshop for the general public on the facts of rape, including its incidence, legal considerations, and methods of prevention. Most of her audience were females between the ages of 17 and 30. The workshop took place in 1975.

18    Irving Spitzberg, Dean of the College System at SUNY-Buffalo, was delivering a speech to dedicate the Ellicott Complex, a series of buildings in a living/learning center on the new North Campus of SUNYAB. The audience of 500 was surrounded by angry protestors. The speech took place in May 1976 at an open mall area in Ellicott Complex.

19    An unidentified speaker was giving a briefing to 100 members of a management club of a large manufacturing organization. The audience was assembled for its monthly meeting and dinner was preceded by cocktails and light social talk. The meeting took place on the second floor of a private hall in a small Pennsylvania town in January 1976.

20    Robert Mulligan, Deputy Commissioner of Public Works, was introducing a representative of the Niagara Mohawk Utility Company to a group of consultants assembled prior to submitting bids for a project financed by the utility company. Mulligan's purpose was to set the stage for the Niagara Mohawk briefing, which took place on April 20, 1976, in the Syracuse offices of Niagara Mohawk Company.

21    John Bakas was addressing the Greek congregation in Albuquerque, New Mexico, and the Archbishop of North and South America, on the occasion of his ordination as a deacon of the Greek Orthodox Church.

22    Anita Gonzales, Field Manager Skin Care Clinic Presentation at client's home, was speaking to client and neighbors. July 25, 1976.

23    Rosemary Mecca was making a series of announcements over the loudspeaker system of a student union building in March of 1975. She was never aware of the size and type of audience that heard a particular message.

24    An unidentified desk sergeant was giving a walking police-station tour to a group of elementary school children in May 1976. The location of the speech varied from floor to floor in the station.

25    Alice "Rosie" Hampton, was giving a demonstration speech to the delegates at the Park and Recreational Convention in Shreveport, Louisiana, in Spring of 1976.

26    E. Zannes, Analysis of Mondale/Dole Debates for the *Albuquerque Journal*, November 14, 1976.

27    G. M. Goldhaber, D. T. Porter, J. K. Frye, and M. Yates, Department of Communication at the State University of New York at Buffalo; Analysis of *Verbal and Nonverbal Differences in the Ford-Carter Debates*, 1976.

# INDEX